The American House

The American House

By Mary Mix Foley

Drawings by Madelaine Thatcher

Foreword by James Marston Fitch

HARPER COLOPHON BOOKS

Harper & Row, Publishers

New York, Cambridge, Philadelphia, San Francisco

London, Mexico City, São Paulo, Sydney

To my father
Charles Melvin Mix, M.D., F.A.C.S.
for his scientist's mind
and
To my mother
Margaret Tracy Mix
for her artist's eye
with love and gratitude

A hardcover edition of this book is published by
Harper & Row, Publishers.

First HARPER COLOPHON edition published 1981.

ISBN: 0-06-090831-9

81 82 83 84 85 10 9 8 7 6 5 4 3 2 1

Contents

Foreword

James Marston Fitch

When John James Audubon set out to record the wondrous variety of native American birds, he brought to the task an endearing mix of affection for his subject matter and scrupulously objective standards for recording and describing it. He also was recording—though he did not recognize it in those days before Darwin—the results of aeons of evolutionary development. Mary Mix Foley is squarely in the great Audubonian tradition in her determination to record with immaculate accuracy every type, variety and hybrid of the species *Domus Americana*. But unlike that earlier great explorer, she belongs to a culture which takes as a basic fact of being the evolutionary development of all organisms across time. Moreover, she understands (as Audubon could not) that this evolutionary process is still very real, moving at the same accelerating pace as contemporary society and not at Audubon's humanly imperceptible pace of geological time. The result is a work that raises our comprehension of the development of American domestic architecture to qualitatively new levels. The study of *Domus Americana* will never be the same after the publication of this book.

The significance of *The American House* springs not so much from the discovery of new, never-before-seen organisms in the American cultural landscape (most of these houses have already been published in a bewildering variety of sources) as from the conceptual perspective from which they are viewed. This is a unified point of view, both cognitively and perceptually. That is to say, Foley's dazzling exposition of the history and typology of American houses is umbilically connected to Thatcher's unified style of graphically depicting them. Together, words and pictures give us a much clearer—and hence, an incomparably more fascinating—view of the subject than the conventional history with its miscellany of woodcuts, watercolors, engravings and photographs.

Although the provenance of each house is established, along with the source of the illustration, this book is refreshingly free of all the usual apparatus of historiography. The author and the artist approach their subject matter more in the fashion of, respectively, a cultural anthropologist and a medical illustrator than as architectural historian and delineator—i.e., typologically rather than historically or esthetically.

This conceptual perspective permits *all* the houses to be handled with exactly the same admirable mixture of fondness and objectivity. Thus a high style urbane artifact like Hunt's *The Breakers* is dealt with in precisely the same clinical fashion as Fuller's High Tech *Dymaxion* of 1944 or the primitive stockade house of Wenlocke Christison of 1670. One is irresistibly reminded of such field studies of animal behavior as Farley Mowat's of the Canadian wolf or Jane Goodall's of the African gorilla; for here one finds that an authentic identification with the object of study—far from being romantic or obscurantist—actually permits a truly scientific analysis of the species in its habitat.

The years of painstaking research and plain hard work which have gone into the making of this book will, perhaps, be obvious only to scholars. Thus when Foley writes of grand New Orleans ladies wading barefoot through the muddy streets on their way to a ball, carrying satin slippers and lace stockings in their hands; or when one sees the scrupulous care with which Thatcher records every last preposterous wooden detail of the Carson House at Eureka, California—then it becomes clear that one is face to face with scholarly work of the highest order.

The average readers of this book may find it too large (or too valuable) to carry in the pocket on their travels around America, although it could serve as an excellent field guide to our cultural landscape. But, once having read it, it is certain that their conceptual grasp of that landscape will have been both broadened and enriched. Orthodox art and architectural historiography, despite its obvious utility, too often suffers from the self-imposed limitation of dealing only with those artifacts (usually upper-class and urbane) whose owners and architects have become embedded in the written record. This shallow perspective prevents the historiographer from observing the vast submerged base of anonymous vernacular activity—illiterate or pre-literate, a-historical or pre-historical—on which all elite activity is ultimately based. Such historiographers will profit, as much as will the general reader, from a study of this book. Not only will they find a wealth of carefully distilled information on a wide range of isolated buildings. Even more importantly, they will find a field of rich and complex relationships, interactions and illuminating analogies which have hitherto largely escaped their attention.

J.M.F.

Graduate School of Architecture and Planning
Columbia University in the City of New York
April 1979

Introduction

This book is a novel guide to American houses. It is neither a scholarly history of domestic architecture nor a coffee-table collection of museum mansions. Rather, it is a guide to style itself—an attempt to sort out the American architectural past so that a house, like a bird, can be recognized in passing.

It was originally inspired by bafflement and confusion on the part of the author. For many years, I had been examining (and admiring) the beautiful photographs in the beautiful picture books of American houses. But always I was left with nagging doubts.

Why did this house, labeled Georgian, look less like the Georgian mansion on the following page than it did like the seventeenth-century homestead several pages before it?

Just what, really, was a Greek Revival house? What made this one—lacking a pillared portico—Greek Revival?

What did the word "Victorian" mean? There seemed to be dozens of "Victorian" styles, ranging in character from turreted castle and gingerbread Gothic through the classic Italian villa, to the lesser-known simplicities of the "Shingle Style."

Could sense be made out of Georgian subtlety and Victorian bedlam? I decided to try.

As saner minds could have told me, it turned out to be an heroic job—even more difficult than tracing, for four hundred years and more, the genealogies of dozens of families all noted for intermarriage, cross-country migration, and the periodic importation of brides from foreign lands.

What I found, eventually, were two dominant strains in American domestic architecture: (1) the formal period styles; and (2) a substratum of folk building, a persistent vernacular brought over in the minds and skilled hands of the earliest settlers and perpetuated by their descendants.

The latter were native traditions—English, Dutch, German, Swedish, French, Spanish—with roots going back through the medieval period to even more ancient origins. These folk-building traditions were intertwined with the ways of life in the old countries from which the settlers came, and they proved remarkably sturdy in the new.

The formal styles, on the other hand, were fickle and changeable, representing at each new period a break with the immediate past. Large and elegant mansions were built in these styles or as close to the Georgian, Greek or Gothic ideal as American money could make them.

But a house is a house is a house. Alongside the newest import, the old familiar ways of building persisted. These vernacular types—here embellished by Queen Anne or Adam details, there crossed with one another to create a new regional idiom, and again surfacing as the basic form of an imposing period mansion—presented a confused, and confusing, picture.

How to sort out such complexities? Could one capture, not a static moment in time, but the process of architectural development itself? In all its ramifications, this is of course impossible. But I have devised a system that I think may come close, and one that has not been used before.

Part I is devoted to the transplanted European houses of early America and to the vernacular architecture that derived from them. In addition, some of these house types are shown as they progress through a variety of later styles.

Parts II, III, IV and V move from the classic period styles through Victorian and twentieth-century revivals, ending with a capsule history of modern architecture. These sections concentrate on the new. But a bit of the old vernacular past also is included, showing that house types might vary while the style of a given period remained the same. In addition, a few new types entered the vernacular and these—as in Part I—are shown moving forward in style.

The sequential system also helps to chart a path through late Victorian confusion. During the post-Civil War years, revival styles were broken apart and recombined into a kaleidoscope of motifs. Our illustrations trace—for the first time—this complicated pattern of change.

By the same method, related illustrations show how modern domestic architecture developed out of Victorian types, and how new ideas traveled from one architect to another, changing and evolving in the process.

If this sounds like architecture made easy, that is indeed the idea. However, an equally important goal is simply to show the astonishing range of quaint, beautiful, splendid, fanciful and functional houses that make up the American past, present and possible future.

Among the houses illustrated, many are open to the public; a list at the back of the book indicates when this is the case. Many, however, are privately owned and many more no longer stand. These can be seen only on the printed page.

For illustration the book uses a more explicit technique than photographs—beautiful and faithful line drawings by Madelaine Thatcher. With rare exceptions, these include the whole house, rather than artistically selected eaves and corners. This approach, so different from the usual photographic essay, permits one to see what a house really looks like.

The use of drawings instead of photographs is basic to my system of organization, and in fact created it. For in line drawings essential form and detail stand out, and the relationship between houses comes across clearly.

I hope that this book will inform and give pleasure in several ways—as a convenient manual of style; as a house-watcher's field guide for travelers; as a traveling architectural tour for stay-at-homes; and as an enjoyable popular history for all those who care about the houses in which they and other Americans live, have lived, and may live in the future.

Mary Mix Foley
Washington, D.C.
April 1979

Part I

The Medieval Echo

America is a nation of immigrants. And the story of its early architecture is largely an immigrant's story. The Spaniard, the Frenchman, the Dutchman, the German, the Scandinavian—and, of course, the Englishman—all brought to the New World the building traditions of their native lands.

These settlers came from countries that were in the process of change from their own distinctive medieval architecture to the imported classicism of the Italian Renaissance. But the new classic influence was at first little more than surface ornament, applied to houses still essentially medieval in plan and structure. Moreover, these decorative changes took place almost exclusively in the palaces of royalty and the manor houses of the wealthy. Rural cottages and the row houses that crowded against each other in busy market towns continued in familiar patterns.

Though settled during the architectural period known historically as the High Renaissance, this country's earliest houses were, therefore, anything but classic. Most colonists were of humble origin: small farmers, artisans, traders. They brought with them the old native building traditions as yet scarcely touched by Renaissance fashion.

Their dwellings, so different from the formal Georgian architecture of the eighteenth century, were an echo of medieval Europe. That echo comes forward to us in the New England farmhouse, the stone dwellings of the Pennsylvania Germans, the southern plantation house, and other familiar examples. It is these houses—both the primitive early prototypes and their later adaptations—which make up the first section of this book.

1

Chapter 1

An English Tradition

In the English settlements, as elsewhere, the need for quick shelter in a hostile wilderness at first compelled a return to the most primitive of dwellings. The earliest houses were no more than dugouts, tents, and roofed-over pits called "cellars." Colonists in Massachusetts Bay added "English wigwams" of bent saplings covered with bark.

But as soon as they were able, the settlers built houses like those which they had known at home. And, in the English colonies, these were not log cabins. Once assumed to have been the first home of Englishmen in America, the house of saddle-notched, horizontally laid, whole logs has now been recognized as the native tradition of Scandinavian, Finnish, and German settlers. A few hewn log blockhouses and garrisons of a defensive nature were built by the English, but these were rare and specialized dwellings. The type of log cabin which would become the pioneer home of a later America was unknown to seventeenth-century Englishmen.

The determining factor in the English, as in other traditions, had been the building material at hand. The log cabin was developed out of the great evergreen forests of northern Europe, with their lightweight, easily worked woods. By contrast, the English technique was based on oak, a strong but extremely hard and heavy wood. From this recalcitrant material there had evolved, over the centuries, the timber-framed house, the dominant wood building system of England.

The first real houses built by the English in America were of this type. Moreover, there was a logical reason why the early settlers were able to use such comparatively advanced construction techniques. Later pioneers, traveling west by horseback or covered wagon, could carry with them only the most rudimentary tools. The ax was their jack-of-all-trades. But the original colonists, arriving as they did by ship, could store bulky equipment in the hold. They brought pit saws and other tools with which to shape their timbers. From the first, they were able to carry on traditional English ways of building even in a wilderness setting.

The "faire framed house" which they constructed might be any of a number of variations on the timber frame system. Those most like the typical English house were "half-timbered." In such dwellings, the wooden framework was exposed and its wall spaces filled with brick nogging or wattle and daub, i.e., a primitive basketry daubed with mud, clay, or plaster. However, in the harsh climate of New England, such fillers proved a frail protection.

An alternative was the plank-framed house, in which vertical boards were mortised into the frame. The houses of the Pilgrims are believed to have been plank-frame (or at least sheathed in planks)—a system dating back to Saxon times in England. Old houses on Cape Cod and elsewhere have been discovered which incorporate this ancient building technique.

For further protection against the harsh climate, colonists added a surfacing of shingles or weatherboard (i.e., clapboards) to their half-timbered or plank-framed dwellings, giving us, very early, the American look in wooden houses. Exposed half-timbering remained the dominant system in England; but the clapboard or shingle covering, a warmer and more weathertight construction, rapidly became the American norm.

As early as Jamestown and Plymouth, colonists built timber-framed dwellings like those described above. Kilns for brickmaking were also established surprisingly soon. But in New England, the wooden house prevailed. Brick was used mainly for fireplaces and chimneys, with soft, sun-dried brick sometimes employed as nogging behind clapboard or shingle outer walls.

There were reasons for this. Most of New England lacked lime for proper mortar so that even walls of kiln-dried brick would have been perishable if exposed to the weather. In addition, many of New England's early colonists had emigrated from the southeastern counties of England where the yeoman farmer's house traditionally was built of wood.

The clapboard house predominated in Virginia, too, while a few brick houses eventually were built in New England. But when he could, the southern colonist used brick. Such dwellings, north or south, reflect the brick manor houses of England's eastern counties. However, brick was the more practical building material in the humid southern climate, where wood rotted easily. Moreover, at least a few Virginians were of a higher social class than New Englanders. For both status and permanence, the southern colonists preferred brick, though it was limited to the prosperous few even there.

Whether of wood, brick, or, much more rarely, stone, and whether built in the North or the South, these seventeenth century dwellings reflected a common English tradition. Distinguishing characteristics included a single file of rooms, sharply angled gables, steep (usually thatched) roofs, tiny casement windows, lean-to additions, and a general air of asymmetrical picturesqueness, all part of the medieval inheritance.

Such timber-framed and brick houses were uppermost in the colonists' minds. But other systems, including the English method of hewn log construction, occasionally were called upon as well. Writing in 1615, Ralph Hamor reported, in Henrico, Virginia: "five faire Block houses, or commaunders, wherein live the honester sort of people, as in Farmes in England . . ." Log blockhouses and garrisons were also built in Maine and New Hampshire as a refuge against Indian attack, and a few still remain today. These defensive structures were two stories in height, often with an overhanging upper story; and they required great skill in the making. Their carefully hewn logs were butted into corner posts or given dovetailed corners.

Such houses may have had their origin in the log "castles" erected in eleventh-century Britain by its Norman conquerors, before they could afford the leisure to build castles of stone. If so, their ancestry would reach back through Norman France to Scandinavia, ultimately deriving from the same tradition—a highly developed and varied one—that gave us the pioneer log cabin.

Though outside the mainstream of English architecture, log houses of this "castle," or garrison, type had continued in occasional use in England as an indication of status in farming communities. They were also built in isolated parts of Ireland and Scotland, where a defensive dwelling had long been the better part of valor; and they were recalled for a similar purpose in America.

However, when a house was needed in a hurry, and there were no proper tools for shaping timbers, the Englishman turned to another remembered type of log construction: the palisade. This method was even more ancient, its roots reaching back beyond history to paleolithic Europe. As a stockade surrounding a settlement, it had been called upon throughout the ages. Julius Caesar's Roman camps, William the Conqueror's early log castles, His Royal Majesty's colony at Jamestown, and Daniel Boone's Kentucky fort, all were protected from unfriendly natives by a palisade of upright logs.

But the system also was used in building houses. This method had entered Britain in the fifth century with Anglo-Saxon invaders, who preferred their own crude palisaded huts to the villas of departed Romans. The system lingered on in isolated backwaters throughout the British Isles, employed for huts and outbuildings long after it had passed from common usage in the architecture of the day.

Because it was so easy to build—simply, logs set upright into the ground to form walls and roofed over with thatch—it was revived as a crude shelter when English colonists pushed inland in early America. A book by George Scot, published in 1685, describes a settlement in New Jersey: "Most of the country houses are built of wood, only trees split and set up on end on the ground." No doubt, if they had known how, these first inland pioneers would have built the now-familiar log cabin; but when they lacked appropriate tools, they reverted to the ancient English type of primitive log construction.

This fact takes us full circle to the beginning of English architecture. For the "palisadoed" hut was the distant ancestor of the seventeenth-century timber-framed house. Thus, in America, the end product of years of architectural evolution existed in the same time frame with the primitive building system from which it sprang. In fact, one glimpses virtually every stage in the development of the English house repeated haphazardly in colonial America.

A brief summary will show this progression. Beginning with the palisade, the next step was the puncheon wall, a system devised to save both wood and labor. Whole or split logs, called

"punches," were set upright like a palisade, but spaced apart from each other. The void was approximately the same width as the log and was filled with wattle and daub. With this system, only half as many timbers had to be used for a wall—hence, the name which would continue in use to its quite different descendant: "half-timber." Houses of "punches sett into the Ground" were mentioned at Berkely, on the James River, in 1619. Though no English example of a puncheon house is shown, we do illustrate the similar French system (Figure 94) known as *poteaux sur solle*.

Another primitive method, thought to have been used for a few houses at Jamestown, was cruck (or crutch) construction. Here, the house was framed by a series of "gothic" arches made from sections of curved tree trunks which met at the ridgepole. The thatched roof of such buildings reached nearly to the ground, a primitive A-frame. In larger cruck houses, roof thatching stopped a few feet above ground; and the lower walls were made of vertical logs and filler—the puncheon system.

In the evolution of the house, it was but a short leap from the cruck roof with puncheon walls to the box-frame with hewn wooden sills and beams, wall posts, and roof trusses. The Tudor cottage was the first box-framed English house. Despite a frame skeleton, this type reveals its puncheon lineage with walls of heavy, closely spaced vertical timbers, filled between with wattle and daub. Tradition dies hard, and builders were not yet sure of the strength of the new framework.

Early in the Tudor period (1485-1631) brick had become popular in England for the first time since the Roman occupation more than a thousand years before. This standardized, man-made material was reintroduced from Holland in the fifteenth century and manufactured in East Anglia. So lively was the trade across the Channel that, on the east coast of England, it became cheaper to build with imported Holland brick than with English timber hauled from 50 miles inland.

Where plentiful, brick was used to build entire houses. It also was substituted for wattle and daub as a filler for the timber frame, set in her-ringbone and other decorative patterns.

Sometimes, the lower story of the Tudor house was built of brick or stone, with a timber and plaster upper structure.

Another feature of the Tudor house was the overhanging upper story known as a "jetty." In crowded towns, where land was at a premium, builders snatched at air space. Each succeeding story, sometimes four or five of them, overhung the one below, until opposing attics nearly met above the street. Since the jetty also was used on farmhouses, where crowding was not a factor, it may have been borrowed from the log garrison.

The Tudor period also saw the widespread adoption of the brick chimney. For centuries, the smoke from English fires had escaped as best it could through a louver in the roof, through primitive wood and clay hoods, or, in Norman times, through slits in the stone castle wall. Now a new fuel—coal—with a heavy, unpleasant smoke suddenly produced the chimney stack. Tudor chimneys were fantastic affairs, great stepped pyramids at the bottom with corkscrew stacks of patterned brickwork, capped by crenellation.

The combination of red brick with the famous black and white half-timbering, the jutting upper stories, the thatched roof, and decorated chimneys gave the Tudor cottage a fairy-tale quaintness. But few of these characteristics made their way to the New World. The jettied upper story appeared briefly in New England; the pyramidal chimney became characteristic of the South. There was a faint Tudor echo in the small Virginia village of Henricopolis. Writing in 1612, one Robert Johnson notes the existence there of timber-framed houses, "the first stories all of bricks."

However, it was the more recent Elizabethan half-timbered house which underlay most colonial wooden building. As English forests diminished, experiments had been made reducing the size and quantity of nonsupporting wooden timbers. Thus called upon, the oak frame performed nobly. *Voilà:* the Elizabethan half-timbered house with its heavy wooden skeleton and lightweight curtain wall. Tie beams and the new diagonal bracing were comparatively thin and spaced widely apart. The much larger voids thus created were filled, as before, with wattle and daub, brick, or other nogging.

It is interesting to note that—like the twentieth-century steel-framed skyscraper—Elizabethan houses in sixteenth-century England often were very glassy. Windows were many and large, even though individual panes of glass were small. Contemporary comment called them "more glass than wall,"[1] and their interiors remain unusually bright and airy even by today's standards.

The combination of cheap glass and a mild climate, plus the separation of frame and wall structure, had produced this innovation. But in the colonies, the weather was severe, glass scarce, expensive, and subject to taxation; hence, small windows in the transplanted houses.

The Elizabethans had kept the jetty which was such a popular feature of the Tudor house. But in the Jacobean period (1603-25) the overhang was outlawed in the cities as a fire hazard; and the half-timbered town house acquired a flat front. Brick nogging or plaster remained the usual filler, but sometimes the house was plastered over in its entirety, including the frame itself. Also used were tile and lapped weatherboarding (both introduced from Holland) as well as vertical and horizontal flush boards and board-and-batten. Thus, the colonist had a full range of surfacing upon which to call for his wooden house.

So far we have not considered that other traditional building material: stone. In England, wood has the more ancient lineage, though a few small stone churches remain from Anglo-Saxon times. Not until the Norman period did stone construction come into its own; and even then, wood was, as we know, used for the earliest Norman castles behind their log stockades. But soon the massive, towering stone keep became the refuge of king and baron, while the wooden house was relegated to lesser folk.

This split in tradition was joined once more with the appearance of the manor house, which began to replace the castle in the thirteenth and fourteenth centuries. Gradually, wood, stone, and brick construction came to be used for dwellings more and more alike. Stone

sometimes was employed for fairly small houses; half-timbering, at least by Elizabethan times, for very large ones. Plans were based on the traditional hall and had much in common, though differing in size and the number of wings. By the time of American settlement, one can speak of an English vocabulary of architecture common to both masonry and wood, to manor house, farmhouse, and crofter's cottage.

This brief outline also shows that architectural change, especially as it applied to the dwelling, was very much an evolutionary process. A new feature was added here, an old one eliminated there, until the Jacobean house became recognizably different from its early Tudor predecessor.

This same process was active in America. The pressures of climate and new ways of living went to work at once on the traditional dwelling. Inappropriate methods of building were abandoned and useful devices borrowed from other settlers. Houses were simplified and adapted until, well before the eighteenth century, regional types began to emerge in the northern and southern colonies. On the other hand, certain familiar features might persist through centuries; for example, a Tudor chimney, still part of a Greek Revival farmhouse in nineteenth-century America four hundred years after its original appearance in England.

An English Tradition

The English Hall

1. The Half-Timbered Hall: *A Cavalier Dwelling, Jamestown, Va., ca. 1608.*

2. The Weatherboarded Hall: *Plantation House, the Tidewater South, early 17th c.*

3. The Brick Hall: *Resurrection Manor, Anne Arundel County, Md., ca. 1653; enlarged to two rooms, 18th c.*

"But Halls we build for us and ours to dwell in them whilst we live here."[2]

So wrote William Strachey, first secretary of the Jamestown colony in the year 1610, conjuring up, in twentieth-century minds, a vision of baronial living in the American wilderness.

Historian Henry Chandlee Forman discovered this couplet and has described what it meant to seventeenth-century Englishmen. The word "hall" then had few of the large associations that cling to it today. It was used interchangeably with "house"—and "house," in turn, derived from the Norse *eld-hús,* meaning "fire-house" or "hearth house," i.e., a single heated living space.[2]

The hall was, in fact, the basic unit of the English dwelling, to which other rooms, if they existed at all, were merely attachments. The lord of the manor might build subsidiary wings to enlarge his great hall. The English crofter knew no such luxury. He made do with a hall only and a small one at that: the one-bay English house, approximately 16 feet in length. It was this tiny, one-room hall that was the first permanent dwelling built by English colonists in America. In this single room, as in the halls of old England, the entire family lived, worked, cooked, ate, and slept.

1. This one-room hut from the reconstructed Jamestown settlement shows the type of house that the first English colonists in America must have built. It was a primitive version of the Elizabethan half-timbered hall, with a heavy wooden frame and walls of wattle and daub, diagonally braced.

This tiny dwelling was a vast improvement over the caves and dugouts that had preceded it—even though it had a dirt floor, its "wind-hole" was closed only by shutter, and its stick chimney was a fire hazard. Some of the early huts had no chimney at all; only an opening in the thatched roof.

Though a makeshift structure, its method of timber framing was to prove long-lived. Disguised by a covering of planks, clapboards, or shingles, it would remain the characteristic wood building system in America until the invention of balloon framing in the nineteenth century.

2. This could have been the "manor house" of a Tidewater plantation in the early days of colonial settlement. Though only a one-room hall, its refinements included a stepped Tudor chimney, a glass window, and weatherboard walls (southerners still call clapboards by this English name). Though weatherboarding was traditional in only a few counties in England, this minor vernacular gave us the American clapboard house.

Already, this is a typical southern dwelling. The end chimney, transplanted by colonists from England's eastern counties, became characteristic of the American South. As there was a plentiful amount of lime for mortaring in the Tidewater region, an outside chimney could withstand weathering there. The end chimney also helped dissipate heat during southern summers. Families had to keep a small fire burning in the house at all times, even though much of the summer cooking took place out of doors, as it had in the courtyards of England. Note the freestanding chimney stack, a protection against firing the thatched roof.

3. This tiny colonial hall once belonged to the son of the Earl of Albion. It is a miniature of the English great hall, which would have had a chimney at the other end as well. Sulgrave Manor, the ancestral home of the Washingtons in England, is a large, two-story example of the type. This one housed a family in a space only 12 by 16 feet.

A notable feature is the combination of gable wall and chimney into one continuous element, a treatment that rapidly became part of the southern vernacular. Like many early brick houses, this one originally was plastered over. However, our drawing leaves a corner exposed to show the type of brickwork underneath. The front of the house is Flemish bond (alternating headers and stretchers); the end is English bond. Plastering an entire house, whether brick or half-timber, was a Jacobean innovation, as was the flat gable itself. Dormer windows were added earlier in the South than in New England, but the first ones were very small.

4. This little hall, believed to have been the type built by the Pilgrims, is another version of the timber-framed house. Walls are of vertical planks, mortised or pegged to the timber frame,

an ancient system dating to Saxon times in England. Plank-frame walls have been found beneath shingles and wainscoting in old Cape Cod houses. The Pilgrims had only the planks for walls, a thin covering, but warmer than wattle and daub.

The roof illustrated here is of crude shingles or "shakes" (thatch was outlawed as a fire hazard in Plymouth in 1629). There was no glass; but windowpanes were made of oiled paper brought by ship from England. Note also the wood-framed clay chimney. In effect, this was a hood, extending down through the loft and ending as a hole in the loft flooring. The fire was built directly below, on the earth floor of the downstairs room. Chimney fires were so frequent that seventeenth-century households always kept a filled water bucket next to the chimney in the loft.

5. The essence of seventeenth-century New England is expressed in this stark little cottage, with its tiny diamond-paned casements, plank door, and high peaked roof (the source of its name). Such a steep pitch indicates that the roof once was thatched.

This house contains only one downstairs room—the hall—plus a second-story chamber (the medieval word for bedroom) and a minuscule loft. Next to the fireplace are a narrow, winding stair (some houses had only a ladder) and a tiny entry, called a "porch." The inside chimney was traditional in the southeastern counties of England from which most of these colonists came. Soft brick and lack of good mortar, plus the cold climate of New England, ensured its survival as a regional type.

Shingles may have been an American translation of the Dutch tile that had become fashionable for walls and roofs in Jacobean England. Or they may have been a vernacular survivor from the Saxons, who had used oak shingles more than a thousand years earlier.

An English Tradition

The Hall-and-Parlor

6. This two-room dwelling, known as a "hall-and-parlor," was the yeoman's approximation of an English manor house. In that much larger dwelling, wings were sometimes added at either end of the great hall: one a buttery or "bottlery" for storing wine and food; the other a parlor, or "conversation room," for the private use of the family. In the cottage version, one end of the hall was simply partitioned off to create a parlor, or a second small room was added to the original house. The parlor was the "best room" as compared to the utilitarian hall. Nevertheless, it probably contained a bed, as did most rooms in those early houses, where families were large and space at a premium.

Our example also illustrates a familiar Maryland vernacular: the use of brick for gable ends with front and rear walls of wood. These are vertical board-and-batten, more weathertight than plain planking and of equally ancient origin. Later houses used horizontal weatherboards. A brick hall-and-parlor house, the finest remaining example of the type, is shown in Figure 20.

6a. The dotted line shows how a second partition was added to create the "central passage" house, a later eighteenth-century type.

7. Though not usually called by that name, the early two-story New England house—like its one-story Tidewater cousin—was based on an English hall-and-parlor plan. However, in New England, a great central chimney block separated the two rooms.

A house might grow to this size simply by adding rooms to the original hall. This was the case with the Howland house, home of a second-generation Pilgrim, which still stands in Plymouth today. The hall, with bedchamber above (known as the hall chamber), was built in the seventeenth century; the parlor and parlor chamber were added eighty-four years later. Each part has been restored to its original appearance. The hall has diamond-paned casements and a simple plank door; the parlor, eighteenth-century sash. Note the vertical strip of wood that seals the joining of the two parts. To reveal the narrow "medieval" silhouette of the typical single-file dwelling, a later lean-to, at the rear, was omitted in this drawing.

6. Board-and-Batten: *The Ending of Contro-versie, Wenlocke Christison House, Talbot County, Md., ca. 1670.*

8. Some two-story hall-and-parlor houses were built all at one time. However, doors and windows still were off-center, revealing the large hall and smaller parlor within. The finest among them reproduced all the furbelows of English tradition, including the Tudor "jetty," or overhanging upper story, with "corner drops," or "pendills," as seen here.

Today, every dwelling with a jettied upper story is popularly known as a "garrison house." But the true garrison was built only in frontier out-posts. Not all had the overhanging upper story. Some were brick. Wooden garrisons were of hewn logs (Figure 72). Later, these were sometimes covered with clapboards or shingles, creating an appearance much like their frame counterparts—hence, the confusion in name. The garrison's overhanging upper story—when it did exist—was given loopholes for shooting down on attackers, just as legend tells it. But the usual jettied house was not defensive. Like this one, it was simply a copy of the better Tudor farmhouse.

6a. Hall-and-Parlor Plan.

7. The New England Farmhouse: *Jabez Howland House, Plymouth, Mass., hall 1667; parlor ca. 1750; restored 1941.*

8. The Jettied House: *Parson Capen House, Topsfield, Mass., 1683.*

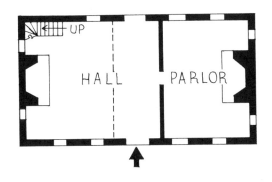

An English Tradition

The Cross House

9. The Southern Manor House: *Bacon's Castle, Arthur Allen House, Surrey County, Va., ca. 1655; seized by Nathaniel Bacon, 1676.*

9a. Cross Plan.

9. Though looking very much grander, Bacon's Castle is fundamentally a hall-and-parlor dwelling. It is known as a ''cross house''—turned into a cruciform by adding a porch at front, a matching stair tower at rear, and a passage between the two. The cross plan was well known in England, and the projecting two-story entrance was a typical feature of many Elizabethan dwellings. The little bedroom above the vestibule was known as the porch chamber.

The house was called a castle, or fortress, because of its use as a fortified refuge during Bacon's Rebellion in 1676. It also has been called the finest example of Jacobean architecture in America. As such it illustrates the way in which a new fashion (i.e., the Flemish gable with its Renaissance steps and cusping) was applied over an old tradition. Such a mixture was typically Jacobean—a transitional style between the medieval and the classic.

The little kitchen cottage at right is a medieval remnant, retained as an outbuilding to a great house, stylistically more advanced. It is attached to the main dwelling by a ''penthouse'' or ''curtain''—names deriving from the sheltered walkways that had connected court-yard structures in England since the twelfth century. Not visible are stables and little ''factories''—work buildings for everything from baking to blacksmithing—that were placed about the rear courtyard. In effect, the southern plantation was a feudal manor, using bond-servants or slaves instead of serfs.

9a. Rooms in the cross house were based on the traditional hall-and-parlor. In the more pretentious houses, the hall became the drawing room, with cooking and other utilitarian chores relegated to outbuildings.

10. This remarkable restoration drawing shows one of this country's rare examples of exposed half-timbering: truly a piece of Elizabethan England transplanted to America. It reveals what colonial frame houses would have looked like without their clapboard or shingle ''skins.'' A thatched roof and catted clay chimney add to the medieval effect.

The name ''cross house'' commonly refers to the southern colonial type, and, in structure, this half-timbered New England dwelling could

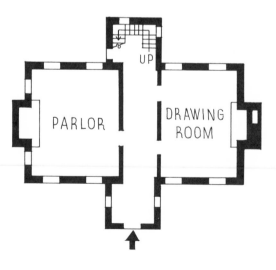

PARLOR   DRAWING ROOM   UP

10. A New England Parsonage: *Springfield Parsonage, Springfield, Mass., 1639.*

11. A Magistrate's House: *The Witch House, Jonathan Corwin House, Salem, Mass., ca. 1675; lean-to addition, 18th c.; restored 20th c.*

hardly present more contrast to the brick house of Virginia. In plan, too, it differs: minus a rear stair tower and plus a center chimney. But the same porch and porch chamber give it a form strikingly similar to the southern example. Obviously, this is the same house, modified in plan and wearing different outer clothing.

11. Here is the Elizabethan tradition in full panoply. If the understructure were exposed, rather than clapboarded over, this house would look very much like the half-timbered Springfield Parsonage (Figure 10). However, with its jettied upper stories, carved corner drops, and Tudor arch above the doorway, it is a more elaborate construction.

The projecting porch and porch chamber relate this dwelling to the cross house. But the similarity of form is obscured by large luçome dormers, an Elizabethan means of lighting the loft, borrowed from the French. Also modifying the basic house is a typical New England addition: the lean-to. This shed-roofed attachment adds another row of first-floor rooms to the original hall and parlor and turns the house into an incipient saltbox. The Witch House was owned by Jonathan Corwin, a magistrate of Salem and one of the commissioners at the famous witchcraft trials.

An English Tradition

The Wing House

12. The L-Plan: *The Rev. Henry Whitfield House, Guilford, Conn., 1639; 20th-century restoration.*

13. The Continuous House: *Benjamin Abbot Farmhouse, Andover, Mass., 1685.*

12. Restored to its seventeenth-century appearance, this 300-year-old house still rears its massive stone walls in the Connecticut countryside. It was the home of Guilford's minister, designed also as a "bawn," or fort, in case of Indian attack. The dwelling is the only remaining colonial example of the English "great hall," the large manorial version of the tiny yeoman's hall (Figure 2).

Fortified manor houses like this evolved during the Tudor period, when the open medieval hall, with its central hearth, acquired a second floor of bedrooms and stepped end chimneys. Here the hall also has been enlarged with a wing, the traditional way of adding to the English house. This is the L-plan, with the wing extending toward the rear from one end of the hall. The T-plan, with a wing at the center, and the U-plan, with wings at both ends, were variants. Stone construction was rare in the colonies, and the stepped end chimney rare in New England. But the Whitfield house shows the coherence of English architecture, despite size, material, or region.

13. As time went on, New England farmers adopted a special way of enlarging the house,

creating in the process a familiar regional type. This is the "continuous house," in which dwelling, shed, and stables connect, allowing stock to be cared for without venturing out-of-doors in winter. The kitchen is snugly inside the house itself. This scheme was an adaptation to a cold climate, quite different from the southern arrangement, even though both added wings to the side of the house (Figure 9).

The continuous architecture of New England was not entirely a clever Yankee invention. A covered corridor between outbuilding and house had been a widely used medieval feature. Another echo of the Middle Ages is the U-shaped placement of buildings to form a court. Though the windows of the Abbot farmhouse are new sliding sash instead of casements, the entry remains traditional in form: a miniaturization of the medieval porch.

14. This cozy room was the principal living-dining-work space of the early colonial dwelling. Typically medieval are the beamed ceiling, the immense cooking fireplace with its hewn "mantel tree," casement windows, and walls of whitewashed plaster—features common to

early houses, north and south. Pine planks, vertically set as wainscoting, also were a typical seventeenth-century wall treatment. Note the massive "summer beam," the central support for the upper story, characteristically joining the fireplace at right angles.

There were no closets. Instead, clothes were hung on pegs. The wooden chest, paneled in a Jacobean design, stored linens and out-of-season apparel. It probably was brought from England, but the simple cradle and high-backed "settle" were homemade.

Most meals were cooked in the big stew kettle that hung from a trammel or crane in the fireplace. Roasts were turned on a spit and bread baked overnight in the Dutch oven. Herbs, handy for seasoning, were strung from a nearby beam. Toasting forks, gridirons, spiders, saucepans, teakettles, and tankards attest to the variety of food and drink that colonists could prepare. However, even the huge fireplace could not heat the room adequately. At any distance from it ink is said to have frozen in inkwells in winter. The only truly warm spot was the "cubby seat" within the fireplace itself.

14. Typical Seventeenth-Century Hall:
A Composite Drawing.

An English Tradition

The Lean-to House

The preceding pages have shown the architectural inheritance that seventeenth-century colonists brought with them from England. The pages that follow show what happened to these traditional houses in America.

Some, especially in isolated areas like Cape Cod, remained close to the English original. Others, particularly in the South, were dramatically changed by the climate of their new land. Such houses became regional types, persisting through the centuries and lending a special flavor to the local architecture of which they were a part.

However, it is precisely such vernacular dwellings that have caused so much confusion. For as they adjusted to different geographical and cultural conditions, they also moved forward in time. In an attempt to decode the process of architectural change, we show a sampling of typical northern and southern houses and of the styles that some of them passed through during 350 years of American history.

15. One of the first changes to appear in the colonial dwelling was the addition of a lean-to across the rear of the lower story. It was the easiest method of enlarging the house, and it soon became a New England type. The example shown here started as a one-room hall but a lean-to kitchen was added at the rear. The result: a tiny seventeenth-century saltbox.

The "stone-ender," so-called because of its massive exterior chimney, was a Welsh type that took root in Rhode Island. In Massachusetts, inside brick chimneys were the rule, though fieldstone could be had for the taking. In Connecticut, stone was used for chimneys, but these were interior affairs. The reason behind the stone-ender is simple: only in Rhode Island was there plentiful lime for mortaring and of a quality to resist weathering.

Note the triple chimney stack, indicating that there were three fireplaces, one in the major room, one in the lean-to, and one in the loft. The break in the roofline reveals the tall, narrow silhouette of the original house.

15. The Rhode Island Stone-Ender: *Thomas Clemence House, Manton, R.I., ca. 1680.*

16. Typical Connecticut Saltbox: *18th c., a composite drawing.*

17. Typical Saltbox Plan.

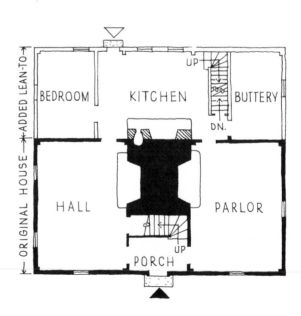

18. Nantucket Whale House: *Shanunga, or Betsy Carey House, Siasconset, Nantucket Island, Mass., original hall ca. 1682; lean-tos ca. 1700.*

19. The Out-Shot House: *Cushing House, Hingham, Mass., 1720.*

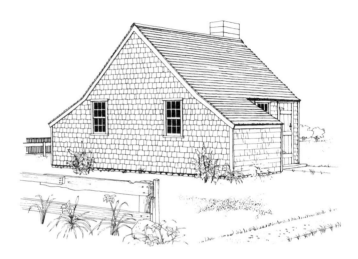

16. The saltbox is seen here in a later and larger version, with eighteenth-century sash windows and shingled outer walls. Now there is no break between house and lean-to; the long, sweeping roofline, like the lid of a colonial saltbox, gives the type its familiar name. In houses like this, the lean-to might be part of the original structure. So popular was the type in Connecticut that it came to be known as a Connecticut saltbox, even though it was found in other states.

Americans once believed the saltbox to be their own clever invention, but now it is recognized as English in origin. Historian Margaret Wood writes: "By the later 16th and especially the 17th century, the English farmhouse had become a rectangular block . . . with a lean-to 'outshut.' . . . It was sometimes off the end of the hall, but usually at the back, often under a long 'catslide' roof."[3] The New England saltbox was such a house.

17. This plan shows how a standard hall-and-parlor dwelling was turned into a saltbox. In addition to adding space cheaply, the lean-to had other advantages. Small rooms, partitioned off each end, provided insulation by air space for the central portion. With the immense cooking fireplace serving a compact and

sheltered pocket, this inner room was the warmest in the house. It acted as kitchen, dining, and work room for the entire family throughout the bitterly cold winter. In reverse, as a "summer kitchen," it kept heat out of the hall and parlor during the warm months. Food was conveniently stored in a buttery partitioned off the cold north end of the lean-to. At the southern end was the parents' bedroom, sometimes called the "borning room," since it was here that the many children who filled these houses were born. Above the lean-to were two more small bedrooms known as the "lean-to chambers."

18. Built as a whaler's hut, this tiny cottage is a Nantucket type, reflecting a way of life long gone from the island. It is one of many variations of the lean-to house that was not a saltbox. The original dwelling was a one-room hall, only 12 by 15 feet, open to the rafters. The hearth was against one wall, sleeping space at the opposite side of the room. Semiprivacy was afforded by a low board partition or curtaining.

As shown here, the house is in a later stage, after enlargement by identical lean-tos at front and rear. These were used as extra sleeping cubicles, opening off the original "bedroom." Additional sleeping space was provided by an

open platform hung above the main bed-chamber. So equipped, a whale house slept a crew of six or a family of eight. Henry Chandlee Forman has traced the "hanging loft" to the Middle Ages in Britain. It still exists in Wales, where it is called a "crogloft." On Nantucket, it now typically is partitioned off, creating a tiny bedroom still reached, as in the old days, by a ladder.

19. Here, a lean-to helps produce a typical cluster of sheds at the rear of a New England dwelling without making it into a saltbox. In this case, the lean-to has been placed below the main roofline and is cut into by a small wing, creating an asymmetrical silhouette. Unseen from the front, these sheds offered handy storage for such necessities as firewood and a winter's supply of staple food. A wing like that at the left might be a summer kitchen, removing this source of heat from the main house during dog days.

These attachments illustrate the medieval English practice of adding "out-shots" to the main body of the house wherever needed. Different placement of wings could create an L-plan (basically that seen here), a U-plan, or a T-plan—all well-known English variants.

An English Tradition

The Tudor Chimney

20. Most seventeenth-century Virginia dwellings were of wood, but few, if any, have survived. This little brick manor house sums up the early type. The outside chimney was characteristic and, as these drawings show, remained part of the southern house throughout the centuries.

Early plantation houses were small. The Thoroughgood House—the outstanding example of a hall-and-parlor dwelling—was a typical size. It was built by a former bondservant who worked out his passage money and rose to become a member of Virginia's House of Burgesses.

The pyramidal chimney and T-shaped stacks are Tudor in origin. Trim is of wood, but it is colored light tan—not white—to simulate the stone trim used with brick in Tudor England. Glazed header bricks that edge the gable trace back to eleventh-century Normandy. American features include second-story loopholes for firing at Indians, "hideyholes," and a secret passage leading underground to the James River.

21. This brick town house, with its pyramidal Tudor chimney, is basically the same dwelling as its seventeenth-century predecessor; but eighteenth-century details are in the new Georgian style. Windows are now sash instead of casements, and flat, splayed lintels have replaced brick arches above windows and door. The door itself is paneled. A "jerkinhead" roof is halfway to the Palladian hipped roof—slanted on all four sides—that accompanied formal Georgian architecture. A further attempt at classic dignity is seen in the raised first floor: a doll's version of the *piano nobile,* in which the main floor occupies the second story, reached by a commanding flight of exterior stairs.

Though built as an 'ordinary,' used primarily by plantation owners when attending the Provincial Assembly, it follows one of the typical Virginia house forms of 1725-50. Such houses often aped the mansions of the English aristocracy, while the cottage types, of both the South and New England, reproduced the English farmhouse.

20. The Tudor Manor House: *Adam Thoroughgood House, Princess Anne County, Va., 1640.*

21. The Georgian Town House: *The Red Lion, Williamsburg, Va., 1730.*

22. The Georgian Cottage: *Typical Maryland Vernacular, early 18th c.*

23. The Southern Plantation House: *Skinner House, near Hertford, N.C., ca. 1800.*

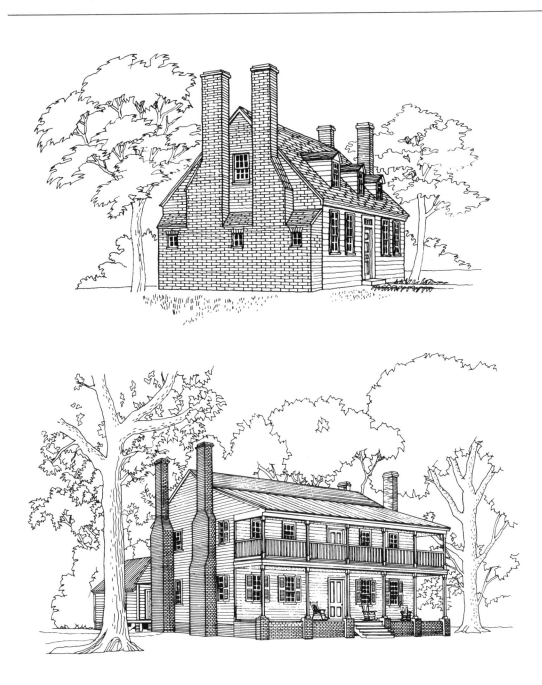

22. The outside Tudor chimney was attached to all sorts of houses, small and large, brick and wood. This example illustrates an evolution from the small, early hall-and-parlor cottage, with its single-file medieval plan (Figure 6). To enlarge that minimum dwelling type, a second file of rooms has been added at rear and chimneys doubled to accommodate the additional fireplaces.

Traditionally English are the little "chimney pents," miniature lean-tos of brick, placed between and on either side of the stacks. Opening to the interior, they provided cubbyholes for wood or other storage or cozy fireside seats. Sash windows and a paneled door with ribbon lights show that this cottage is of the Georgian period. But stepped chimneys remain, an echo of Tudor England, unchanged within the changing fabric of an American house.

23. More than two hundred years after it appeared in seventeenth-century Virginia, the Tudor chimney still persists on this vastly changed American dwelling. The house itself has made a major adjustment to climate. A double-tiered porch across the whole of the front transforms it into a typical southern plantation house.

The verandah seldom, if ever, appeared on English houses until after the Revolution. This postwar example is in North Carolina, a meeting ground for the English from Virginia and French settlers from South Carolina, where the galleried house was a French vernacular type. Settlers of different backgrounds often borrowed from each other in the process of creating a new regional architecture. Though two stories in height, the Skinner house remains a simple farmhouse. But it is a forerunner of the stately Greek Revival mansions that would become the pride of the antebellum South.

An English Tradition

The Gambrel Roof

24. A Medieval Echo: *Jonathan Brooks House, West Medford, Mass., mid-18th c.*

25. A Southern Variant: *Lord Mayor William Ramsay House; original house of one room per floor, ca. 1724.*

24. The shift to Georgian architecture took place in a variety of ways. Here, a gambrel roof helped transform the traditional English house. This feature, which appeared in England in the seventeenth century, was largely an eighteenth-century phenomenon in America. It had a double function: to enlarge the upper story of the gabled house and to lower its sharp, medieval peak toward the classic lines of the Palladian villa.

This gambrel caps a house that otherwise retains its narrow medieval silhouette, reflecting the single file of rooms within. Also medieval are its "watershed dormers," gabled porch, and enlargement by an ell at the rear. Yet the house has become a Georgian "center hall colonial." Even the little medieval porch has been given a classic treatment. The Brooks house is of interest as a transitional type. But it suggests the problem faced by the observer of architecture. As one historian put it: "The biologist never finds the tail of a lion grafted to the body of a cow."

25. The Ramsay house, oldest dwelling in Alexandria, Virginia, is the southern counterpart of the Brooks house and a textbook example of the way in which climate can remodel a dwelling. Obviously, the basic house, including the gambrel roof, is the same; but outside chimneys, raised basement, and especially the open porch are responses to the southern climate.

The Ramsay house also demonstrates one way in which this new type of porch—very rare before the Revolution—may have become attached to the English dwelling. The entrance facade (not visible in this view) remained formally Georgian and flat-fronted. The porch was in the rear, turned toward the Potomac River. Here, William Ramsay, who was a merchant as well as mayor of Alexandria, could enjoy a cooling breeze while keeping an eye on his shipping. The conservative English maintained appearances at the front of the house even when they succumbed to the uses and pleasures of a verandah at the rear.

26. Early Georgian (The Queen Anne House):
Deputy Governor Jonathan Nichols, Jr., House (Nichols-Wanton-Hunter House), Newport, R.I., 1748; exterior and interior details ca. 1756.

27. Late Georgian (The Federal House): *Col. Ruggles Woodbridge House, South Hadley, Mass., 1788.*

26. This house, one of the finest in eighteenth-century Newport, is a seacoast interpretation of the gambrel, with significant differences from its inland cousins. The slopes of the roof have been adjusted to accommodate a widow's walk. In addition, the medieval single file of rooms has been doubled, creating a deeper house and a broader roofline. Though deriving from the vernacular, this dwelling is a mansion. Its spacious, high-ceilinged rooms, elegantly paneled and furnished, reveal how early coastal prosperity changed the simple colonial house.

The doorway is of unusual interest. Its deeply carved Baroque pediment is characteristic of the late Stuart or Queen Anne Style which ended about 1714 in England. Because of a time lag between England and her colonies, the Queen Anne house was built in America during the Georgian period and usually has been called Georgian in this country. Like many early colonial dwellings, the exterior of this one originally was unpainted and weathered gray.

27. Here, the modest medieval farmhouse has been all but obscured by elegant new clothes. Characteristically Georgian are the quoins at the corners, pedimented dormers, a Palladian fanlight, and a doorway framed by piers in the Ionic order. The fully developed gambrel roof, covering a double file of rooms, achieves a proportionately lower, more classic silhouette. Outside shutters also are part of this later fashion.

In England, the classic vocabulary had been expressed in houses of red brick with pale Portland stone trim. In New England, inventive carpenters turned masonry quoins, pilasters, piers, columns, and pediments into wood. By this route, the elegance of the Italian Renaissance was transferred into a wood vernacular in the small towns of eighteenth-century America. However, it was a little late in arriving. As sometimes happened, this typically Georgian house was built after the Revolution, during the period known in America as Federal.

An English Tradition

The Gabled House

28. Early American (The Medieval Echo): *Typical Elizabethan Farmhouse, 17th c.*

29. The Queen Anne House (Late Stuart or Baroque): *from ca. 1700-50; Mission House, Stockbridge, Mass., 1739.*

The simple gabled house is such a familiar type that it is almost a synonym for home. It is the child's first drawing of a house, the advertisement in the Sunday newspaper, and the clever invention (in primitive stake and thatch) of Bronze Age Man.

Like that of other species, its survival has been based on adaptability. The saltbox and the gambrel were superior solutions to specific problems. But changes of style and circumstance cut their development short.

By contrast, the gabled house proved to be the always-flexible dwelling. It has survived, chameleonlike, as an Elizabethan hall-and-parlor, a Georgian colonial, and a modern house. Inside the basic form, old plans have given way to new as patterns of living changed throughout the centuries. Seldom the darling of the times, it demonstrates the victory of the generalist. The illustrations which follow show the gabled house from the seventeenth century into the twentieth.

28. Distinguishing features: massive central chimney; casement windows; inside shutters; asymmetrical hall-and-parlor plan with off-center doorway; plank-framed doorway or small gabled porch; plank door; narrow clapboards or shingles weathered gray or dark brown; single file of rooms; sometimes jettied upper stories, corner drops, and brackets.

29. Distinguishing features: symmetrical facade with centered entry; pilastered doorway with deeply carved Baroque pediment; elaborately paneled door; sash windows with small panes, 9 in top sash, 6 in bottom; inside shutters; double file of rooms; twin chimneys with fireplaces between front and rear rooms; exterior usually weathered gray.

30. Distinguishing features: sash windows with small panes, 12 over 12 (18th c.), larger panes 6 over 6 (late 18th, early 19th c.); outside shutters after ca. 1740; center chimney (early 18th c.; occasionally as late as 1780); center hall plan with twin chimneys (rarely before 1740); simple, paneled door and pilastered doorway with triangular or curved pediment or flat architrave and ribbon lights (18th c.); fanlight (late 18th, early 19th c.); exterior weathered gray or painted muted, usually dark colors, with buff trim (early and mid-18th c.); pale yellow, pinkish tan, pale gray, or gray-blue with white trim (late 18th and early 19th c.); white with dark green shutters (19th c.).

31. Distinguishing features: central pavilion, delicately pedimented and pilastered; pedimented doorway with fanlight and sidelights; Palladian window; pedimented gable with attic fanlight; pilastered corners; splayed window arches; modillioned cornice; symmetrical center hall plan; large sash windows with small panes 12 over 12 or larger panes 6 over 6; pastel painted clapboard with white trim, white or dark shutters.

32. Distinguishing features: gable end usually turned toward street to emphasize temple form; heavily pedimented gable with wide, plain entablature; gable wall sometimes pilastered; entry pillared or pilastered; pavilionlike, one-story wings at one or both sides; window sash 6 over 6; latticework trellises; entire house painted white in imitation of marble, with dark green shutters or no shutters.

33. Distinguishing features: gable end usually toward the street; round-headed attic window; other windows occasionally round-headed; deep moldings and heavy bracketing under the eaves and above windows; canopied, bracketed doorway; service rooms usually indented from main body of house; painted buff or gray to simulate stone with light or dark trim.

34. Distinguishing features: one or more verandahs; gingerbread trim in Gothic motifs; house and trim painted in a monotone color scheme of stone gray, slate blue, fawn, or moss green to blend with the landscape (white was considered vulgar); shutters in a muted dark color.

35. Distinguishing features: overhanging upper story, borrowed from the seventeenth-century New England farmhouse (Figure 28), erroneously supposed to have been a garrison; eighteenth-century Georgian colonial styling in shuttered windows; often factory fabricated clapboards of vinyl or enameled metal in nineteenth-century Federal colors (white or pastels); ''picture windows'' adapted from modern architecture; sheets of brick veneer or artificial stone typically applied as trim at front of lower story (simulating the brick lower story of a Tudor house); attached garage.

30. Georgian Colonial (A New England Vernacular): *Composite drawing of typical 18th c. Early Georgian House, built, with minor changes, to ca 1840 or 1850.*

31. Late Georgian or Federal (The Palladian Echo): *from ca. 1790-1810; Joshua Monroe House, South Shaftsbury, Vt., ca. 1800.*

32. Greek Revival (The Temple-Form House): *from ca. 1825-50; Jonathan McFarland House, Chagrin Falls, Ohio, ca. 1825.*

33. Italianate (The Bracketed Style): *from ca. 1845-75; Lambertson House, Pittsfield, Mass., ca. 1855.*

34. Carpenter's Gothic (The Gingerbread House): *ca. 1840-80; Summer Cottage, Cape May, N.J.*

35. Garrison Colonial (Builder's Subdivision House): *Greenbriar, Fairfax County, Va., 1968.*

An English Tradition

The Cape Cod Cottage

36. One-Bay Cottage: *The "Half House," Provincetown, Mass., early 18th c.*

37. One-And-One-Half-Bay Cottage: *The "Three-Quarter House," Brewster, Mass.*

38. Two-Bay Cottage: *The "Full-Sized House," Chatham, Mass.*

39. Two-Story House of One-And-One-Half Bays: *The "Nantucket House," Hezekiah Swain-Maria Mitchell House, Nantucket, Mass., 1790; lean-to addition, 1850.*

Soon after their bitter first winter in Massachusetts, the Pilgrims built what was to become the typical American small house: a one-story, gable-roofed dwelling, the most famous descendant of which is known as the Cape Cod cottage. As most commonly seen in its native habitat, the cottage was a stark little house, its shingled surface left to weather variable gray, like fish scales, in the salt Cape air. The eighteenth century had brought with it sash windows and a simple classic doorway, sometimes substituted for the old plank-framed entry. The steep medieval roofline was lowered to what Cape Codders call "a short hoist and a long peak." Otherwise, its elements remained virtually static. In this New England region, an essentially medieval house has persisted—not as a museum piece but as a live and lived-in tradition.

36. Among the antique characteristics of the Cape Cod cottage, none is more evocative than size. This quaint little dwelling, with its single downstairs room, is the smallest of the type, popularly known today as a "half house." But until late in the nineteenth century, it was called simply a "house," while the two-room cottage was called a "double house."[4] Without knowing it Cape Codders were perpetuating the old English meaning of the word "house," synonymous with "hall," i.e., the all-purpose room that had once been the basic unit of the English dwelling.

The modular system, of which the "half house" is a part, traces back to the fourteenth century, when oxen were stabled under the same roof with the family. Because it took approximately 16 feet to house a team of oxen, this became the standard length for a room—the "bay"— multiples of which made up a larger dwelling.[5] Cape Cod's "half house," approximating that dimension, is thus a distant echo of the English "ox-house."

37. Popularly nicknamed a "three-quarter house," this was the type most frequently built on Cape Cod. It had one large and one small front room, the latter only a half-bay in width: obviously a Cape Cod version of the seventeenth-century hall-and-parlor (Figures 6 and 20).

38. Today's "full-sized house," with two large

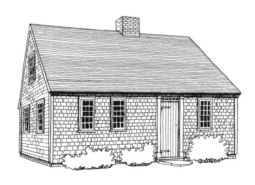

front rooms, was formerly called a "double house," that is, a doubling of the basic one-bay cottage. Today's "double house" on Cape Cod (not shown) is in effect two full-size houses end-to-end, or a four-bay cottage. Ships' carpenters are said to have devised the bowed "rainbow roof."

39. The "Nantucket House" is a two-story dwelling visibly kin to the Cape Cod vernacular. Note the identical shingled exterior, door framing, and window placement. This example is popularly known as a "three-quarter house," like its one-story Cape Cod cousin. There also were two-story "half houses." The widow's walk was a seafaring touch, here used by the famous astronomer Maria Mitchell who at one time owned this house.

An English Tradition

The Half House in the City

40. Flounder House: *John Fitzgerald House, Alexandria, Va., ca. 1799-1822.*

41. Father-Son-And-Holy-Ghost House: *Bladen's Court, off Elfreth's Alley, Philadelphia, Pa., ca. 1830.*

40. Rural Cape Cod was not the only region to perpetuate the medieval bay system of building. The city developed a different version, building up instead of out. A famous example is the "Flounder house," in Alexandria, Virginia, so called because its single-sloped roof was supposed to resemble the head of a flounder. A similar house by the same name was built by Germans in St. Louis. Both are examples of the "half house" that is actually a one-bay hall, though multiplied by two stories, a loft, and a cellar. Because such dwellings were considered half finished, taxes were correspondingly low. Few ever were doubled. However, embellish-ments often were added to the basic house. This one is quite an elegant little pied-à-terre, with a Regency bay window and a piazza overlooking the garden. It is very like the galleried houses of Charleston, South Carolina (Figure 108), from which it may have been copied.

41. Philadelphia, too, had its one-bay house, pushed into verticality by the high price of land. This is an alley dwelling, originally a minimum home for a working family. It was three stories plus basement, one room to a floor, and nicknamed, because of its triplicate upper stories, the "Father-Son-and-Holy-Ghost" house. The raised basement was the kitchen; the main, or first floor, the living room; the second floor, parents' bedroom; the third floor a loft, divided into two small bedrooms for children.

The narrow silhouette of this house creates the effect of a miniature tower or keep. But the slanted roofline—a distinguishing feature of the urban half house—is the same as that of the Flounder. Here, resemblances end. Instead of a southern piazza, there is merely a stoop leading up to the raised first story. The only ornament is a classic frame for the doorway.

2

Chapter 2

A Dutch Tradition

The colony of Nieuw Nederland, chartered in 1621 by the Dutch West India Company and taken over by the English in 1668 without the firing of a shot, was little more than an interlude in American history. Yet during its brief period of ascendance, the Dutch colony left an imprint on our architecture that is still visible today.

However, this imprint is anything but clear cut. Unlike the almost totally English New England, Nieuw Nederland was never wholly Dutch. The people and architecture of Holland predominated, even after the colony had come under English rule. But from the first, Nieuw Nederland—like the cosmopolitan city of New York which sprang from it—was a haven for settlers of diverse origin.

Particularly in evidence were the Flemish, the French Huguenots, and a sprinkling of Walloons from both Belgium and France, many of whom had fled religious persecution in their homelands. Living in tolerant Holland for varying periods of time, they absorbed Dutch architectural tradition or passed their own on to the Dutch, emigrating with them to America. Here, they intermingled, intermarried, and built houses that have been confusing architectural history ever since. It is disconcerting to find, as one often does, that what seems to be a typically Dutch farmhouse actually was built by a French or a Flemish settler.

This confusion, however, is not totally colonial. It reflects an overlapping of tradition in Europe itself. The peasant cottages of France, Germany, Holland, and the other Low Countries—despite regional and national accents—often were strikingly similar. The town houses of Amsterdam, Cologne, Bruges, and even Copenhagen had much in common. Each belonged to a distinct tradition of urban or rural building which encompassed most of the countries of Europe.

These differences and likenesses were preserved in the Dutch colony. On the outlying farms, or *bouweries,* of Long Island and northern New Jersey and in the rural villages and patroonships of the Hudson River Valley, one finds mainly the low, solid cottages of peasant Europe. Along the busy streets of Nieuw Amsterdam and Beverwyck (later renamed New York and Albany), the tall,

narrow, gable-fronted merchant's house predominated. Variants of the urban types might be used as country manor houses and cottages might appear inside the village proper, but the types themselves remained distinct.

These two very different kinds of Dutch houses are shown in separate sections in this chapter. In addition, because of the mixed character of Dutch settlement, we include houses built by colonists of other nationalities which were part of a common tradition in Dutch America.

A Dutch Tradition

The Town House

42. Klokgevel Gable: *Early Row House, Nieuw Amsterdam, after the Dewitt View, 1653.*

Dugouts and bark huts excepted, the town house was the first dwelling type to be built by the Dutch in their American colony. The remarkable seventeenth-century drawings of Nieuw Amsterdam show tightly packed rows of houses, like a fragment of a Dutch city set down on the shores of America. Even in this wilderness outpost, houses were placed gable end to the street, with the gable wall brought up above the roofline and ending in Dutch curves or crow steps—as near a replica of their native habitat as transplanted Hollanders could make it.

This way of building, though characteristic of the seventeenth-century Dutch city, was part of a tradition of great antiquity. In fact, the row house is at least as old as Rome. In the form shown here, it was a development of the early Middle Ages, when trade increased, causing the rapid growth of the medieval city. First built as a mansion for the new merchant princes or as a meeting place for powerful craft guilds, it rapidly became a vernacular type, often combining dwelling and shop, and designed to use the least possible amount of precious street

frontage. Thus, the length of the house was extended into the block while the entry was shifted to the gable end facing the street. This placement led to a tall, proportionately narrow silhouette and to the decorated gable.

We have come to think of this house as typically Dutch, and so it was. But it was not limited to Holland. In every country that sent settlers to America, the traditional city house belonged to this basic type. The English colony at Jamestown was planned as a village of row houses, and two such rows actually were built. In France, the saying "to have a gable on the street," meaning to own a house, shows that this placement had become part of the language.

Nevertheless, it was along the canals of Amsterdam and the streets of Leyden and other Dutch cities that the row house reached its most intense development. And it was the Dutch who transplanted the type, like an image of home, to their American settlements.

42. This little row of town houses shows what a

street in New York City looked like when it was still Nieuw Amsterdam. Houses were faithfully Dutch, set gable end to street, the gable wall brought up above the roofline. The *klokgevel*, or concave curve, is the graceful gable illustrated here. One of four major Dutch types, it echoed the city of Leyden, where this roofline predominated.

Because of the scarcity of brick, the favorite Dutch building material, most of the earliest houses were made of wood from the seemingly endless American forests. Even the brick dwelling in this row is only a brick front for a wooden house, a thrifty combination typical of Dutch settlements.[6] As elsewhere, thatched roofs predominated at first but red and black Dutch pantile gradually replaced them. Later still, inexpensive wooden shingles edged out tile, to the distress of the more conservative colonists. Characteristically Dutch was the use of vertical or horizontal planking, or clapboards, over a timber frame. In fact, English clapboards—and thus our familiar American clapboard house—probably derive from Holland.

43. The Crow Step: *Typical Dutch House, Nieuw Amsterdam, early 17th c.*

44. The Tuitgevel or Flemish Gable: *John Ellison House, New York City, N.Y., ca. 1717.*

43. Shown here is the crow step, corbie, or corbeled gable, a type so popular in Holland that it has become very nearly a symbol of the country. In Nieuw Amsterdam, the crow step was the choice for the finest brick dwellings; and it grew more common as brick replaced wood for building.

Unlike the New England Puritans, the Dutch had come to the New World primarily for trade; and Dutch architecture reflected that fact. They built their brick houses two to four stories and a "cockloft" in height to accommodate the shop, home, and warehouse that made up a typical merchant's dwelling.

The attic was the warehouse. Merchandise was hauled directly from street to attic window by rope and pulley—a "Dutch elevator." The shop was at the front of the house. Directly behind it was a spacious kitchen—the family living quarters—giving onto a rear garden. With walls of red or salmon brick and dark green painted doors and shutters, these were rich and handsome houses for seventeenth-century America.

44. The *tuitgevel*, or Flemish gable, is a series of convex curves, sometimes simple, as here, sometimes extravagant and convoluted, as in the famous town houses of Brussels and Bruges. Though a native of Flanders, the Flemish gable was a favorite also in Belgium and Holland. The English borrowed it during their Jacobean period (Figure 9). As part of the Spanish tradition, it reached America in the colonial missions of California and the Southwest.

However, the Flemish gable was not recorded in Dutch America until the 1721 Burgis View of New York supplied the lone example seen here. A later development than the medieval crow step, its curves have a Baroque quality that reflects the Italian Renaissance. Note the balcony with its classic balusters. Though a Dutch house in what was still overwhelmingly a Dutch city, this dwelling seems not to have been built by a Dutchman. The influence of Holland was so strong in the early eighteenth century that houses entirely Dutch in design often were built by other colonists.

A Dutch Tradition

The Straight-Edge Gable: The Dutch Original

45. The Straight-Edge Gable: *Ferry House Kitchen, Van Cortlandt Manor, Croton-on-Hudson, N.Y.*

45. This little kitchen building reproduces one of the most popular Dutch gables of colonial America. Usually the front for a town house, set gable end to street, it was a common type in the 1721 Burgis View of New York. Seen here is a rural adaptation with the *stoep,* or raised entry, on the long side. Also typical of the country version is the lean-to at the rear. In the gable wall, a Dutch "beehive" oven projects outside the house but opens into the fireplace. In two-story size, this was the characteristic Dutch farmhouse of Albany County—more like a manor house than like the peasant cottages that dotted other areas of the Hudson River Valley.

Its gable is variously known as a "straight-edge," a "straight-line," or a "straight-edge gable with square elbows," a reference to the single crow step at either eave. Of the four distinctively Dutch gable types, this one probably had the most lasting influence on American architecture. It entered England from Holland and traveled on with English, as well as Dutch, colonists to America. The Dutch colonial form has survived only in isolated examples. But the modified English version, embodying, as we believe, a Dutch ancestry, became a widespread American vernacular (see Figures 46-49).

A Dutch Tradition

The Straight-Edge Gable: An Anglo-American Translation

46. Georgian: *The Telescope House, Carvel House, Kent Island, Md., 17th and 18th c.*

47. Federal: *Belmont, Baltimore, Md., early 19th c.*

48. The Double Chimney (Georgian): *Archibald Macphaedris House, Portsmouth, N.H., 1718-23.*

49. The Double Chimney (Greek Revival): *Henry Chouteau Mansion, St. Louis, Mo., 19th c.*

46. The smallest house in this continuous dwelling is the earliest. It is also the one most like the Dutch original. The straight-edge gable was widely used on English houses, sometimes extending above the roofline with Dutch elbows, more often with the roof capping the wall, as seen here. This is a ''telescope house,'' so called for the way in which the parts ''telescope'' together: a regional type on the Eastern Shore of Maryland. Both Dutch and English examples also are found in New Jersey.

47. Here is the Anglo-Dutch manor house looking a bit overdressed in the costume of the early American Republic. A fanlight above the door, a Palladian window to light the upper hall, and splayed window lintels with central keystones were marks of the Federal period circa 1780-1820. The wing has been given a typical southern porch. Rear wings had been a traditional way of enlarging the narrow, medieval English house. The method persisted in America beneath new architectural fashions.

48. This famous Georgian mansion, the first brick house in Portsmouth, New Hampshire, shows a new way of enlarging the traditional dwelling. Instead of adding a wing, its single file of rooms has been doubled, and chimney stacks doubled to match, providing the necessary fireplace in every room. The resulting chimney form, called a ''curtain,'' became increasingly popular after 1760.

This early example reveals its origin as a double house with two separate gabled roofs parallel to each other under a later covering. In England, where weather was less severe, these double roofs commonly were exposed. Note also that chimney walls extend above the eaves line in the original Dutch manner. Clustered chimney stacks are a carryover from the Jacobean period.

49. This house, the pride of St. Louis in its day, is close to the end of the road for the Anglo-Dutch ''straight-edge gable.'' With the addition of an enormous portico, the immigrant from Holland through Jacobean England had become an imposing Greek Revival mansion in the new-sprung American West. On formal classic houses, the Greek entablature carried around the entire house, creating a pediment at each gable. Here, because of the continuous chimney wall, it ends at the corner.

A Dutch Tradition

Patterned Brickwork:
The Dutch Original

50. Dutch Cross Bond: *Nicholas Vechte-Jacques Cortelyou House, Gowanus, N.Y., 1699; destroyed 1897, reconstructed 1934.*

50. Patterned brickwork was another tradition shared by the Dutch and the English. An ancient type of gable decoration, its roots trace back to medieval France. It entered England in the fifteenth century and—as might be expected—by way of Holland. The pattern of repetitive diamonds in the center of this gable is known as "Dutch cross bond" (the English

called it "diaperwork"). Zigzag edging was *"muizetanden,"* or "mousetooth," to the Dutch; "tumbling" to the English. Initials and the date of construction often were displayed in the brickwork too.

Patterns were made by inserting "headers" (bricks with the small end out) among the

"stretchers" (bricks with the long side out). Where brick was hard to come by in outlying areas, the Dutch used fieldstone for the body of the house, limiting brick to the gable. However, the stone walls of the Cortelyou mansion, several feet thick, were built to protect the owners from pirates, then believed to frequent Gowanus Bay.

A Dutch Tradition

Patterned Brickwork: An Anglo-American Translation

51. Diaperwork: *Abel Nicholson House, Elsinboro Township, Salem County, N.J., 1722.*

52. The Chevron: *William and Sarah Hancock House, Salem County, N.J., 1734.*

53. The Inverted Chevron: *Keeling House, Princess Anne County, Md., ca. 1700.*

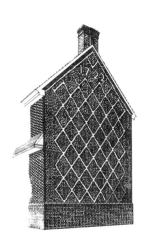

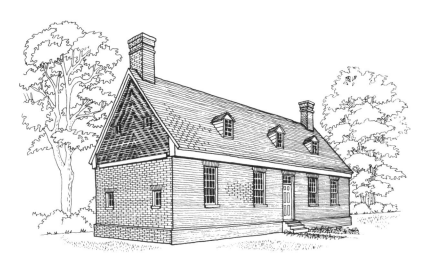

51. This English colonial example is of diaperwork or diapering, identical in pattern to Dutch cross bond. It is located not far from Philadelphia, in Salem County, New Jersey, a region uniquely noted for the decorative brickwork of its early houses. Diaperwork, chevrons, triangles, and checkers, as well as geometric flowerlike designs, can all be seen in this one small area. The houses are of red brick with patterns characteristically picked out in dark blue glazed headers, though gray or purple headers sometimes were used.

The front of this house is the checkerboard of Flemish bond, created by alternating headers and stretchers of different colors. It was common not only in Salem County but also in the English colonies of Tidewater Maryland and Virginia. By contrast, the gable end is English bond, in which a course only of stretchers alternates with a course of headers. Usually, there was no color change in this bond, and it was used as a neutral background for another pattern.

52. This Salem County gable illustrates the chevron, another typical brickwork pattern transplanted from the Old World. Prototypes for the many variations of Salem County brickwork can be found in Essex and other parts of East Anglia in England. Just why the full range was reproduced in a single American county no one knows. Surmise assumes a family or group of craftsmen who passed their skills on through many generations, for the brick houses of Salem were built from the late seventeenth century well into the nineteenth. The Hancock house and the Nicholson house (Figure 51) are eighteenth century, costumed in the famous "pent roof" of Philadelphia and its environs (Figures 128 and 89). Note the raised entry, which may or may not originally have had a stair. Some early dwellings had no steps at the rear in order to allow women to mount a horse or enter a carriage directly from the house without muddying shoes or skirts.

53. This early eighteenth-century plantation house shows one more of the many patterns that decorated colonial gables. Here, lines of black header bricks follow the slope of the roof to meet as a series of inverted Vs, or Chevrons. There were many such examples of Anglo-Dutch brickwork in the Tidewater English colonies.

The Keeling house also is one of the finest examples of the "central passage house" which developed from the seventeenth-century hall and parlor (Figure 20). Two partitions instead of one now separate the major room, or hall, from the parlor, creating a passage through the house from front door to rear. Room sizes have become larger; the passage is lighted by a transom; windows are classic sash rather than medieval casement; and lintels are set in a straight line instead of an arch—changes that identify this house as an eighteenth-century dwelling. Its decorated gable shows how ancient practices can persist in the fabric of a house, even as it advances in style.

A Dutch Tradition

The False Front:
The Dutch Original

54. Brick-Front House: *Harmanus Wendell Shop and House, Albany, N.Y., 1716.*

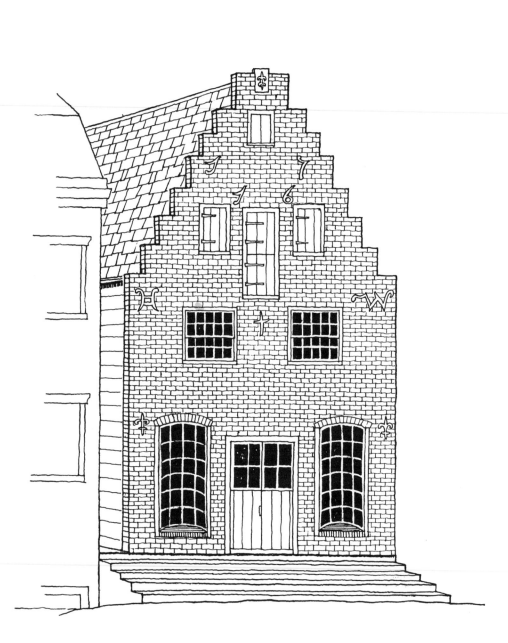

54. A town house in eighteenth-century Albany, with its crow-stepped gable brought up above the roofline, shows once more the typical Dutch combination of brick front and clapboard sides. This Dutch separation of the frontispiece from the rest of the house may well have been the source of that famous American building type, the false front. Though virtually a symbol of the Wild West, the false front was not in fact limited to frontier towns. It had been a well-known way of building in the East before the pioneers left home. Examples can be found almost anywhere, but it is perhaps significant that they are common in the villages which fan out from Albany in what once was an area of Dutch influence.

To reach the nineteenth-century false front, one must leap across an undocumented void from a lingering Dutch tradition to Victorian revivalism. Only field work beyond the scope of this book may someday prove a connection. But our illustrations offer visual evidence for an intriguing possibility.

A Dutch Tradition

The False Front: An American Translation

55. Corbeled and Bracketed False Fronts: *"Bad Shot Gulch," Bodie, Calif., town established ca. 1870; ghost town early 20th c.*

56. Greek Revival False Front: *House and Shop, Charleston, S.C., ca. 1840.*

57. Queen Anne False Front: *House owned by Jacob Kochevar, Crested Butte, Colo., ca. 1890-1900.*

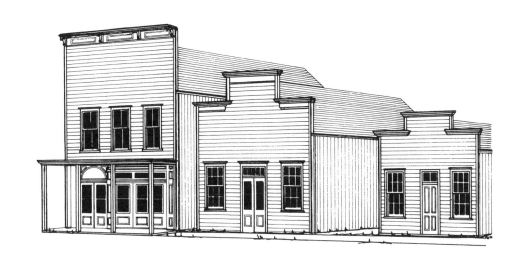

55. In the raw cow towns and mining camps of frontier America, the false front gave a make-believe dignity to a jerry-built Main Street. If our theory is correct, the corbeled fronts are direct descendants of the Dutch crow-stepped gable. In fact, stepped wooden fronts similar to these still may be seen in Holland. But whatever their type, the important point was the extension of the front above the roofline. With this as a base, American false fronts simply echoed the styles of the day. One of the most popular was the Italianate, distinguished by heavy brackets under the cornice, as seen in the last house of this row. Shop (or saloon) and living quarters typically were combined as they had been in the Dutch town house.

56. The false front was found in many an unlikely corner, including the gracious southern city of Charleston. Here, superimposed orders of the Greek Revival have been applied as frosting to a wooden box. This is a store front, but living quarters could have been included. The shop-house combination was a typical false front scheme and a persistent echo of the mercantile Dutch town house. This is a wooden example. Later, such false fronts might have been prefabricated of cast iron and shipped knocked down from New York or another manufacturing city—part of the new technology of late-nineteenth-century America.

57. This fantasy from Crested Butte, Colorado, is in the "Queen Anne" Style, a nineteenth-century revival first used for enormous country houses in Victorian England. Part Jacobean and part classic in inspiration, the style still echoes those sources in the false front of a western mining town. The half-circle atop the gable retains a faint resemblance to the real Jacobean gable (Figure 9) and to its Dutch cousin, the Flemish gable (Figure 44). In America, a wall covering of shingles was characteristic of Victorian Queen Anne, substituting for English tiles. This house was built to be, though never used as, a brothel.

A Dutch Tradition

The Dutch Farmhouse

58. The Dutch Cottage: *Pieter Bronck House, West Coxsackie, N.Y., 1663; later west wing and brick house not shown.*

59. The Franco-Dutch Farmhouse: *Jean Hasbrouck House, New Paltz, N.Y., 1712.*

During the seventeenth and eighteenth centuries, the farmers who settled rural Nieuw Nederland and its successor colonies transplanted to America the traditions of peasant Europe. Squat, sturdy stone and wood dwellings, great barns, and neat garden patches appeared within the forests and along the waterways of what are now New York State and suburban New Jersey.

These unpretentious farm and village houses were entirely different from the Dutch town house and from the often imposing country manor houses related to it. They boasted no stepped or curving gables and no patterned brickwork. Rather, these simple houses gained distinction through a straightforward use of native wood and stone.

Nevertheless, within the confines of a cottage architecture, they were by no means all alike. Diversity was inevitable, given the conditions of Dutch settlement. Great numbers of Flemings and French Huguenots—as well as other migrants—had entered Holland to escape religious persecution. As a consequence, Dutch colonial settlements were often an ethnic mix. But it was not unusual to find little knots of diverse nationality within the Dutch fabric. The French Huguenot village of New Paltz, New York, was one of these areas and there were French enclaves in New Jersey's Bergen County. Evidence indicates that the Flemish settled in New Jersey and on Long Island, where the type of dwelling known as the Flemish farmhouse proliferated.

As national types, the houses of these colonists are quite distinct from each other. Flaring eaves are Flemish. Typically Huguenot is the in-line plan of two or more rooms, each with its outside entry door and no interior hallways. Characteristically Dutch is the broad, deep plan, organized around a center hall, its roof rising high and sweeping low over a capacious attic.

But finding these houses in pure ethnic form is all but impossible. Settlers of one nationality have perversely built houses belonging to another. There is an imperceptible melding of several traditions. At the same time, regional American materials give quite different dwellings a family resemblance. In the area of Dutch colonization, nothing is ever precisely what it seems.

58. True to the mixed Nieuw Nederland heritage, this very Dutch house was built by a man believed to have been of Danish or Swedish descent. Pieter Bronck's immigrant father had purchased land north of Manhattan in what is now the Bronx (which was named after him). But he was killed in an Indian raid and his young son was taken west, eventually becoming a pioneer in the Hudson River Valley. There, on Indian lands which he bought for "150 guilders in beaver," Pieter Bronck built a house for his Dutch bride in the prevailing Dutch manner.

Like most seventeenth-century houses, it was very small, simply one room with bedchamber above and a loft above that, both upper floors tucked beneath the steeply sloped, medieval roof. This picturesque little cottage with its thick stone walls, casement windows, and half-shutters was a relative to the later and larger stone farmhouses which would become a Hudson River Valley vernacular type.

59. This thoroughly Dutch house was put up by a Dutch builder for a Huguenot owner in a French-speaking village in the Dutch-dominated Hudson Valley. Of gray fieldstone with gable ends of weathered clapboard, it was part of a vocabulary shared by both nationalities. However, its broad form and ample proportions are strikingly Dutch. In fact, its appearance is similar to the peasant house of central and southern Holland, itself an offspring of the Lower Saxon *Bauernhaus* of North Germany. Those compact but capacious buildings combined under one roof the dwelling and the farmhouse, as the barn then was called. In the Hasbrouck house, an unusually large garret, like the mow of the barn for hay, was used for food storage, including hogsheads of grain, hams, herbs, and other staples. The loft also was a weaving room accommodating the cumbersome loom with which the colonists made their own cloth. The first floor has the eighteenth-century center hall plan found also in English Georgian houses. However, these Dutch and Huguenot dwellings, neither formal nor classic, were virtually untouched folk architecture.

60. The Dutch Manor House: *Van Cortlandt Manor, Croton-on-Hudson, N.Y.; lower level 17th c.; upper stories 18th c.; verandah 19th c.*

60. The double-tiered porch added to this Dutch dwelling in the early nineteenth century gives it the appearance of a plantation house in French Louisiana (Figure 96). But behind it, the Dutch colonial vernacular is unmistakable. Though a two-story mansion with elegantly paneled interiors, Van Cortlandt Manor bears a striking resemblance to the sturdy fieldstone dwellings which were its farmhouse cousins. The en-circling porch, typically French and typically southern, is an architectural anomaly. It may have resulted from family trade with the West Indies, where the southern type is thought to have originated.

In the early eighteenth century, the wealthy Van Cortlandts lived in New York, using this house (then much smaller) as a hunting lodge and tenant office. Not until 1749 did the third Lord of the Manor move to his country estate for year-round living. From that time on, the house became a center of social life and political history. Benjamin Franklin, the Marquis de Lafayette, and, of course, George Washington were among the notables lavishly entertained at Van Cortlandt Manor.

A Dutch Tradition

The Dutch Interior

61. The _Doten-Kammer_: _Freely based on photographs of the restored Jan Martense Schenck House, ca. 1675._

61. The _Doten-Kammer,_ or parlor-bedroom, was the "best room" in a Dutch house. It was cheery and bright, with large casement windows, a garnish of pewter or Delft plates on the mantel, and a table covered with intricately patterned "China carpett" (in those days, carpets were not used on the floor). "Turkey work," a fashionable eighteenth-century fabric resembling tapestry, upholstered the chairs. Furniture was massive and elaborately carved, like the _kas,_ or wardrobe, in which the Dutch family stored its clothes.

The Dutch parlor fireplace was quite different from the English (Figure 14), simply a hood, a hearth, and a decorative firebacking mounted flat against the wall. The hood was edged with a pleated linen ruffle, changed daily. Jambs typically were faced with blue and white Delft tile.

Contemporary visitors to Dutch houses noted with surprise that there seemed to be no beds. The Dutch slept in "cupboard beds" or "bed-boxes," i.e., heavy pieces of furniture with doors which closed like cupboards, or built-in sleeping nooks with doors or curtains, as seen here. Whenever possible, these were placed next to a fireplace for added warmth.

A Dutch Tradition

The Flemish Farmhouse

To most Americans, Dutch architecture begins and ends with a single dwelling: the clapboard, shingle, or stone house with the bell-shaped gambrel roof and flaring eaves which was revived in the twentieth century as "Dutch Colonial." From the preceding pages, it is obvious that this familiar style was not the only type brought by colonists to Nieuw Nederland.

More surprising, perhaps, is the fact that this synonym for Dutch Colonial may be neither colonial nor Dutch. It is, indeed, something of an architectural mystery, the subject of speculation and controversy for well over 40 years.

In its fully developed form, this modest but graceful cottage was not built until the late eighteenth century, long after the Dutch colony of Nieuw Nederland had ceased to exist. Its greatest popularity occurred near, or after, the American Revolution. On the basis of these facts, historian Rosalie Fellows Bailey has called it "a distinctive architecture and our only indigenous form until the coming of the modern skyscraper."

This resolute statement was quickly challenged by another historian, Thomas Jefferson Wertenbaker, who argued that the Dutch Colonial house was not Dutch, nor yet an American invention, but instead a Flemish farmhouse, as true to its old-world prototype as any other transplant.[7] He traced its flaring eave to Flanders, where it is known as a "flying gutter."

In Flanders, the overhang had been a functional necessity, acting to protect perishable walls of clay, mixed with lime and straw, that were a regional way of building. In America, the argument goes, abundant stone and wood were substituted for clay walls, but the traditional flaring eaves retained. The stone houses typically were plastered over and whitewashed, perpetuating a visual resemblance to the Flemish prototype. Also cited as evidence is the mortar used between stones: a mixture of clay, lime, and straw or hogs hair, unlike the usual hard American mortar, but identical to the wall material of Flemish houses.

Though the Flemish in America are difficult to trace, some historians estimate their numbers as high as two-thirds of the total immigration to Nieuw Nederland. Unlike the Dutch, most of whom came originally as traders, the Flemish typically were peasant farmers. A great many are believed to have settled in rural Long Island and New Jersey, two areas in which this type of house proliferated.

With such persuasive evidence, the Flemish farmhouse has long since become an article of faith among historians. Just the same, it is unlikely that any national type could remain untouched and pure in Dutch America. The flaring Flemish eave appears on otherwise typically French Huguenot houses in Bergen County, N.J. Some verifiably Dutch houses in Brooklyn and on Long Island acquired the "flying gutter" as part of enlargement and remodeling. It seems likely that the Flemish roofline became a colonial fashion, incorporated into houses built by families of varied nationality in the areas of Dutch settlement.

As time went on, new influences acted upon the Flemish type. A gambrel roof was added, and later a porch, neither of which are found in the Flemish original. The gambrel was part of the Renaissance influence that modified traditional ways of building in both English and Dutch colonies. The porch was a French colonial feature, a regional type in Louisiana, Missouri and the Carolinas. It may have originated in the West Indies, with which the Dutch, too, had a brisk eighteenth-century trade.

Though the initial impetus undoubtedly was Flemish, it is fairly certain that what one sees, after 150 years of American development, is not a Flemish farmhouse. One would have to destroy the very fabric of these houses to sort out the contributions of the nationalities which they contain. Perhaps, after all, this can be called an indigenous American architecture.

A Dutch Tradition

The Flemish Farmhouse

62. The Flemish Eave: *Pieter Wyckoff House, Brooklyn, N.Y., 1639-41; enlargement and addition of Flemish eaves, late 17th c.*

63. A Dutch Contributor: *Kost Verloren (Money Thrown Away), Tenant House, Van Renssalaer Manor, East Greenbush, N.Y., ca. 1708-33.*

64. The Added Gambrel: *Jacobus Demarest House, Bergen County, N.J., wing 1693 or 1717; main house ca. 1719.*

62. The flaring eave, which became so much a part of Dutch colonial architecture, has been traced to the "flying gutter" found on cottages in Flanders. This example, built by a Dutchman, originally was a tiny cottage with a gabled roof. Flemish eaves were added when the house was enlarged. Round-ended shingles were a Dutch type resembling the tile that was used as a wall surfacing in Holland.

63. This Dutch house shows the type of gambrel roof that was added to the Flemish farmhouse to create a new American type (Figure 64). It was a very early gambrel, breaking just below the ridgeline, and only slightly modifying the peaked gable of medieval ancestry. English as well as Dutch houses used this high-breaking gambrel. Later houses of both traditions dropped the gambrel's breaking point to its final and typical Anglo-Dutch position.

64. Considered the most beautiful of all gambrels, this graceful bell-shaped roof combines the flaring Flemish eave with the early Dutch gambrel that breaks near the ridgeline (Figure 63). Once adopted, this gambrel never progressed to a lower breaking point like its Anglo-Dutch counterparts.

The original dwelling of the Demarest House was the tiny wing, later turned into a kitchen. Often, a second wing was added at right for grandparents or for the eldest son when he married, producing a three-part composition of great charm. This way of enlarging a house is typically Flemish. However, the Flemish farmhouse also may have had antecedents in France. This example was built by a Huguenot, and houses with a similar kick to the eaves were built by French settlers in Canada.

65. With the addition of a verandah, the "Flemish farmhouse" completed its American development. Possibly of French or West Indian derivation, this porch extends the Dutch *stoep* the length of the house, roofed by an extension of the flying gutter. Pillars, fanlighted doorway, and dormers are in the delicate new Federal Style. This fully developed "Flemish farmhouse" was one of those happy blendings which occur now and again in architecture. Together, its Flemish eaves, Dutch gambrel, French-West Indian porch, and English classic styling add up to one of the most graceful and livable small houses in America.

65. The Added Porch: *Richard Vreeland House,
Leonia, N.J., original small house ca. 1786;
main house 1818.*

3

Chapter 3

The Log Tradition and the Pioneer House

The log cabin is the house of American myth. Chopped from the forest with an ax, erected without nails or sawn timber, this pioneer homestead symbolizes the courage, frugality, and independence of a lost America. Seven of our presidents were born in or at one time lived in a log cabin. During the nineteenth century, at the peak period of settlement, it was the predominant building type all along the western frontier.

At first it had been the isolated forest home of a single pioneer family or one of a group huddled inside the stockade of a wilderness fort. As time went on, whole towns were constructed of logs, including not only log houses and barns but log churches, log schools, log taverns, log courthouses, and, in Tennessee, a log cabin college (Martin Academy). As late as the 1950s, a geographic survey of Georgia revealed that 10,000 to 12,000 log dwellings were still standing in that state alone.

Projected backward by sentiment and faulty history, the log cabin came to be thought of as the home (and the invention) of the earliest English colonists at Jamestown and Plymouth. Painstaking research has shown the facts to be otherwise.

The log cabin as we know it was brought to America by Swedish and Finnish colonists in 1638 with the founding of Fort Christina at the site of what is now Wilmington, Delaware. Log construction, a native tradition of Norway, the northern part of Sweden, and Finland, was employed for village buildings and for the complex of houses, barns, storage sheds (and, in Finland, the sauna) which made up the peasant homestead. It was part of a pine and fir tradition, i.e., soft, lightweight woods, the logs having straight, smooth trunks which were easily shaped and handled.

The origin of the log cabin is lost in the mists of prehistory, but some archaeologists believe that it developed with the forest culture of northern Europe in a transitional period between hunting and agriculture, probably during the Bronze Age.

Whatever antique structural genius first thought of saddle-notching logs and criss-crossing their ends, the log house had become a tradition in Scandinavia by the Viking period, A.D. 800 to 1000. The earliest Viking cabin was a primitive log dwelling of a single room, with a packed earth floor, a central "fire place" (in the literal meaning of the two words), and a roof vent for the escape of smoke and the admission of dim light. It had no windows. The old Norse name for this basic shelter was eld-hús—literally "fire house" or "hearth house"—from which the English word "house" is derived.

The "hearth house," the heated communal living-eating-sleeping room, remained the basic unit of log construction long after respectable floors, windows, fireplaces, and chimneys had superseded the crude early arrangements. Under a later name, the Vardagstuga, or common room cabin, was the first log house to be built in seventeenth-century America and remained the basic type as pioneers pushed westward.

With logs, a single room is, of course, the easiest to build, for size is limited by the length of the logs and the weight a man can lift. As a result, the one-room log unit became the essential building block, used almost like a module. For a large house, two or more "cabins," or "pens" as they were called, might be built abutting each other, or two pens might be built apart but joined by a roofed passage which served as an entry porch to both. Two-story houses were, in effect, four cabins placed two on two. Larger and more complex houses developed from these basic types. But because of the discipline imposed by the length of the log and the joint, the method was quite similar in most countries having a log tradition.

In seventeenth-century America, English settlers built a few hewn log blockhouses and garrisons as strongholds against the Indians in Maine and Vermont. French and Spanish colonists in the Middle West and Southwest built their own vertical log types. But on the Eastern Seaboard, log construction remained the almost exclusive property of the Swedes and the Finns until the eighteenth century, when Germanic colonists from the Rhine Palatinate, the Swiss Alps, Silesia, Moravia, Bohemia, and Saxony began flooding into Pennsylvania. The first farmhouses and barns of these German-speaking immigrants (loosely grouped together as the Pennsylvania Deutsch or Dutch) were built almost invariably of logs.

Though they shared a basic building system with each other and with the Swedes, there was great variation in the detail of these houses. Quite small regions within each parent country had, over the centuries, developed characteristic methods of notching corners or of fitting logs together, and these were reproduced in great variety in the new world. Roofs, plans, and chimneys also varied, a central chimney usually indicating a German house and a corner chimney a Swedish.

Scandinavians and Germans carried their own traditions with them as they moved deeper into the hinterland. Added to them during the eighteenth and nineteenth centuries were waves of Scots-Irish who settled in Delaware and nearby New Jersey or passed rapidly on to challenge the Germans for the backwoods of Pennsylvania. These rugged newcomers, lacking an appropriate building tradition of their own, quickly borrowed the log cabin from their Scandinavian or German neighbors, depending on their place of settlement.

In this way, the Americanization of the log cabin began. For though borrowing log construction, the Scots-Irish retained their own type of chimney and other features. English and French pioneers later borrowed the log method, adapting it to their own traditional house types.

From New Sweden and the Dutch country of Pennsylvania, log building spread out along familiar routes of settlement—south into Maryland, Virginia, and the Carolinas; north to New England; west by northern, southern, and central routes—hybridizing as it went. Even before the Revolution, the log cabin had become a familiar sight in newly opened territory from Vermont to Kentucky: the chosen home of an already advancing frontier.

The Swedish-Scots-Irish combination probably was the most popular frontier cabin and the type which has come to mean "log cabin" to most of us. However, American log construction is not one type but many: large and small, crude and meticulously crafted, of both pure and hybrid ancestry. This chapter gives but a sampling of its variety.

The Log Tradition
and the Pioneer House

A Swedish Tradition

66. Swedish Two-Room Cabin: *"The Lower Swedish Log Cabin," Darby Creek, Upper Darby Township, Pa., on land that was once part of New Sweden, ca. 1654.*

66a. Plan, *Vardagstuga* with *Gang*: *A typical Swedish two-room plan.*

67. Swedish Common Room: *Based on "The Lower Swedish Log Cabin," Darby Creek.*

68. The Pioneer Log Cabin: *Characteristic Scots-Irish Type, Georgia, the 1840s.*

66. New Sweden existed as an independent colony for only 17 years, but it gave America its most famous house. This Swedish colonial homestead, still standing after more than three centuries, is the prototype of the American log cabin. It shows the simple structural system—round logs, notched and crossed at the corners—which would become the typical way of building all along the frontier. Logs were either saddle-notched or V-notched (the joining used here). Characteristically Swedish is the treatment of the ends of the logs, hewn at a slant to facilitate the runoff of rainwater. Thin, lapped boards, laid vertically over a layer of birch bark, surfaced the roof. Chimneys were set down from the ridgeline, another distinguishing feature, indicating Swedish corner fireplaces inside the house.

This was a woodsman's home in a primitive wilderness. Glass was unavailable, and windows were closed by sliding boards or animal skins. Door height was low and the sill was raised. One had to stoop and step up to enter—a scheme calculated to put an unfriendly visitor at a disadvantage. A wooden cross bar bolted the slab door on the inside, but could be lifted from the outside by a latch string threaded through a small hole—a Swedish device which would become the symbol of frontier hospitality. If the "latch string was out," guests were welcome.

66a. The *Vardagstuga*, basic unit in the Scandinavian log tradition, is the living-dining-sleeping room of this typical two-room plan. Figure 66 shows an American variation, with a fireplace for each room. But it was usual to heat only the common room, or "hearth house." When the Swedish log cabin was enlarged to two rooms, the second traditionally was smaller and unheated: a *gang*, or vestibule, which served also for storage and as a milkhouse—a kind of Swedish refrigerator. Sometimes, a tiny bedroom was partitioned off the *gang*, backing up to the fireplace for warmth. If so, an additional door was cut, leading directly from common room to bedroom.

67. This "common room" shows the typical Swedish corner fireplace, so different from English or Dutch types. Fieldstone commonly was used in New Sweden, though brick sometimes was substituted after 1655 when the Dutch took over the colony. Some of the cruder cabins had only a clay fireplace with a stick and clay chimney, little more than a hood built across one corner of the room.

This interior is shown with a typical Swedish log bed, filled with straw, over which animal skins have been laid. Out of sight at right there would traditionally have been a corner cupboard. Tucked into the remaining corner

were built-in benches and a table. The Swedes apparently liked corners and filled up every one. As in Viking days, floors usually were of packed earth. This puncheon floor—split logs with the round side down—was a luxury. Note the sliding wind-board, pushed back from the open window.

68. The frontier log cabin was, more often than not, a Scots-Irish translation of the Swedish original. The major change was an exterior chimney, built against the gable end. Usually of sticks and clay, it sometimes was built of stone, or it might combine a stone fireplace with a stick-and-clay stack. Saddle-notched corners and a roof of split saplings, both Swedish, were typical of the frontier.

Describing the hundreds of log cabins in the Allegheny Mountains which he saw on his trip to America in 1842, Charles Dickens wrote that most had an "utterly forlorn appearance, the windows being stuffed with old clothes, boards and paper." Dickens saw the log cabins from a distance. Philip Fithian, a Presbyterian circuit rider in the Shenandoah Valley, had spent many a night in them. In 1775, he wrote: "But o the Fleas! Some mornings at some Houses, I rise spotted and purple like a person in the Measles. . . ." The reality of the frontier may not have been quite so picturesque as history has painted it.

The Log Tradition and the Pioneer House

The New Immigrants

69. Norwegian *Tommerhus* (Gallery House):
John Bergen Homestead, built by Osten Gullickson Meland, Racine, Wisc., ca. 1842-47.

By the time the Americanized version of the log cabin reached Wisconsin and Minnesota, it was met, so to speak, by its own ancestor. Great numbers of new settlers from Scandinavia, Finland, and Germany traveled overland from eastern ports during the mass immigration of the nineteenth century. There they built their frontier homes according to uninterrupted Old Country tradition. The early log house types which had been part of seventeenth-century New Sweden and eighteenth-century German Pennsylvania reappeared, virtually unchanged, in the new settlements of these western states, as seen in these examples.

69. Built by a Norwegian pioneer in nineteenth-century Wisconsin, the Bergen homestead shows the two-story Scandinavian log house, no seventeenth-century example of which has survived from New Sweden. Logs are crossed at the corners, the system typically used by both Swedes and Norwegians, even with hewn logs. These have been split in half, a method developed in the oak regions of Scandinavia since whole logs of hardwood are too heavy to handle.

Sash windows and a small "stove chimney" show this to be a nineteenth-century dwelling. Though native-born pioneers still used the fireplace, new immigrants preferred the more efficient cast-iron stove.

Rare in America is the gallery, or *sval,* across the front, or far side, of this house. A shallow, two-story porch containing a stairway, it gave access to every room. Here, it is enclosed with plank panels, some of which could be removed in summer. Except for doors to the gallery, the only upper-story ventilation was a tiny roof hatch called a *skyveluke.*

The gallery house was an exceptional type even in Scandinavia. It appeared during the Viking period after those far-ranging marauders had penetrated the Mediterranean. One historian[8] suggests that it may have been a log copy of the galleried Mediterranean farmhouse, itself a prototype for our southern plantation house (Figure 102).

70. This neatly hewn log house illustrates yet another tradition which spanned the centuries. Built in Wisconsin around 1900 by a newly arrived Finnish immigrant, it echoes a type built in New Sweden 250 years earlier, where Finns are now known to have been as numerous as Swedes.

The Finns' special gift to the American log vernacular was the multiple cabin. Since the size of a log house was limited by the length of the log, adding another room meant, in effect, building another cabin. These one-room units were known as "pens" or "dens," and the Finnish tradition included well-defined ways of putting them together. Shown here is the triple-pen house, but a double-pen variant (Figure 71) became one of the most popular log cabins on the American frontier.

However, though copying the Finnish model, few backwoodsmen could match Finnish skill. Seen here is plank-form construction in which logs were split and hewn so smoothly that they resembled boards. Dovetailed corner joints also were precise. Chinking was unnecessary in a house built by a Finn. These master woodsmen hollowed their logs along the bottom but left them rounded at the top so that they fitted into each other, becoming tighter as they aged. The best houses were allowed to settle for a year before doors and windows were cut.

71. The "dog-trot," "dog-run," "possum-trot," "double-pen" or "double-den" cabin, or "two-pens-and-a-passage"—as it was variously called—was long thought to have been an American invention. But its plan—like that of the closely related triple house—is Finnish.

In Finland, only one of the pens was heated, the other used for storage. In America, except in the deep South, both usually had fireplaces or, later, stoves. One pen typically was used as the kitchen-dining room; the other as a living room and bedroom. The breezeway served as entry, outdoor sitting room, and as a convenient place in which to set tubs, kettles, and pails. It also was the dog's domain, a fact from which the popular name for the house derives.

The dog-trot represented luxurious accommodations for the American backwoods, where a man, his wife, eleven children, two overnight guests, and assorted animals have been recorded as sleeping in a cabin of a single room. Because of the breezeway, it was especially popular in the South.

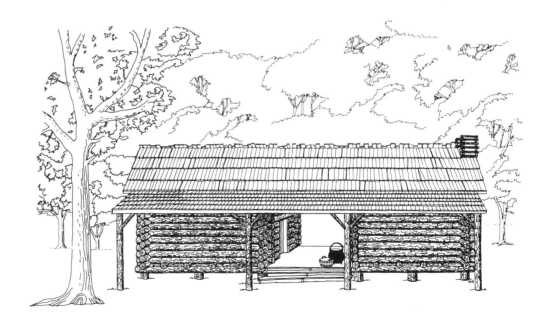

The Log Tradition
and the Pioneer House

National Types

72. The English Garrison House: *Freely based on the Micum McIntire Garrison, Scotland, Maine, ca. 1640-92.*

73. German Blockbau: *Bertolet-Herbein Cabin; Berks County, Pa., between 1737 and 1745.*

72. Though outside the mainstream of English tradition, a specialized type of log dwelling was known in the British Isles. It was the famous "garrison house," built of massive timbers, neatly hewn and closely fitted, the logs dovetailed, lapped, or butted into corner posts. These defensive structures were used on the New England frontier during the seventeenth and eighteenth centuries as strongholds against Indian attack.

The most prominent citizen typically built a garrison in which his neighbors took refuge during raids. The great, solid logs were hard to set on fire and made it difficult for marauders to hack their way in. Windows were tiny and barred; doors thick and strong. The overhanging upper story contained slots through which defenders could fire down on attackers. One garrison even had a portcullus to lower behind the door.

Though New England frontiersmen probably were unaware of it, they were living in reasonable facsimiles of eleventh-century Norman "castles"—also made of logs—which had been hastily thrown up after the Conquest as a protection against unfriendly Saxon natives, before there was leisure to build castles of stone.

73. In Germany, log construction had been a widespread peasant vernacular with numerous variations. Shown here is a house of *Blockbau*, or hewn logs, with V-notched corner joints. Logs typically were spaced apart and the voids chinked with stones and clay, while the gable end was surfaced with vertical boarding. Small casement windows, the double door, and the hood, or pent, above it, all are faithfully German.

Another characteristic feature was the slightly off-center chimney—distinct from the corner fireplace of the Swedes, the center chimney of an English garrison, and the exterior stack applied to log construction by Scots-Irish and English borrowers. It created the typical German plan (Fig. 83a), dividing the lower story into two major rooms, the *Kuche*, or kitchen, running the depth of the house, and the slightly wider *Stube*, or parlor, from which, at the rear, a small bedroom usually was partitioned off. Variations on this German log tradition are shown in the following chapter: a one-room cabin (Fig. 78), a two-story farmhouse (Fig. 84), and a saltbox (Fig. 88).

74. The Southern Log House: *Cade's Cove,*
Great Smoky Mountains National Historic Park,
Tenn., early 19th c.

74. The American frontier was one of the world's most effective architectural melting pots. Illustrated here is a solid, skillfully built two-story house of German *Blockbau*, combined with a stone chimney of English Tudor ancestry. Yet another culture—the French—contributed the twin porches which run the length of this frontier dwelling. The resulting silhouette is strikingly similar to that of frame houses in the South (Figure 107), a region pervasively influenced by the French–West Indian tradition.

Log dwellings as large and finely made as this were not temporary shelters but permanent homes. They reflect the social distinctions which operated even on the frontier. The line was firmly drawn between settlers who continued to live in makeshift cabins of rough logs and those who went to the considerable effort of building neatly hewn and dovetailed log houses.

This one is part of Cade's Cove, a virtually untouched log village in the Great Smoky Mountains, settled by English pioneers who pushed inland after the Revolution. So stable and successful was Cade's Cove that descendants of the original settlers were, until a few years ago, still living in the log houses built by their Revolutionary ancestors.

The Log Tradition and the Pioneer House

The Great Plains Dwelling

75. Homesteader's Dugout: *Custer County, Montana, 19th c.*

76. The Soddie: *Homesteader's Dwelling, Nebraska, late 19th c.*

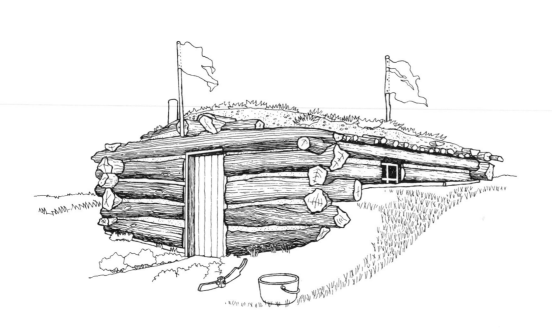

75. As the pioneers left the eastern forests, they began to feel the scarcity of timber for building. The Great Plains opened up to them a treeless expanse of prairie, stretching on for limitless miles. Cottonwoods grew along the rivers but nowhere else. To the north, in the rolling tableland of eastern Montana, trees were scarce, sagebrush the common vegetation. The dugout was a typical solution that used far fewer logs than a normal house. Settlers sometimes brought stock sash windows west with them in their covered wagons, and one is seen here. The ragged flags atop the dugout were neither a patriotic nor a decorative touch but a practical necessity. After a buffalo hunt or a trapping expedition, they allowed the returning owner to find the hillock which was his home amid the vast expanse of endless prairie.

76. This house was built of "Nebraska Marble," the name homesteaders in that state gave to prairie sod, the only available building material on much of the Great Plains. In a method copied from the Pawnee and Mandan Indians, settlers cut the deeply compacted sod into building blocks to construct their dwellings.

The soddie was the typical pioneer home of the land rush, when the Great Plains were opened up to homesteading after the Civil War. Some were no more than dugouts, but many were freestanding sod boxes. This example is characteristic of the better sod house, with blocks neatly squared, a paneled door, and stock window sash, precious luxuries brought from the civilization that homesteaders had left behind. "Lace curtains" at the windows were cut from old newspapers. The only fuel for the stove was "buffalo chips," "cow chips," corn stalks and cobs, or bundles of dried prairie grass. Nearly every house, however, had its trophies of buffalo horns and a cage or two of birds at the doorway.

The soddie was cool in summer and warm in winter, but it was dirty and full of bugs. Cloths often were hung above tables and beds to catch the dirt sifting down from the sod roof.

The Log Tradition
and the Pioneer House

Millionaire's Log Cabin

77. The Camp Beautiful: *Sagamore Lodge, Camp of Alfred Gwynne Vanderbilt, Adirondack Mts., New York, 1893. William West Durant, designer, builder, and first owner.*

77. While westward-moving pioneers were taking shelter in rude cabins, dugouts, and soddies, a very different type of log house appeared in the Adirondack Mountains of New York. It was the north woods lodge, designed for the leisure of a new American upper class and christened by contemporaries "The Camp Beautiful."

The idea of rustic luxury had been conceived by William West Durant, president of the Adirondack Railroad and developer par excellence of the north woods he loved. Durant created a distinctive school of Adirondack architecture, combining a glorified log construction with the airy balconies of the Swiss chalet. On the exterior, logs were left with the bark on, but interior surfaces were peeled, planed, sanded, and rubbed with beeswax, creating a wall appropriately rustic yet smooth and sweet-scented.

Durant pioneered the year-round use of these woodland retreats and set their lavish tone. But no one outdid Alfred Gwynne Vanderbilt, owner of Sagamore Lodge. He and his entourage traveled to camp by private railroad car and private yacht (or, in winter, horsedrawn sleighs). Christmas dinner at Sagamore was a feast à la Delmonico, eaten in front of a roaring fire under the sweet-scented beams. Twenty-two servants made sure that roughing it was not too rough. Had he known of its existence, the American backwoodsman would have marveled at log cabin life as played out in Adirondack baronies by some of the most powerful men in America.

4

Chapter 4

A German Tradition

Like tolerant Dutch Nieuw Nederland some 40 years earlier, Pennsylvania's experiment in political freedom drew colonists of many nationalities and of varied religious beliefs. As an English Quaker and founder of the colony, William Penn extended an open invitation to pacifist and persecuted sects wherever they might originate.

The Welsh barony near Philadelphia was established as a haven for Baptists, leaving its memorial in the famous name of Bryn Mawr. Swedish and Finnish Lutherans had been on the banks of the Schuylkill before Penn. Later, Scots-Irish Presbyterians would pour into the colony. But in the early eighteenth century the most notable migration, other than the English itself, was the German. There were Lutherans and a few Catholics among them; but many were of the small "heretic sects" that had been persecuted alike by Roman Catholics and orthodox Protestants: the Quakers, Mennonites, Moravians, Amish, United Brethren, Dunkers, Schwenkfelders, and others.

The background of these people was a tangled one. At the time of American settlement, there was no German nation in the sense that we understand today. Instead, there were a number of small, independent, German-speaking states, still entirely feudal in their ways. It was from a group of such little principalities, situated west of the Rhine and known collectively as the Palatinate, that the majority of settlers came.

Some of the emigrants were not German at all, but were Swiss or Dutch Mennonites or French Huguenots who had fled to the Palatinate years before, during a brief period of religious tolerance there. These people were included among the German colonists. Thus, more than one ethnic tradition contributed to German architecture in America.

The first group of German and Dutch-German Mennonites arrived in Pennsylvania on the ship Concord—the German Mayflower—in the year 1683, just two years after the founding of the colony. But it was not until the second decade of the eighteenth century that the trickle became a flood, giving Pennsylvania what remains, even today, the largest population of German descent of any state in the Union.

One of the first settlements was an ethnic enclave of German Quakers named Germantown, not far from Philadelphia and now a part of that city. However, it was toward the outlying countryside, especially today's Lancaster, Berks, York, Dauphin, and Bucks Counties and into the Lehigh Valley, that the German settlers migrated in ever-increasing numbers. This part of America, so like their homeland in its equable climate, rich soil, and dense forests, beckoned irresistibly to the displaced German peasants.

This is what we know today as "Pennsylvania Dutch" country from a corruption of the word *Deutsch* meaning German. It is one of the few areas of America in which old-world customs, dress, language, and architecture have been at least partially preserved. Here, the bearded Old Order Amish in their sober, collarless black suits and broad-brimmed hats, can still be seen at market or on back-country roads driving their horse-drawn buggies. And here, too, may be glimpsed the solid stone farmhouses and decorated bank barns that have made the region famous.

However, what we see today represents a revolution in the pattern of life of the original German settlers. Though the individual farm had been common in Switzerland and occasional in the Germanic states, life in the Palatinate was based mainly on the agricultural village. Peasants lived close together in a compact community, farming small outlying fields under the harsh laws and taxes of the local overlord.

In the best of times, this tenure exacted punishing toil as the price for subsistence. But during the religious wars of the seventeenth century, these people had been the victims of alternating Protestant and Catholic rulers, experiencing with each change the most brutal oppression: homes burned, family and friends killed, crops and orchards devastated.

In the safe haven of Pennsylvania, in a colony dedicated to religious freedom, and allowed for the first time to own property outright, the Palatinate refugees satisfied a long-repressed land hunger. Sacrificing everything to enlarge their holdings, these frugal and hard-working people, within a short time, possessed themselves of much of the richest farmland in Pennsylvania. The agricultural village that had

been the traditional pattern transplanted to America thus gave way to the large, individual farm, with the village acting only as a trading center.

Starting with a small log cabin and barn, over the years (and sometimes generations), these farms grew to include an imposing stone house, an even larger bank barn, and a whole complex of related buildings sited around one or more courtyards. The German peasant, now a free man and master of his own acres, had remembered and copied his former overlord.

In the same way, he clung to a traditional architecture that was largely medieval. Many of the houses built in Pennsylvania during the major years of settlement would have looked at home in the Black Forest or in a village on the Rhine during the Middle Ages.

However, the Germans had settled in an English colony at a time when English architecture already had turned to the classic. Almost from the beginning, German houses were an amalgam. Stock windows, for example, were immediately available through English carpentry shops in the new eighteenth-century sash which was all the rage in Philadelphia. These, as well as other stock details, were incorporated in the German house.

In a separate trend, a few colonists imported handbooks direct from their homeland, building German versions of the Renaissance styles. Medieval, Anglo-German, or German Renaissance—all were included under the heading of Pennsylvania German architecture and all were built during the eighteenth century.

The result is a regional architecture of unusual variety, here medieval, there thoroughly classic, in size ranging from a log or stone cabin to near-mansion proportions. Yet all were recognizably part of the same tradition with deep roots in the past. This family resemblance maintained itself even a state or a continent away. German houses in North Carolina, Maryland, Wisconsin, and Texas illustrate the durability of folk tradition across time and space.

A German Tradition

The Medieval Echo

78. *Blockbau* or Hewn Log Construction:
Georg Mueller Spring House, Milbach, Pa., 1752.

79. The Stone Cabin: *Hans Herr House, Lancaster County, Pa. Built for his father by Christian Herr, 1719.*

78. Unlike those of the English, the first homes of German colonists really were log cabins, though few remain today. This little spring house on the Mueller property perpetuates the tradition. It may have served as a temporary home while the main house was under construction, a common practice in German Pennsylvania. Note the tiny barred window, typical of a frontier dwelling, and the primitive wooden door latch.

For his first crude shelter, the German might leave his logs in the rough and cross them at the corners, but for any permanent structure, he preferred to dress his timbers. This spring house, therefore, was built of *Blockbau,* or hewn logs, in the best German tradition. Typically, logs were spaced apart and the void between filled with nogging. Vertical siding surfaced the gable. There were various types of corner joint. This one is the *Schwalben-schwanzen,* or swallowtail, a type that required great skill to hew. Each surface of the notch was cut to slope both out and down so that rainwater would drain to the exterior.

79. The Hans Herr house was the home of the Mennonite Bishop of Pequea Creek, the first German settlement in Lancaster County. It is a textbook example of the early German-Swiss stone dwelling. The steep pitch of its roof and the stone walls, nearly 2 feet thick, are thoroughly medieval. So are the tiny wooden casement windows, board shutters, and V-patterned door.

In characteristic German fashion, the house was built on a hillside over a spring, providing a continuous supply of ice cold water through a trough in the cellar. The flow served not only as a water source but as a coolant for milk and other perishables.

This down-slope room also may have been designed as a refuge against Indian attack. Its ceiling is a massive stone barrel vault and its windows, 30 inches wide on the interior, narrow to 6 inches on the outside, like firing slits. However, relations between the Indians and the kindly Mennonites turned out to be friendly. After a snowstorm, the Herr family often awoke to find Indians asleep around the fireplace. As the Indians had discovered, the German stone house was a snug retreat. Warm in winter and cool in summer with "running water" and built-in "refrigeration," it offered the most convenient and comfortable living of any early colonial dwelling.

80. This little stone house with its red tiled roof, flowered shutters, and whimsical animals on the cellar door is straight out of Hansel and Gretel—a quaint and cozy fairy-tale cottage.

The front of the house and the lower doorway are sheltered by "outlookers," as these slanted German hoods were called. Also Nordic is the *Vorschuss,* or gabled hood, over the loft window. When the shutters were closed, their flowered side showed on the interior as "pictures" against the whitewashed walls.

The roof is surfaced with flat, round-ended tile, a German type, ingeniously functional. Rows were laid vertically and each tile slightly grooved down the center for a vertical runoff. Despite occasional daylight between rows, the roofs did not leak. Though not built over a spring in typical German fashion, this house was conveniently near a backyard brook.

A German Tradition

The Medieval Echo

81. *Fachwerkbau* **or Half-Timbering:** *Third House, Old Salem, N.C., 1767.*

82. Brick and Stone House: *Winkler Bakery, Old Salem, N.C., 1800.*

81. This house is of *Fachwerkbau,* the German name for half-timbering. Although a medieval system of construction was employed here, the large sash windows, broad form, and comparatively shallow roof peak of this house mark it as an eighteenth-century dwelling.

The "Third House" is one of six nearly identical dwellings built along the main street of the village of Salem, a Moravian religious settlement in North Carolina. Following old-world custom, houses fronted directly on the street. On this steeply sloping site, rear access to the main living quarters is by exterior stairway placed parallel to the wall and creating a side approach to the door which was typically German. Also Germanic is the stone lower story.

As in other devotional communities, the Salem church directed both spiritual and business activities, ordering a daily schedule of work, worship, and music by which the Moravians lived their lives. The "Sisters House" and the "Brothers House" were communal homes for single men and women. Families dwelt separately; but their houses, like this one, reflected the communal life. The main floor was organized around a central kitchen with a private living room and bedroom on one side and a large "assembly hall" on the other.

82. This brick and stone dwelling illustrates the old-world custom of combining home and business in a single structure. The lower story is the bake shop with family living quarters above. The small shed attached to the house at the right is the bake oven, and to the rear of the bakery is a woodshed for storing the large quantity of fuel necessary.

The house is a traditional German type which retains its steep, medieval roofline despite up-to-date sash windows and outside shutters. The deep door hood is a Baroque version of the *Vorschuss.* Note that this German house has a "saltbox" roofline, though its rear lean-to (unlike that of the English saltbox) is made of different material than the main body of the structure.

A German Tradition

The German Interior

83. The German *Stube*, or Parlor: *Based on the Mueller House, Milbach, Pa., 1752.*

83a. Typical German Plan: *Mueller House, Milbach, Pa.*

BEDROOM

KÜCHE

STUBE

83. The German parlor was alive with color and pattern. Deep green, rust red, a muted blue and mustard were favorite colors, combined in the floral and animal motifs that decorated furniture and pottery. Unlike English colonists, the Germans ate in the parlor and the heavily carved dining table was part of its furnishings. Note also the straight chair with its scalloped back and heart-shaped cutout. A black cast-iron stove was embellished with scenes from the Bible in bas relief.

The German heating system was both ingenious and practical. A large cooking fireplace opened into the kitchen, but the parlor was equipped with the "five-plate stove." It had a top, a bottom, two sides and a front, ie., five plates of cast iron. The back of the stove had no plate,but opened through the wall into the kitchen fireplace. Every now and then the housefrau would shovel a few coals into the stove, which warmed the parlor by radiation. There was no wood supply in the parlor and no

mess, a typical tidy German arrangement.

83a. The larger German farmhouse typically was divided into two major rooms, the *Stube*, or parlor, and the *Küche*, or kitchen. Often, a small bedroom was partitioned off the *Stube* at the rear. A central fireplace opened into the kitchen, connecting to a parlor stove (dotted lines). The stairway typically was placed in the kitchen, near the entry door. The house from which this plan was taken is illustrated in Figure 86.

A German Tradition

A Pennsylvania Vernacular

84. The German Original: *Log House near Landis' Store, Pa., 18th c.*

85. An Anglo-German Translation: *Squire Boone House, childhood home of Daniel Boone, Baumstown, Pa., original house ca. 1735; addition 1779; restored 1938.*

84. One of the distinctively German features often seen on Pennsylvania houses is the pent roof: a "hood" between the first and second stories which sheltered door, windows, and lower walls. As this drawing shows, it was used even on log houses. In fact, this is a log version of the traditional German plan employed also for the finest stone dwellings. The central chimney, which serves both downstairs rooms, is slightly off-center, making the *Küche,* or kitchen, a little larger than the *Stube,* or parlor.

Typical of German log construction are the trim timbers spaced apart and chinked and the vertical siding at the gable end. A log house as fine as this would be the second dwelling of the German colonist, following his first, hastily built log hut. With such a house, it might be another generation or two before a third, permanent family home was built of stone, the Germans' favored material.

85. This large stone dwelling shares its most prominent feature with the log house in Figure 84. The continuous pent roof was part of the German vocabulary of building that entered the Pennsylvania vernacular. Here it embellishes what once was the boyhood home of Daniel Boone.

However, the famous frontiersman probably would not recognize his home as it appears today. Young Daniel, born in a log cabin on the same property, lived here until 1750, when he was sixteen years old. But the stone house he moved into as a child was only the far portion of the present dwelling, terminating at the central chimney: a small, one-room-to-a-floor pioneer stone cabin.

Today, more than doubled in size and with Georgian detailing and a doorway in classic balance, it has become one of the handsomest mansions in the Anglo-German tradition. Though built by an Englishman and remodeled by another, it is basically a German stone farmhouse—its original cellar built over a spring and its most striking feature the characteristically German pent roof.

86. The Mueller house is the finest example of the German Renaissance still standing in Pennsylvania. Most German farmhouses contemporary with this one were influenced by the English Georgian style. But the Müller house is pure German, the design taken from an imported German builder's handbook of the period.

Its most striking feature is the bell-shaped gambrel roof with a pronounced break at mid-roofline and a "kick" at the eaves. This is a characteristic German gambrel, distinct from both the English type (Figures 24 and 25) and the Dutch (Figure 64).

Quoins of dressed red sandstone contrast with the limestone of the walls, lending another touch of Renaissance elegance to this sturdy country mansion. Heavy oaken doors are paneled in a Germanic version of the classic. At the same time, the house encloses the traditional German plan and retains the wraparound pent roof. Despite its massive dignity and Renaissance features, this remains a vernacular German house.

87. This Federal mansion was built by a German, but virtually the only thing Germanic about it is its thick stone walls. The late English Georgian style has swallowed up German tradition. The German plan is gone, replaced by the classical center hall with its formal symmetry. Typical of the times in Federal America are the sash windows with 12 over 12 lights, the fanlight above the door, the classic trim of doorway and dormer windows, the splayed keystone lintels, the outside shutters, paneled on the first floor, louvered on the second, and a classical cornice which carries across the gable end.

This applied style probably was copied from an English builder's handbook. Gottlieb Drexel, a skilled German carpenter, is generally credited with carving the fine woodwork, and a faint German touch is visible there: the very English moldings have been enriched with German gougework and wood appliqué. However, the basic woodwork may have been bought ready-made in a Philadelphia carpenter's shop and transported to the Fischer farm by flatboat or Conestoga wagon, a common practice.

A German Tradition

A Persistent Heritage

88. The Wisconsin Log House: *Christian Turck House, Germantown, Wisc., ca. 1840.*

89. The Pennsylvania Stone House: *Typical Anglo-German Stone House, late 18th c.*

90. The Maryland Stone House: *Hager's Fancy, Jonathan Hager House, Hagerstown, Md.; original one-story-and-loft, 1739-40, enlarged late 18th c.*

91. The Texas Clapboard House: *The Sunday House, Fredericksburg, Tex., mid-19th c.*

88. This type of German log house with its pent roof only across the front undoubtedly was built in Pennsylvania during the eighteenth century, relating as it does to pent-roofed stone houses there. This example, virtually unchanged, was built in Wisconsin during the nineteenth century.

The Turck house also repeats the characteristic wood technique which Pennsylvania German colonists had used a century earlier (Figure 78). Logs were neatly hewn and widely spaced, the cracks filled with stone and clay nogging. Vertical siding at the gable remains stubbornly German. So does the side placement of the porch steps. The lean-to addition, here used as a summer kitchen and extra bedroom, had been a feature of earlier German houses (Figure 89).

89. The house seen here—reflecting William Penn's mixed colony—is not pure German. The basic type remains German, with a lean-to at the rear and the traditional pent roof like those in the log house (Figure 88). But the English influence has taken over elsewhere. Sash windows, paneled shutters, and the matching paneled door are in the English Georgian style. This combination of the German medieval and the English classic is found on quite early Pennsylvania houses, built as they were when stock elements of Georgian design were readily available. In this house, even the German plan has given way, as seen by the end chimneys, centered doorway, and formal balance in window placement.

90. At some point during the Americanization of the German house, what had been the pent roof turned into a front porch. This characteristically German type was used on Hager's Fancy, a two-story dwelling which grew from a small cottage as its pioneer owner prospered.

To the casual observer, Hager's Fancy hardly looks German at all. Classic details give this traditional farmhouse a certain Georgian elegance. However, German ancestry is revealed in the sturdy stone construction, off-center chimney, projecting hooded porch, and the use of the cellar as a spring house (the stream emerges at right).

Jonathan Hager was a blacksmith, gunsmith, and fur trader who became so successful that the frontier village in which he settled was renamed after him. His was the only stone house in a town of two hundred log dwellings. Though more prosperous than most, he was only one of the many Germans who pushed on beyond Pennsylvania in the eighteenth century to settle in the fertile Piedmont just east of the Appalachian Mountains, where their houses still may be seen today.

91. This little house shows how German farmers in pioneer Texas faithfully reproduced the German front porch and outside stairway built a century earlier in the eastern settlements. It was one of many such small dwellings in Fredericksburg, Texas, a town established in 1846 as a market village from which German settlers spread out to claim land for cultivation.

In order to attend church services on Sunday (and to do their trading the day before), the outlying ranchers and farmers built "Sunday Houses" which they occupied only once a week. They were miniature dwellings, usually one small downstairs room, possibly a lean-to kitchen, a minuscule loft, and a tiny front porch. Here the German family tied up the horses, cooked and ate meals, slept on Saturday night, and visited with friends in a "home away from home."

The Sunday house was not unique to the Germans. Early New England colonists had built tiny "Sabbath Houses" in which to feed and warm themselves during breaks in their formidable all-day church service held in an unheated meeting house.

5

Chapter 5

A French Tradition

For more than 100 years, France controlled the heartland of America, from Canada on the north to the Gulf of Mexico on the south and from the Allegheny Mountains to the Rockies. However, of Louis XIV's original American empire, only a small portion was ever colonized. The French who ventured down from Canada were mostly wilderness men: trappers, Indian traders, voyageurs, *coureurs de bois,* Jesuit missionaries, and soldiers. The fur trade flourished; so did far-flung frontier forts and missions.

But the building of stable settlements below Canada was limited mainly to a narrow, vertical swathe, stretching down through the Great Lakes, along the Mississippi River and its tributaries, to the Gulf of Mexico. On or near these waterways, the French placed little villages, including such familiar twentieth-century names as Detroit, St. Louis, Natchez, Biloxi,and New Orleans.

Very few French houses from the early period still stand today. Only photographs or paintings remain of the riverfront dwellings of old St. Louis. A handful of French examples from the eighteenth century may be found in the bypassed villages of Kaskaskia and Cahokia in Illinois and St. Genevieve in Missouri. In and near New Orleans, there is more than a remnant. Here, the French way of building took root, acting as the base for a regional architecture and giving us, through later houses, an idea of the earlier ones. Canadian houses are not illustrated in this book, but some of the best remaining French examples still exist in that country, especially in such quaint backwaters as the Isle d'Orleans in rural Quebec.

All these houses are part of a peasant vernacular which, at one time, stretched from French Canada on the north to French Louisiana on the south, creating between the two a 1,000-mile corridor marked by a coherent architectural pattern.

That it should be coherent is strange indeed. For this vertical slice of a continent encompassed a range of geography and climate from the frozen north through temperate middle America to the near-tropical Gulf Coast. Added to it were scattered French settlements on the Eastern Seaboard, notably in the lush, warm Carolinas and in the New York-New Jersey area with its pronounced seasonal shifts. The French tradition in the new world accommodated itself to a diversity of place, climate, and condition encountered by no other.

At its extremes, the major line of French settlement shows characteristic houses which seem to have little in common. The usual Canadian house was solid and compact, with a high hipped roof which might be half again as tall as the sturdy walls beneath it. This dwelling had a snug, cozy look—a house for a cold climate.

In Louisiana, the French plantation house often resembled a pavilion, with an umbrella roof that sheltered *galeries,* as the French called them, on all four sides. French doors, rather than windows, could be thrown open all around, inviting the breeze in this near-tropical climate.

Historians believe that the broad roof and encircling porches which appeared on French houses in America were copied from tropical dwellings of the West Indies, with which trade was brisk in the eighteenth century. But the French also had a galleried house of their own—the Mediterranean farmhouse—with porches only across the front. Both types were built in French America, the latter as far north as Canada.

Conversely, the house without porches was built in the deep South. A few examples remain of the small, early dwelling of New Orleans; and it proves to be a compact, often hip-roofed type—a close match to its Canadian cousin.

Similar structural systems also are found throughout the French area of colonization. Most of the early settlers came from the north of France, especially Brittany and Normandy. The traditional building material of Brittany was stone and of Normandy half-timbering, including the ancient *poteaux-en-terre,* a vertical log construction much like the English palisade or puncheon.

These techniques were transported to the American continent, stone becoming the favored material in Canada and vertical logs along the Mississippi frontier, but with examples of both types to be found in either country. *Briquéte-en-poteaux,* a French half-timbering that used bricks as filler between posts, was common in New Orleans. Most Louisiana plantation houses, and many early city houses, adopted a combination of masonry and wood, using brick for a raised basement, topped by a second story of vertical timbers.

Whether of stone, brick, log, or half timber, the French house characteristically was plastered over and whitewashed so that it was all but impossible to tell what was underneath. Stone houses in Quebec presented much the same smooth, white exterior as did the vertical log houses of Missouri and Illinois. Even the combined brick and wood dwellings of Louisiana often achieved a uniform appearance throughout their first and second stories.

A variation, used of course only on wooden houses, or parts of houses, was a surfacing of clapboards. Found in all areas, it seems to have been most commonly employed in South Carolina. Huguenots in Dutch New Jersey combined local sandstone with a clapboarded or shingled gable, plastering only the stone portion of their one-story houses.

The French tradition, though encompassing extremes of climate and adapting to them, maintained consistency even at its farthest outposts. What we find is a vocabulary of architecture common to all French settlements, but used by them in different ways. There are many variations, but all are somehow related, sharing a roofline here, a *galerie* there, achieving partial kinship through form, structure, material, or detailing; and yet displaying in the major areas of settlement, distinct regional types.

A French Tradition

The Mississippi Valley

92. This tiny, hip-roofed cottage was a basic type in the French colonial tradition: an essential house on which elaborations were worked to suit regional climate and terrain. Construction might be of stone, vertical logs, or half-timbering. But whatever the material, it typically was plastered over and whitewashed to create a smooth exterior surface.

Very Norman French is the extreme verticality of the end planes of the roof, which is known as a *pavillon.* The earliest roofs were of thatch, followed by bark and, finally, shingles. Note the little finials at the ends of the roof ridge, a French device to protect the shingling from weather at its most vulnerable points. Another Gallic touch was an apple-green door.

Plaster was the favored interior finish, but some of the frontier houses were lined with birch bark or their log walls were hung with deerskins. The most primitive had dirt floors, with Indian mats as a covering and perhaps a bearskin beside the bed—testimony to the proficiency of the French as hunters and trappers.

93. Here, the same basic French cottage has been adapted to a warm climate by adding a *galerie,* or porch, to encircle the house, and extending the roof to shelter it. The bonnet roof, reminiscent of a troll's cap in a French fairy tale, was a regional vernacular in the Mississippi Valley, though found as far away as Haiti. Some historians believe that this type originated in the West Indies, with which the French maintained a flourishing trade.

Whatever its source, this French plantation house was a brilliant solution to the problems of a warm, moist climate. Its broad roof served not only as an umbrella against the rain, sheltering walls from weathering, but also as a parasol shading the house during hot days.

Also a practical feature was the elevation above ground level. Except for major disasters, the house could ride out rain and flood. Dampness did not penetrate its floor. The passage of air beneath the house helped to keep the underside dry and cool and to dry out the wet ground after rain.

94. This illustration shows what a French vertical log house looked like without its usual

92. The *Pavillon:* *Diagram of typical Hip-Roofed French Cottage.*

93. The Bonnet Roof: *Diagram of typical Galleried French Plantation House.*

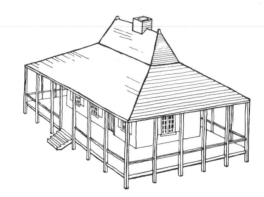

surfacing of plaster and whitewash. Timbering commonly was exposed in the part of Normandy from which many of the settlers came, though rarely so in the French colonies. This type of construction is called *poteaux-sur-solle,* meaning posts-on-foundation, a system superior to *poteaux-en-terre,* in which posts were simply set upright into the ground. Here, a rock-filled trench was topped by a log sill into which the timbers were seated. Logs were hewn flat on all sides and the spaces between filled with broken rock held together by lime mortar, a chinking known as *pierrotage.*

The plan of the house is typically French. Each room had its own entry door. Thus, any part of the house could be reached from the out-of-doors by way of the covered *galerie* which functioned as an exterior hallway.

The Saucier house included many unusually fine touches: casement windows with glass panes, matching glazed French doors, beaded ceiling

beams, plaster-on-lath interior walls, and, wonder of wonders, a floor of split sassafras logs rather than tamped earth.

95. This is the "raised cottage," yet another variation of the basic French colonial house. Typically, the ground floor was built of stone or brick, while the upper part remained an airy, wooden pavilion.

Though this St. Louis example was a city house, the type traces back to a very ancient peasant dwelling in which the lower part of the structure was a stable for animals, with family living quarters on the floor above. In French America, the enclosed ground floor was used as a "service area," containing laundry and other work rooms, slaves' or servants' quarters, and storage. Alternately, it might be turned into a shop or offices. The family lived on the raised and galleried first floor. French houses of this general type may be seen in the Vieux Carre, the Old Quarter of New Orleans.

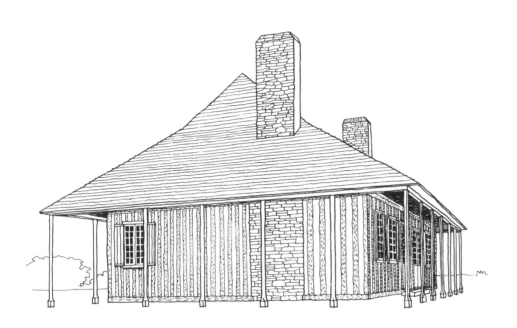

A French Tradition

The Louisiana Plantation House

When French settlers arrived in southern Louisiana near the mouth of the Mississippi River, they found a flat, swampy lowland, laced with muddy rivers, sinuous bayous, and a network of smaller streams. The vegetation was lush, the climate warm and languorous, rain seasonal but copious, the ground marshy, and flooding a commonplace.

This region, with New Orleans at its focus, but including also the nearby bayou country and the river plantations up the Red, the Cane, and the Mississippi, could be compared to a wilderness Venice. Everyone traveled and traded by boat. Planters on the Mississippi sent cotton and sugar direct to Europe from their own docks and received furniture, silver, and brocades at the same place from incoming ships. Lumber and other raw materials from the north were floated down the Mississippi on flatboats.

Except for the river footpaths and, here and there, a cowpath, this countryside had no roads. On the smaller waterways near New Orleans, brown-sailed market barges from each plantation glided past Indian pirogues or the cushioned passenger boats which carried master, mistress, or children on any one of a dozen errands and outings. Visits to other plantations were frequent and lengthy. For the bayou families, Saturday was the great day when everyone took boat for New Orleans for shopping, trading, meeting one's friends, billiards, cockfighting, and fêtes.

Even in New Orleans, however, water was not left behind. City squares, on the grid pattern, were marked off by drainage ditches and were known as "islets," which no doubt they were in wet weather. Until the problem of ground water was solved, the city was too marshy to permit normal paving or building.

These difficulties of terrain are brought out by a young visitor to New Orleans in his description of the unique local method of traveling to a ball, "as hacks and public vehicles were then unknown."

"Everything prepared, [he wrote] the order was given to march; when to my horror and amazement, the young ladies doffed their shoes and stockings which were carefully tied up in silk handkerchiefs, and took up the line of march, barefooted, for the ballroom. After paddling through mud and mire, lighted by lanterns carried by the negro slaves, we reached the scene of action without accident. The young ladies halted before the door and shook one foot after another in a pool of water close by. After repeating this process some half a dozen times, the feet were freed of the accumulated mud and were in a proper state to be wiped dry by the slaves who had carried towels for the purpose. Then silk stockings and satin slippers were put on again, cloaks were thrown aside, tucked-up trains were let down, and the ladies entered the ballroom, dry-shod and lovely in the candlelight."[9]

The conditions which sent proper young ladies barefoot to a ball were the same facts of existence which shaped the houses in which they lived, namely, warmth, water, and mud. The earliest dwellings were simply wooden shells with a *galerie* on one or more sides: the same sort built by French settlers in Illinois and Missouri and shown on the preceding pages. But here they were raised above ground, poised as it were on stilts above the swampy terrain.

Virtually none of these early dwellings remain. The disastrous fires of 1788 and 1794 all but destroyed the old French village of New Orleans. Rebuilt under Spanish edict, it would become a city of brick and tile. The early plantation houses, too, are most of them gone, rotted by damp or swallowed by the Mississippi as its waters gradually ate away the banks on which they stood. But from the eighteenth-century descriptions, old engravings, and a few small houses of later date, we know what the early Louisiana dwellings must have looked like. They were, in fact, simply a primitive version of larger and grander houses which exist today. The basic early type would remain at the core of Louisiana domestic building no matter how modified over the years by wealth and period styles. By adapting their houses to the Gulf Coast's watery, semitropical domain, French settlers had created a unique and long-lived regional architecture.

96. The Louisiana plantation house evolved from the same small cottage as did the French colonial dwellings of the Mississippi Valley. However, the typical roof was different: a broad sunshade, straight from peak to eave, rather than the bonnet roof with its break in direction. Moreover, in the booming corn and sugar cane economy of Louisiana, the French cottage turned into a mansion.

Homeplace was characteristic of these large plantation houses, with service floor below, family quarters above, extra bedrooms under the roof, and porches all around. Slaves cooked the food in a separate kitchen building, carried it to a serving pantry, and thence to the master's table.

Typically, in this hot, humid, rainy climate, the *galeries* acted as exterior hallways. There were no windows; instead French doors gave easy access to and from every room. These were double doors with glass casements opening in, cypress shutters opening out. Lower walls were stuccoed brick but upper walls remained the old Norman-French vertical log system, plastered over and whitewashed to resemble an interior room. This surfacing was typical of Louisiana, where much casual entertaining took place on the *galerie*—the airy outdoor living room.

These late-eighteenth- and early-nineteenth-century houses had been lightly touched by classic fashion. The crude posts of the primitive "raised cottage" were supplanted by Tuscan columns at the lower story and by slender wooden colonnets above, a typical combination. Note also the pedimented dormer windows and ribbon lights over the doors—details shared by American houses during the Georgian period whether of English, Dutch, German, or French extraction.

97. This illustration shows the French plantation house in Victorian dress. Its gingerbread trim is a simplified wooden version of the intricate cast-iron lace that decorated the New Orleans town house (Figure 100).

The basic dwelling remained unchanged. But stairs are centered for classic symmetry and a rococo-Greek motif now caps French doors. Upper walls are surfaced with Gothic board-and-batten (here laid horizontally). In addition, the Spanish influence (Figure 113), which melded with the French in Louisiana, echoes in the brick arcade. This thoroughly eclectic house illustrates the charm and originality with which a traditional way of building was reinterpreted in the Victorian period.

96. Georgian: *Homeplace Plantation, The Fortier-Keller House, St. Charles Parish, La., 1801.*

97. Victorian: *Plantation House, Chalmette Road, La., 19th c.*

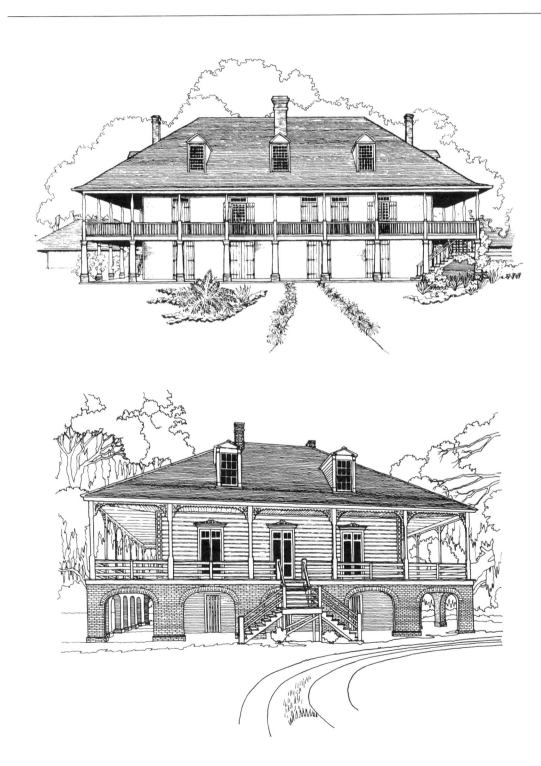

A French Tradition

The Louisiana Plantation House

98. Classic Revival: *Bon Sejour or Oak Alley, Governor Alexandre Roman Mansion, St. James Parish, La., ca. 1830-36. Joseph Pilie, probable architect; George Swainey, builder.*

98. The southern mansion reached its height of luxury during the rich decades preceding the Civil War. The formal classic styles—both the lingering Georgian and the new Greek Revival—reached the plantation country during those same years. The result was spectacular. It was as though a French peasant farmhouse had been waiting for the magic wand which would transform it into a palace. Bon Sejour ("a good visit") was part of this enchantment. Everything is here: a great classic colonnade sweeping from porch to roof; the grace of Federal fanlights and dormers; delicate wooden balustrades, simulating wrought iron, on gallery and belvedere; the balance of verticals and horizontals into a composition of faultless proportion.

The twenty-eight stately Tuscan columns which surround the house are matched in number by the twenty-eight live oaks which have given the plantation its other name, Oak Alley. Contrasting with the dark branches of the trees and their shifting shadows are the pale, pink-tinged walls of the house and its creamy colonnade. Oak Alley is a palatial mansion, a house designed to be serviced by a retinue of slaves. But underneath the grand manner, it remains the sensible, livable dwelling of its vernacular origin.

A French Tradition

The New Orleans Town House

99. The French Original: *Mayor Nicholas Girod House, New Orleans, La., 1814.*

100. Victorian Ironwork: *Le Pretre Mansion, New Orleans, La., 1836. Frederic Roy, builder, for Joseph Coulon.*

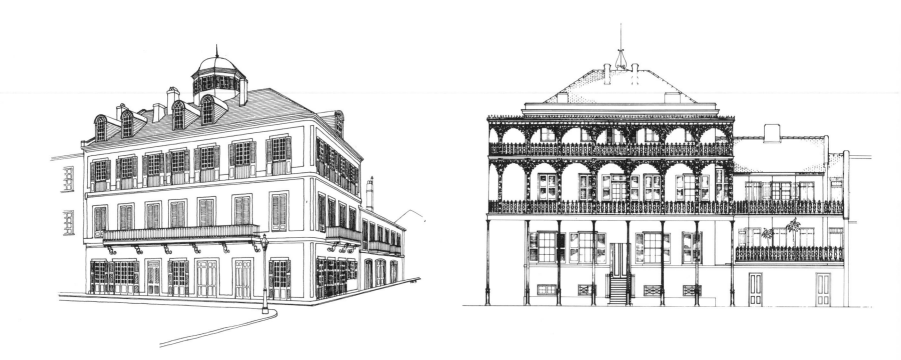

99. Nicholas Girod, a mayor of New Orleans, built this house, the finest French residence still standing in the city. Despite its urban elegance (a touch of the classic à la Louis XVI), it is visibly kin to the preceding French houses in this chapter, sharing with them the hipped roof, blocky form, and smooth, stuccoed wall surfaces which were so much a part of the French tradition.

Like the plantation house, this city dwelling reserved its ground floor for utilitarian purposes (here, offices and shops) with family living quarters above. Other likenesses are less obvious. Fronting directly on the street, this town house presents an aloof public facade. Nevertheless, it is an urban version of the plantation house, in effect turned outside in. Hidden from view at the rear, continuous open galleries overlook a private courtyard, defined by the house and its outbuildings. The carriage entrance, through the courtyard wall, is glimpsed at right. Inside, a splashing fountain, flower beds, perhaps a magnolia, sweet-smelling camellias, and other shrubs make a refreshing haven from the busy street: an ideal scheme for city living.

100. Behind its frivolous dress of cast-iron lace, the form of the traditional French town house can be glimpsed in this drawing. Like the earlier Girod House, the Le Pretre mansion still had its private *galeries* overlooking a walled court. But the new decorative ironwork was too delightful to hide from view. Street-front *galeries* were rapidly added to houses of all sorts, giving New Orleans its unique architectural identity.

Though romantically charming, this iron lacework was a technological phenomenon, part of the industrialization of America. It was cast iron, made cheaply and in quantity by machine, rather than traditional wrought iron, made by hand and therefore used sparingly. In other regions, such ironwork usually was painted black or, occasionally, white. But in New Orleans it was green, a color described as broken and blended by the atmosphere into "hues of emerald, lavender and blue of indescribable charm."[10] This ironwork first appeared during the Greek Revival period and the motifs seen here are Greek. But its intricate tracery expresses the spirit of a new age—the Victorian—in which fanciful decoration, of whatever style, would become the most important part of architecture.

A French Tradition

The Acadians

Late in the eighteenth century, a new group of French settlers arrived in Louisiana. They were Acadians (nicknamed "Cajuns"), so called after the French colony of Acadia in Canada from which they came. Refusing the oath of allegiance to England after the Peace of Utrecht, these French Canadians were forced to leave their homes. Some scattered through New England, others migrated to Georgia, but the most cohesive group ended their long trek in Louisiana, where they established a unique, waterborne culture in the bayous and swampy lowlands of the Gulf Coast.

They brought with them, virtually untouched by their stay in Canada, a tradition of French peasant architecture with roots going back to antiquity in the Mediterranean. This simple building type, with its gabled roof and a gallery across the front, was distinct from the hip-roofed French cottage which originated in Normandy and from which the largest and grandest plantation houses evolved.

The smallest of the Acadian houses was the "Cajun cottage" (Figure 101). In the following letter to the author, Leona M. Guirard, herself a Cajun who lived in such a cottage, describes what life in these houses was like.

"Cajuns are a happy people and their homes reflect a carefree, happy and informal type of existence. As the front room was the main bedroom, sometimes used as a sitting room, the gallery naturally became a year-round sitting room. The floor was just about knee-high.

Families were large and furniture, especially chairs, was scarce. The elder generation sat on the few chairs available and the rest of the family and friends sat at the edge of the gallery and let their feet hang. There were never balustrades on an Acadian house.

"When a person sat on the edge of the gallery with feet swinging just above the ground and a cup of hot coffee in hand he was in paradise. Never mind about looking forward to paradise, he had found it. The art of conversation flourished at that time, and each family had its teller of tall tales. He was called a *raconteur*. In each family at least one member played the accordion, the violin or the harmonica. You didn't have to travel to a night club to dance: wherever Cajuns a-gathered, the gathering usually broke into a dance. Always there was a stair leading to the attic. Should the weather be rainy, dancing was done in the boy's room in the attic.

"Many of the Acadian houses were not ever painted. The cypress used in building the home quickly became a silvery gray. However, the Acadians very often painted only the front door and that only on one side, the inside. You see, if the weather was good, the front door was opened and only the inside of the door was seen. It would have been wasteful to have painted the side which didn't show. If the weather was rainy and a bit cool and the door was closed, then those inside were cheered with the colorful door and no one was noticing the outside of the door when everyone was inside the house.

"The roof is steep which was necessarily so because here we drank rain water, there are no springs and bayou waters were too muddy for drinking. With a steep roof a heavy dew will put at least a couple of gallons of water in the rain barrels or cistern.

"The kitchen was not a part of the main house, but was separated from it by a small walkway (sometimes covered and sometimes not). There was no fire protection and a spark from a fireplace or cookstove falling on a dry cypress floor would have set the whole house afire. In case of fire a man with an axe could quickly destroy the walkway and the house would be safe from the burning kitchen.

"From one of the kitchen windows (or from the passage) there was always a shelf on the outside. This was called *une tablet*. Dishes were washed in a pan and the water was emptied on the ground below. Chickens quickly gobbled the bits of food from the ground and there were no odors resulting from such a practice. Neighborhood news and gossip passed quickly from one house to another while dishes were being washed. There was no need for a telephone. This was just as quick.

"I know you asked only about the house, but being a Cajun myself, and the *raconteur* of my family, I couldn't possibly stop there."

Leona M. Guirard

A French Tradition

The Gallery House

102. The Gallery House: *Typical Acadian Farmhouse, Acadia Parish, La., late 18th c.*

103. The Greek Revival Mansion: *Shadows-on-the-Teche, David Weeks House, New Iberia, La., 1831-35. James Bedell, master builder. Restored by Weeks Hall, 1922-58; Armstrong & Koch, architects.*

104. Triple House: *A multiple dwelling, New Orleans, La., 19th c.*

101. The "Cajun cottage" is a remarkable architectural antique, a vernacular type so little changed over the centuries that one can glimpse in it the primitive ancestor of the French galleried house (Figure 102). In minimum form, it had only one room and a loft; but no matter how small, there was a *galerie* across the front and a stairway in the traditional position at the end of the porch. No more than one room wide, it might be one, two, three, or four rooms deep, with doors lined up front to back for coolness.

The house is built of cypress, weathered gray; and the primitive chimney is constructed of moss and mud. Doors are the characteristic double French shutters. The doorway is curtained rather than screened, a practice which links this cottage to Italy in the Age of Justinian. Sixth-century Roman paintings show doorways with hangings exactly like this, neatly looped back. Surprisingly, they still can be seen in France today where multicolored plastic strips now usually substitute for fabric.

102. This galleried farmhouse, introduced by Acadian refugees from Canada, became a Louisiana type. Though evolving from a primitive

forebear much like the "Cajun cottage," the two-story form is very ancient too. Generations of peasant families along the Mediterranean lived in houses much like this. Cattle or sheep were stabled at ground level, with family quarters above. In America, the animals were moved out of the house; but the ground floor remained a service area. Traditionally, the balcony was known as the "spinning gallery"—the protected spot where the women of the household could enjoy the out-of-doors while working at one of their most time-consuming tasks.

The gallery house was not limited to France or to Louisiana. It was introduced by French colonists elsewhere in the South. Spanish versions appeared in Louisiana, Spanish Florida, Texas, and California. Adopted by settlers of other origin, it became a vernacular type throughout the South and Southwest, a house as suited to the warm regions of America as it had been to its original setting.

103. The Greek Revival transformed the simple French farmstead into an antebellum mansion. Dominating the facade are eight stately Doric columns, reaching unbroken from base to en-

tablature. Behind them, the plan, the *galerie*, the gabled form, all are typical of Bayou Teche. Nevertheless, the house is not entirely French. It was built by an Englishman and is, in fact, an English brick dwelling combined with the French galleried type. The house must once have looked lighter and more Gallic, for it originally was painted white. Through the years, this coating wore away, exposing the brickwork. The house has been left in this state, its color scheme a counterpoint of dull coral brick walls, blue-gray slate roof, green blinds, and cream-colored columns and woodwork.

104. This three-family house in New Orleans has done its best to look like a plantation mansion with the aid of a colonnaded porch and second-story *galerie* across the front. These features also make it a trifle more livable, though individual porch space is small and privacy noticeably lacking. Each duplex consists of two rooms, one to a floor, plus an attic loft. The wooden posts represent a crude attempt at Doric columns; and the plain, wide entablature is typical of stock Greek Revival detailing the country over. But underneath the trim, this multiple dwelling is yet another much-modified descendant of the ancient gallery house from the shores of the Mediterranean Sea.

79

A French Tradition

A Southern Vernacular

105. The French Original: *Louis Bolduc House, St. Genevieve, Mo., ca. 1770.*

106. The Southern Cottage: *Melrose Plantation, near Wedgefield, S.C.*

107. The Trinity House: *Jarrett Manor, or Traveler's Rest, near Toccoa, Ga., original house, Major Jesse Walton; enlarged by Devereaux Jarrett, ca. 1835.*

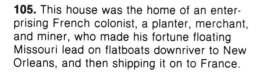

105. This house was the home of an enterprising French colonist, a planter, merchant, and miner, who made his fortune floating Missouri lead on flatboats downriver to New Orleans, and then shipping it on to France.

In those early days, men of considerable wealth often lived in modest houses, little more than cottages. This example shows once more the way in which raised porches and extended roofs transformed the blocky French house into a graceful pavilion.

It also illustrates the typical gabled roof of a small French-Missouri riverfront dwelling. Unlike the straight Acadian type, it breaks from a steep pitch to a gentle slope over the *galeries,* a close relative to the "bonnet roof" of the same Mississippi Valley region (Figures 93-5). In fact, this house—shown here as it appeared before restoration—now has its original bonnet roof. But the French colonial gable is of equal interest. The type lies behind the characteristic small cottage of the American South.

106. This house is the Cape Cod cottage of the South—the characteristic small dwelling of the states below the Mason-Dixon line. French colonists introduced the type to the Carolinas—clearly a relative of the French-Missouri cottage shown in the preceding illustration. However, this one is not a French original but an Americanized descendant. The French *galerie* has metamorphosed into an American front porch. Plastered vertical log construction has given way to frame. The break in the roofline is lower. Nevertheless, the silhouette is unmistakable.

The owner of such a dwelling might or might not be French and might or might not be wealthy. A rich planter in South Carolina, master of thousands of acres, more often than not lived in a plantation house like this. The type was adopted by the English and other settlers. Traveling west and translated into adobe, it became the typical ranch house of Texas. In fact, this modest dwelling type is so much a part of the vernacular that one can hardly travel anywhere in the South without seeing examples.

107. The two-story house of English tradition also acquired a porch in the South. However, instead of a single continuous roof, sweeping out to cover the *galeries,* the house, its front porch, and rear lean-to are distinctly separate elements, separately roofed. The tripartite form was used in Middleburg Plantation (not shown), built by a Huguenot in South Carolina, and dating to 1699, with later wings.

Our Anglicized example was enlarged to its present size and shape by a Georgia settler who came from South Carolina. After noting the traffic which passed his door, Devereaux Jarrett opened his home as a stagecoach inn, post office, and trading post, at the same time turning it into a wilderness fort.

The original owner had been massacred by Indians, and Jarrett did not look forward to the same fate. His doors were massive, his hinges made of heavy wrought iron, his locks imported from England, and his keys as big as tomahawks. The combination was said to be capable of stopping a battering ram. Not content with running a wilderness hotel, Jarrett

also raised silkworms and taught his slaves to weave the silk in a loom house connected to his home. The elevated walkway which joins them is seen above.

108. This is the famous Charleston town house, a unique regional type. Both this city house and the country manor shown in Figure 107 developed from the early French plantation house of South Carolina, with its central block and attached, lean-to porches. City living in a soft southern climate dictated the placement of the house, end to street, its entry reached by a graceful flight of iron-railed stairs and its colonnaded "piazza" (as the French *galerie* now generally was called) overlooking a side garden—an arrangement which, repeated many times, gave the city of Charleston its special character. Renaissance elegance also remodeled this house. Doric and Ionic columns, a delicately detailed fanlight, and a pedimented gable have transformed a country cousin into a classical lady.

This charming regional house and the gracious city it helped to compose owe their development to the malarial mosquito. South Carolina families could not live safely on their plantations during the dread mosquito months. They therefore journeyed to Charleston for the summer, which became one of the social seasons. Planters built elegant town houses for their annual stays in Charleston, a suitable background for the balls and parties which took place within them.

108. The Charleston Town House: *Pelzer House, Charleston, S.C., ca. 1845.*

Chapter 6

A Spanish Tradition

The earliest permanent European settlement in America was the military garrison at St. Augustine, Florida, established in 1565. Except for twenty years of English rule in the eighteenth century, it remained a Spanish outpost on this continent until 1821, when the whole of Spanish Florida was ceded by treaty to the United States. Thus St. Augustine, established fifty-five years before the arrival of the Pilgrims, remained in colonial status until forty-five years after the signing of the Declaration of Independence.

Nevertheless, this oldest of the Spanish colonies has less authentic early architecture than either New England or Tidewater, Virginia. During most of its 256 years of existence, it remained a small military outpost, its inhabitants subsisting mainly on the payroll of a parsimonious Spanish government. No independent prosperity allowed this little garrison to build the substantial homes and occasional mansions which date from the seventeenth century in the English colonies.

In addition, St. Augustine's history has been a tempestuous one. By 1740, it had been sacked and/or burned four times. During the twenty years of English occupation, from 1763 to 1783, the Spanish inhabitants were ousted and the town used as a haven for Tory refugees from the American Revolution. Most of the small Spanish houses were destroyed at that time, and those remaining were extensively remodeled by the British.

A handful of these older houses, much changed, have managed to survive. But few of the quaint dwellings which now line the streets of St. Augustine predate the British occupation. Many were built later still, during the final Spanish colonial period and beyond.

Nevertheless, enough is known from old maps, sketches, and written descriptions to show something of the architecture of the early Spanish days. Recent archaeological work has established the original appearance of some of the houses which do remain. A few have been restored.

From these researches, it is clear that St. Augustine presented a startlingly different appearance during the various periods in its history. The grass shelter (borrowed from the local Seminole Indians) and the wooden hut (shared with the English and the Dutch) were virtually the only houses throughout the first 150 years of St. Augustine's existence. There was little to indicate a Spanish background in these primitive shelters.

What is today called the "St. Augustine look" did not appear until the first part of the eighteenth century, with the advent of masonry buildings. The town was then at its most Spanish, even the smallest houses having *rejas* or gratings over the windows and some of the larger ones including balconies and loggias.

Part of the Spanish arrangement was the placement of houses directly on the street, without steps, yard, or even a front door. Dwellings might form a line along the narrow way; but space was left between them for the gate to a walled courtyard which, in turn, led to a private entry.

The houses themselves typically exhibited broad expanses of smooth, plastered, masonry wall, punctuated by doors, balconies, and window gratings of wood. The contrast of dark against light, of heavily carved or planked door against smooth plaster, of filigreed balcony and latticework against plain surface created a uniquely Spanish character, not unlike country houses in the north of Spain.

During the English occupation, new wooden houses were built, most of them larger than the crude wooden shacks of the earliest Spanish days, often with exterior walls of typical English clapboards. Some small stone houses left over from the Spanish were enlarged by the addition of wooden second stories. New stone houses were constructed, too. Entry doors now faced the street and windows had the sliding sash and outside shutters of Georgian England. Fireplaces and chimneys replaced the charcoal brazier which formerly had heated the house. St. Augustine was no longer a totally Spanish town.

Yet neither was it English. The "St. Augustine look" remained: houses directly on the street, the walled courtyard, the smooth expanse of wall, loggias and balconies on many of the new English houses.

Though Spanish details were gone, these houses clearly showed their origin. They demonstrate the staying power of the underlying Spanish type, so well suited to the region and the climate that it persisted through the English occupation and beyond: a new variant in the age-old Mediterranean tradition.

A Spanish Tradition

St. Augustine, Florida

109. Palma Hut: *St. Augustine, Fla., 16th-19th c.*

110. Tabla or Board House: *St. Augustine, Fla., 16th, 17th, and 18th c.*

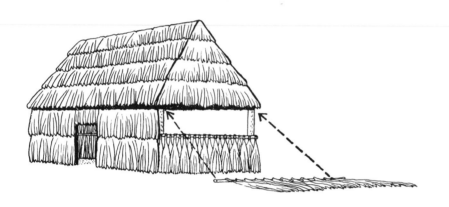

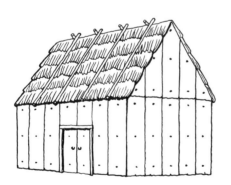

109. The thatched hut of palmetto fronds, copied from the Seminole Indians, was the first home of Spanish colonists in St. Augustine and an emergency shelter throughout its history. After each disaster a new crop sprang up, to be abandoned later for more substantial homes. Newcomers, even in the nineteenth century, still built these primitive shelters.

Though insubstantial, a properly made *palma* hut was remarkably weathertight. Fronds were hung on long poles and the poles hung on the frame of the house so that each "curtain" of thatch overlapped the one below. There were no windows and only a small doorway. Cooking was done out-of-doors, away from the dangerously combustible walls and roof. Barring fire, storm, and sack, a well-made *palma* hut could last for several years.

110. Sir Francis Drake stumbled across the Spanish garrison of St. Augustine on his way home from the Caribbean in 1586 and quickly burned it down. Before applying the torch, he recorded the following description: "a little town or village without walls, built of wooden houses . . . with delightful gardens."

Only seven years later, the drawing was made from which our illustration is copied. The little village had been rebuilt, complete with houses, church, and magazine, all of the same vertically sheathed wooden construction.

Throughout the sixteenth and seventeenth centuries, the board house, or *tabla,* remained the predominant dwelling in St. Augustine. It had one room and not even a loft. Much cooking still took place out-of-doors. For heating and indoor cooking, these houses had a fire on the dirt floor and a smoke hole in the roof.

111. When the Spaniard enjoyed even mild prosperity, he preferred to build in masonry; and during the eighteenth century, he was able to do so. By 1763, when the English took over the colony, 264 houses were made of stone or shell aggregate and only 78 of wood. Most of them were the so-called common house, i.e., one room used by everyone for everything. But even these little dwellings were characteristically Spanish. Windows projected a foot or more into the street screened by a wooden grating called a *reja*. Behind it, the women of the family could sit in safety watching the passersby. Sturdy inside shutters secured the windows when desired. The Spanish house had no front door. Entry was through a gate into the fenced yard and around to the rear or side door. Most of these dwellings were built of "tabby," a local lime mortar mixed with oyster shells, plastered over, and whitewashed to prevent mildew.

112. The "St. Augustine Plan" refers to the regional house type which evolved from the Florida climate, the Spanish tradition, and an admixture of English detail in the late eighteenth century. Two stories in height, with two or more rooms to a floor, this house was a luxurious dwelling by earlier standards. Its distinctive feature was the loggia or two-tiered porch at the rear of the house, giving access by outside stairway to the upper rooms. At front, a wooden balcony substituted for grated windows overlooking the public way. Now, the colonial señorita could look down in Spanish fashion on serenaders in the street below. English influence is seen, however, in sash windows and outside shutters and the chimney at the end of the house—a replacement for the traditional Spanish charcoal brazier. Walls of coquina, the local shellstone, usually 11 inches thick, were a natural regulator of both summer heat and winter cold. The roof typically was of cypress shingles weathered gray.

A Spanish Tradition

St. Augustine, Florida

113. The Spanish Courtyard: *Ribera House, St. Augustine, Fla., 18th c.*

114. The Spanish Interior: *Ribera House, St. Augustine, Fla., 18th c.*

115. Spanish Kitchen: *St. Augustine, Fla.*

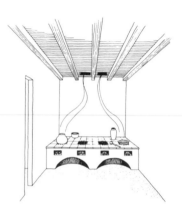

113. Family life in St. Augustine centered on the walled court. The arcaded loggia opened toward it and a recessed balcony overlooked the scene below. At the far end was the separate kitchen building from which food was carried through the loggia to the dining room. Like the *galerie* in a French farmhouse (Figure 102), the loggia was the circulation system of a Spanish dwelling, containing doors to all rooms and a stairway to the upper story. However, arcades and the intricately carved wooden doors, shutters, and spindlework were uniquely Spanish. So was coloration: white plastered walls set off by the dark brown, almost black woodwork.

The St. Augustine loggia was specifically adapted to the Florida climate. Usually oriented toward the south or southwest to catch the prevailing breeze and partially shielded by thick masonry walls, this passage became a shaded summer living room. In winter, the low sun warmed the loggia while the house cut the northwest wind.

This side entry court is only one part of the outdoor area. At the back of the house is a pleasant garden. Low fences typically sub-divided a Spanish property into the patio, or "house yard," a vegetable garden, chicken yard, and orchard.

114. This is the *sala*, the living room or reception hall, in a Spanish house. It fronts on the street, giving a view through the *reja*, or wooden grating, which screens the window. There was no glass in the early days but heavy inside shutters secured the opening. Note the small "peephole shutter" cut in one of the larger ones, permitting a view of the street even when the major pair was closed. The heavily carved double doors lead to the loggia at right. Houses typically were heated by charcoal brazier, a small, low table with a metal-lined "dish" for coals.

Though a luxurious house by St. Augustine standards, the Ribera living room was sparsely furnished with only three spindle-backed chairs, a table, a small desk (not visible), and a low, carved wooden chest. Dark ceiling beams, woodwork, and furniture create a dramatic contrast to whitewashed walls, the same effect indoors as out. Note the chandelier of hand-wrought black iron, undoubtedly brought from Spain.

115. The ordinary St. Augustine family did its cooking out-of-doors. More prosperous families had separate kitchens, occasionally a room attached to the house but, usually, a free-standing building in the patio. The stove was made of coquina with a tile surface. Charcoal was burned in separate chambers topped by grilles, on which the cooking pots were set. Small openings in the roof, directly above the stove, acted as vents for the smoke. The system was not notably effective, and the Spanish kitchen was reported to be "as smoky as an Indian cabin."

116. This famous house, part of which is the oldest still standing in St. Augustine, illustrates what could happen to a small Spanish dwelling over a period of 180 years. Only one room of the lower story was the original Spanish house; but, fortunately, it was built of coquina rather than perishable tabby. During their occupation, the English destroyed most tabby houses but even small stone dwellings were retained.

Presumably, it was during this period that the house was enlarged and the clapboard upper story added. This was a typical British method of remodeling a St. Augustine house. However, the combination also was Spanish. The masonry lower story, coupled with a balconied wooden upper structure, was part of the tradition of both Spain and France (Figure 102) and was transplanted by both to America. The one-story, flat-roofed Spanish house known as an *azotea* (not shown) was most easily enlarged in this way, but the "Oldest House" probably had a hipped roof, replaced by the upper story. In its final stage, this house had an English front door; but the restored courtyard entrances, with their heavily carved doors, are Spanish in type.

Though most early houses were the natural white of oyster shells or lime plaster, this one, finished under the English, is olive green. Crushed brick sometimes was used to color plaster a soft pink. Dull blue, yellow ochre, and a rusty red also have been documented from the British period.

116. An Anglo-Spanish Vernacular: *"The Oldest House," St. Augustine, Fla. Original house, before 1727; wooden second story, British occupation; balcony and two-story rear addition, before 1788; street windows and doors, 1900; restoration begun 1959.*

A Spanish Tradition

New Mexico

117. Fortress Adobe: *Palace of the Governor, Santa Fe, N.M., ca. 1610.*

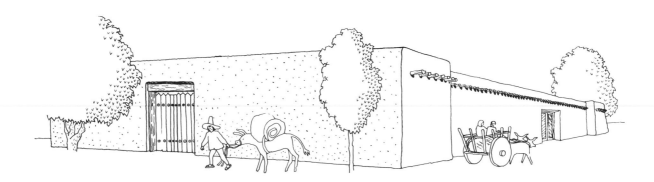

For approximately three hundred years—from the middle of the sixteenth century through nearly half of the nineteenth—the southwestern part of what is now the United States was dominated by Spain or Spanish Mexico. During that period, a regional architecture developed which is unique in America. It was composed of Spanish and native Indian traditions: a flat-roofed, thick-walled, courtyard-centered system as different from houses in most of America as timber framing is from adobe brick.

This is a vocabulary of the Southwest, congenial to any hot, semiarid region, and using stone or adobe with equal facility, according to the material at hand. Colonists in New Mexico, Texas, and Arizona—sharing a Spanish tradition, using Indian labor, and faced by similar climates—built houses which clearly are related. However, in New Mexico, the vernacular developed earlier, persisted longer, and remains very much a part of the region's architecture today. We have therefore chosen the New Mexican adobe house as representative of the Southwest.

Mud-wall construction was indigenous to much of New Mexico, where trees grew only on distant mountains or along the riverbanks and the earth itself offered the only readily available building material. Long before the Spaniards arrived, the Indians of the region had built their pueblos of mud, using a system known as "puddling." Walls were shaped in place, built up in layers of moistened clay, each dried by the sun before the next layer was added.

The Spaniards brought their own technique. "Adobe" is an Arab word meaning "earth from which unburned bricks are made," and it entered the Spanish lexicon during the Moorish occupation, along with the method of construction it described. As made by Spaniards in New Mexico, adobe bricks were a mixture of clay, sand, and straw or other binder, shaped in wooden forms about 1½ feet long, dried in the sun, and stacked to make a wall. Technically, the puddled Indian pueblos were not adobe at all.

Wooden doors and door frames were another Spanish innovation, as was the *portal,* or porch, across the long side of the house. But the flat roof was traditional with both cultures. *Vigas,* or beams, placed across the width of the house, were covered with a mat of smaller poles, called *latias* in Spanish. Above these, the roof was finished with a layer of mud or tamped earth.

The completed house was plastered over inside and out with a coating of mud which dried to a hard finish. Though a protection for adobe walls, it was not impervious to rain and had to be continuously renewed on the exterior. Without such frequent replastering, an adobe house would literally melt away in the rains over a period of years. Even with the best of care, the corners were rounded by the weather, producing the typical softened contours.

Trees were scarce in New Mexico and *vigas* were hard to cut with the stone axes of the Indians. It was therefore Indian practice to salvage the roof beams when an old home was abandoned. Sometimes the *vigas* did not match the dimensions of the new house and were allowed to project beyond the wall line, a system adopted by the Spanish and characteristic of their early New Mexican architecture.

The length of the *viga* determined the maximum width of the room which it spanned, usually 13 to 15 feet. By adding more *vigas,* the room could be lengthened indefinitely or other rooms added at either end. The New Mexican colonial house was, therefore, always an in-line plan. The largest houses, accommodating related families of parents, grandparents, aunts, uncles, and cousins, each in its own quarters, typically formed a continuous square around a *placita,* or courtyard, with an adjoining walled *corral* for the stables.

Such adobe construction was an effective shelter against the desert climate. The thick clay walls acted to absorb solar heat during the day and to release it at night. Small windows, deeply set and shaded by an extended roof over the *portal* (a continuous porch), prevented the entry of direct sunlight and the searing desert breeze. The continuous system of construction minimized the surface area; and the quadrangular plan acted as a windbreak, adding to the cooling effect during the day and to warmth at night.

Like primitive building everywhere, adobe

118. The Spanish Pueblo Style: *Palace of the Governor, Santa Fe, N.M., restored to its appearance in the early 19th c.*

represents a condensed solution to multiple problems of environment, worked out with the materials at hand. But another decisive factor in shaping the early architecture of New Mexico was the danger of Indian attack. In this isolated region, the gracious walled courtyard of Spanish tradition was changed into a fortress, a massive enclosure, windowless on the exterior. The focus of the house was entirely on the inner courtyard, entered by only one opening, a gate of wooden timbers heavy enough to withstand a battering ram.

The Palace of the Governor, focal point of the plaza in the little Spanish colonial village of Santa Fe, was the largest and most impregnable of the "fortress adobes." A vast establishment, it served as living quarters and offices for the Spanish Governor, as a military barracks, and as a place of final refuge for all colonists in the dangerous early days of New Mexico.

The houses of the ordinary townspeople which clustered around the plaza near the Governor's Palace usually contained only two or three rooms and depended for safety on the walls of the town itself and on the inner citadel of their fortress neighbor.

But in outlying areas, Spanish *patrones* to whom the King of Spain had granted vast estates along the Rio Grande built smaller versions of the Governor's Palace—each home its own fortress against attack. Despite the dangers which surrounded them, these favored

colonists lived spacious lives, much of it on horseback, their great farms and ranches worked by Indian peons and profits rolling in from Mexico City and Chihuahua 1,500 miles away. In exchange for hides, tallow, raw wool, and Indian blankets, the *patrone* was able to acquire luxuries which contrasted strangely with the whitewashed walls and packed earth floor of his adobe dwelling. It was not unusual to find a Mexican silver service, embroidered shawls and chests from China, and metal and leatherwork from Europe. The King of Spain had hoped to set up a vast feudal empire in America, and the Spanish in New Mexico did their best to make his dream come true.

117. This restoration sketch of the Governor's Palace, the oldest colonial building in the United States, shows it as a "fortress adobe" during the Spanish Colonial period. At its largest, this compound contained the Governor's private apartments, offices, reception rooms, servants' quarters, stables, granaries, an arsenal, a chapel, and a military barracks, disposed around a number of courtyards and corrals. Its massive adobe walls saved approximately one thousand Spanish colonists from massacre during the Indian uprising of 1680.

The portion illustrated here is not much larger than one of the fortified farm or ranch houses which the great landowners built on their thousands of acres along the Rio Grande—and the type is the same. In both palace and hacienda, rooms were aligned like boxcars around the perimeter of the compound, facing

an inner court. The common outer wall, windowless, many feet thick, and "battered" or slanted for strength and stability, formed the enclosure. In this drawing, the *vigas*, or beams, which support the flat roof of the inner dwelling are seen as they project beyond the wall line. Note the *Zaguan,* the heavy wooden gate which could swing wide to admit a Spanish coach-and-four or a two-wheeled Mexican cart but, when closed, was proof against the strongest attack.

118. Here is the Palace of the Governor restored to its appearance in the Mexican Colonial period. As the Indian threat receded, blank fortress walls were opened up. A *portal* was added across the front, leading to reception rooms within, and functioning as a grandstand facing the plaza. Here, trading caravans were unloaded, parades held, and fiestas celebrated. From his *portal* the Governor could both observe and hold court.

No longer a fortress, the palace had become an excellent example of the "Spanish-Pueblo Style." Posts of the *portal* were characteristic: trimmed and smoothed logs, connected to the beam above by a corbel bracket known as a *Zapata.* This was a primitive version of the capital of a classic column, carved by Indian woodworkers. The entrance gate, or *Zaguan,* now had two leaves. These swung open to admit horses, carts, and carriages but remained closed for pedestrians, who entered through the small door in the right leaf.

A Spanish Tradition

New Mexico

119. This view from inside the *placita,* or courtyard, shows the traditional adobe house decked in a new Greek Revival colonnade. In earlier days, the inner *portal,* or porch, would have had round posts of weathered wood with hand-carved *Zapatas* like those of the Governor's Palace (Figure 118). By contrast, these are simplified Doric columns, sawn at the mill and painted white. *Canales,* or drain spouts, also were mill sawn. Large sash windows and windowed doors attest to the passing of the Indian threat and to the availability of stock parts. It all adds up to the "Territorial Style"—a variety of changes brought by the Anglos when New Mexico became a Territory of the United States in 1850.

Otherwise, the Delgado house perpetuates the traditional New Mexican dwelling: a continuous in-line arrangement of rooms, forming a quadrangle. The *portal* acts as a sheltered walkway, giving access to all parts of the house. With a well to supply water and a barrel for storing it, this was a convenient and self-contained living space. Note that the courtyard is bare, hard-packed earth. Grass was a mark of bad housekeeping in a New Mexican *placita.* As part of a working cattle ranch or sheep farm—administered by men on horseback—the courtyard was for use, not show.

119a. The contiguous rooms which formed the early New Mexican farm or ranch house faced inward toward the *placita,* or courtyard, which they defined. All rooms were fronted by a roofed walkway, known as a *portal.* This was the New Mexican equivalent of the French *galerie* or the Spanish loggia—both a sheltered porch and a circulation system which tied together all parts of the continuous dwelling. Stables were placed at the far end of the *placita.* In a large establishment, stables and servants' quarters defined a separate but connected stable yard, known as a *corral.*

120. This dwelling is a traditional Spanish-adobe town house. Its end faces the street and its long side gives onto a private patio, reached by way of a gate in the low courtyard wall. But details show that it was remodeled during the Territorial Period.

Typical of the Territorial Style is the brick *pretil,* or coping, which tops the courtyard wall. Soon

119. The Territorial Style (Greek Revival): *Courtyard, Felipe Delgado House, Santa Fe, N.M., ca. 1872.*

119a. Plan, Typical Early Adobe: *Based on the Pascual Martinez House, near Taos, N.M., 1824.*

after their arrival, the Anglos established brick kilns. The durable, kiln-fired brick was too expensive for entire houses, but it was quickly seized upon as protection for adobe at its vulnerable points. The pattern is meant to represent classic dentils: a faint echo of the Greek Revival which was beginning to penetrate isolated New Mexico. Note also the "pointed lintel" above the window, a standard piece of millwork almost everywhere in America during the Greek Revival period (Figure 164).

121. Victorian whimsy came even to New Mexico, as seen in another example from the Territorial Period. The scrollwork fascia board is like a light-hearted valentine applied to the sober adobe dwelling.

Underneath the gingerbread, however, this is neither a Victorian house nor a typical Spanish Colonial one, but a New Mexican version of the Greek Revival. Its wide, flat cornice; porch posts, with their hint of capital and base; and paneled door and window trim are vernacular Greek. So is the classically symmetrical plan—a complete break from the narrow, in-line arrangement of Spanish rooms. This is, in fact, the familiar center hall type, inherited by the Greek Revival from the English Georgian and transplanted across a continent. The Yanquis introduced the plan and, with their sawmills, made it possible, since large sawn beams can span greater distances than small *vigas.*

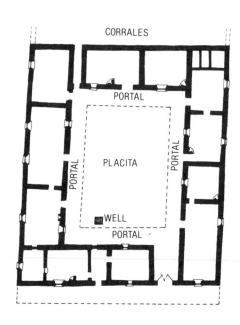

120. The Territorial Style (Greek Revival): *Roque Tudesqui House, Santa Fe, N.M., before 1841; Territorial Style Trim after 1865; window restored to 19th century appearance.*

121. The Territorial Style (Victorian Gingerbread): *Leandro Martinez House, Ranchitos District, near Taos, N.M., 1862.*

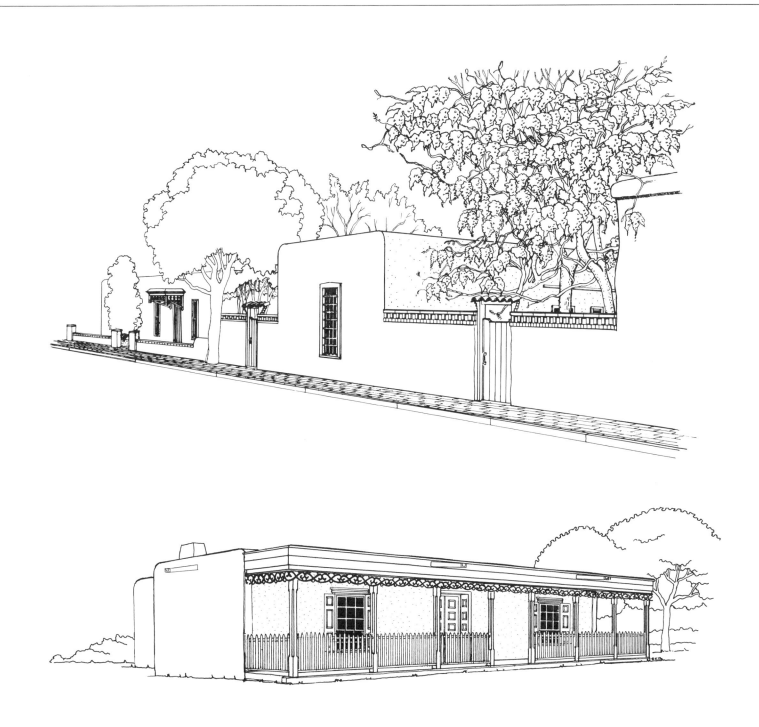

A Spanish Tradition

California

122. The California Ranch House: *Typical Early Adobe, Los Angeles area, Calif., ca. 1825.*

123. The Greek Revival Ranch House: *de la Guerra Adobe, Santa Barbara, Calif., 1819-90.*

Spain did not colonize California until almost time to give it up. The first settlement, the presidio and mission of San Diego de Alcala, was established in 1769. Just fifty-two years later, Mexico took California from Spain, along with her own newly won independence. Twenty-nine years after that, in 1850—as part of the spoils of the Mexican War—the United States of America added another star to its flag and spanned a continent.

During the greater part of these eighty-one years, the Spanish missions were dominant in California, occupying vast lands, building superb churches, but offering little more in the way of domestic architecture than monastic quarters and huts for Indian laborers.

The presidio, or military fort, was the other official establishment. A walled quadrangle lined with barracks for officers, storerooms, a chapel, and stables, it resembled the Governor's Palace of New Mexico. Large individual land holdings were virtually nonexistent during this period and homes were crude minimum shelters.

In 1834, Mexico expropriated the missions, dividing their vast holdings into estates of thousands of acres as land grants to colonial favorites.

The earliest California houses had been rude shelters, sometimes no more than tents of "tule," a local bulrush. Where wood was available, the settlers built *palizado* houses of logs set upright into the ground and roofed with thatch or sod—a primitive system used in different parts of America by the Spanish, the English, and the French. In the cattle country of California, the palisades were laced together with rawhide, a regional touch.

In the southern part of California, however, trees were extremely scarce, forests nonexistent, while the red clay hills and black loam valleys offered material for a familiar way of building. The adobe house rapidly became the typical colonial dwelling of the last Spanish frontier.

The original California ranch house was simply an adobe box with a dirt floor and no fireplace, much like those of the Spanish southwest. Windows were small, unglazed apertures, barred

against marauders in frontier fashion. The usual flat roof prevailed.

The first slight shift from tradition was an entirely practical one, the result of the discovery of the La Brea tar pits near Los Angeles. Soon the roofs of the southern California adobes were surfaced with black tar and gravel, hardly aesthetic but far more weatherproof than the tamped earth used in New Mexico. Pits were soon developed in San Diego, Santa Barbara, San Luis Obispo, and Santa Clara. Though it goes against the grain of romantic myth, the flat asphalt roof was a staple of California's colonial architecture.

However, California's climate, unlike the hot, dry, semidesert of New Mexico, is mild in temperature and subject to seasonal rain. Under such conditions, a pitched roof is better than a flat one, in which problems of drainage are bound to occur. Both roof types were familiar to the Spanish. The red-tiled gabled roof had been used by the Spanish missions. Now, the thick-walled adobe ranch house acquired a roof of low pitch and wide eaves, and the California look was born.

The other major change was the virtual abandonment of the walled courtyard, at least in the small early houses. Occasionally, a little yard was fenced with wooden rails or with a low adobe wall 2 to 3 feet in height. Otherwise, all was open and clear.

Several factors had combined to produce this very un-Spanish way of building. They were, mainly, horses, cattle, and Indians. Like New Mexico, this was a society on horseback, and the area near the house—like the New Mexican *placita*—was used as a mounting and dismounting yard. Outside the towns, cattle ranching was the occupation, with Indian or Mexican vaqueros, the original cowboys, doing the work. Houses typically were placed on high ground, without trees, in order to survey ranching operations and keep an eye out for cattle rustlers and possibly an Indian attacker. The practical necessity of the long view, coupled with the comparative safety of the region and reinforced by the constant coming and going of horses, virtually eliminated the traditional walled court.

A few houses were enlarged horizontally in

traditional Spanish fashion; but, typically, they enclosed no more than three sides of what was known in California as a patio. There was no need to turn the house into a fortress and good reasons not to. California under Mexican rule was wide open country and its architecture the opposite of New Mexico's inward-turning, walled, and barricaded type.

122. This ranch house shows the California adobe after it had changed from a flat roofed dwelling, much like that of New Mexico, into a new regional type. In response to California's winter rainy season, it had acquired a gabled roof and a *corredor,* the California name for the porch across the front. It also had expanded from the early one-room house into a larger dwelling, its rooms aligned in typical Spanish fashion.

The roof of the early ranch house, whether flat or gabled, was surfaced with black tar. Its floor was of tamped earth. Doors and small, barred windows were closed by hangings of rawhide or by wooden frames over which rawhide was stretched. There were no fireplaces. Cooking was done out of doors or in a separate kitchen building. A low adobe or rail fence might be used to define the patio or house yard, but often there was only a corral for horses and a pen for smaller animals.

123. This delightful Greek Revival ranch house shows what could happen to the Spanish adobe in changing times. With American prosperity, it has grown to define three sides of a patio, a traditional scheme of the large California ranch house.

Originally, this dwelling was of exposed adobe, with a ground-level *corredor* and plain porch posts (Figure 122). During the late nineteenth century, the porch was raised and the wings and tower, subject to weathering, covered with Yankee clapboards. The new Greek Revival style can be glimpsed in simple Doric columns and latticework screening. The formal row of small trees in their neatly latticed skirts, possibly an attempt at classic landscaping, bestows on the patio a whimsical charm. Nevertheless, hitching posts show that this was a utilitarian yard for a ranching family. The latticed boxes no doubt were a necessary covering for young trees, protecting them from the nibbling, rubbing, and trampling of horses.

A Spanish Tradition

California

124. The Monterey Style: *Thomas Larkin Adobe, Monterey, Calif., 1835-37.*

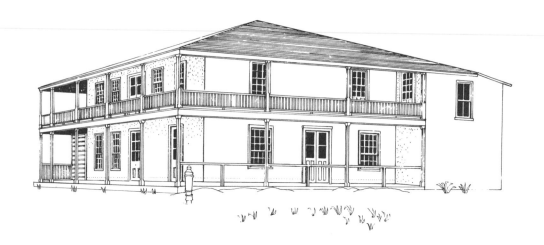

125. An Anglo-Spanish Vernacular: *La Casa Grande, General Mariano Guadalupe Vallejo Adobe, Petaluma, Calif., 1834-44.*

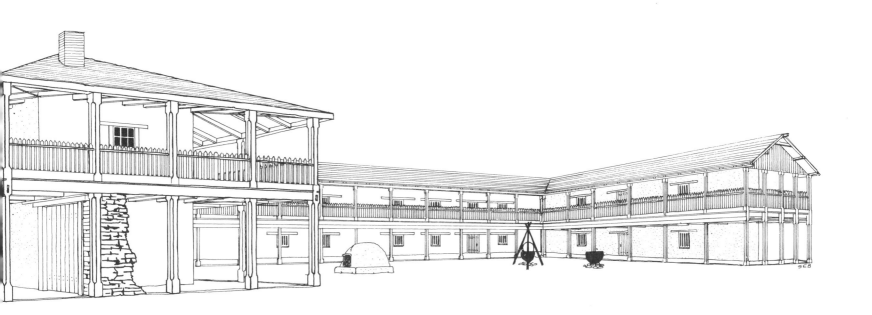

124. This town house and store was built during the Mexican Colonial period by a Yankee merchant, U.S. Consul to California when it was a colony, and a leading citizen after it became a state. Thomas Larkin from Boston made his adobe house two rooms wide and two rooms deep, with a hallway down the middle and a hip to its shingled roof. It had a fireplace in the living room and wallpaper over its adobe walls. There had never before been anything like it in California. It was, in fact, a New England center hall colonial, the Georgian type which had been new on the East Coast a century earlier.

Distinctly not Bostonian, however, were the *corredor* and balcony with which Mr. Larkin faced his house. It took the ingenious Yankee to combine adobe with a wooden frame capable of supporting an upper story, thus fusing the Spanish and the English traditions. So influential was his two-story balconied house that its many variations came to be known as the Monterey Style.

This house can be seen today in lavishly land-scaped "restored" condition. In its original state, it fronted on the dirt road with a hitching rail along one side, supplemented by a Spanish cannon for a hitching post. Where shrubs now grow, Thomas Larkin's friends and customers tied their horses. Our illustration shows the house as it really was.

125. In the Vallejo adobe, the same fusion of traditions which made up the Larkin house are weighted on the Spanish side. Rooms are a single depth, aligned end to end, each giving into the next and each with a separate entrance from the *corredor*. But this otherwise typically Spanish ranch house is two stories in height with shallow hipped roofs—the contribution of Larkin's New England. Mixed elements also include machine-cut nails, factory-made glass, and cast-iron hinges used side by side with the wooden pegs, rawhide thongs, and hand-forged hardware of Spanish tradition.

This largest of California adobes (only half of it remains today) was the ranching headquarters for a 66,000-acre grant to the north of the San Francisco presidio. It was the home of a Mexican ranchero who was also a general in the Mexican colonial army and the military and civil commandant of his provincial territory. His ranch was, in effect, a feudal village, its work crew composed mainly of Indians but including Mexicans, Yankees, and even a few Kanakas from Hawaii. At its peak, the Vallejo establishment employed two thousand men working to produce hides, tallow, and wheat for the Yankee trade.

A ranch such as this was at once the creation of the American merchants and the base upon which their trading depended. For a brief moment, the alien Spanish and Yankee cultures were bound together in a precarious balance, just before the one overwhelmed the other.

Part II

The Classic Period

The eighteenth century brought to America something radically new in colonial architecture. It is visible not only in the formal Georgian mansion but in modest farmhouses and cottages as well. What one sees, expressed in building, is the awakening known as the Renaissance, the shift from the medieval to the classic set of mind.

This represents far more than a change in style. The Renaissance was one of the great breaking points in human history. In its new way of approaching the world, the Renaissance changed architecture as it changed everything else which then existed.

The old medieval ethos had been one of accommodation to an overwhelming environment. Things happened *to* the ordinary man and he adjusted accordingly, with little comprehension or question.

The houses of the first settlers in America echo this medieval spirit, even though the men who built them were passing rapidly out of its range. The very act of coming to a wild, new land, of ordinary people daring to take destiny into their own hands, was an unmedieval thing to do. It indicated a freedom and self-reliance which were the opposite of the principle of the Middle Ages.

But architecture is slow to change. Seventeenth-century English houses in America were medieval houses shaped by tradition and necessity. In a system evolved over the centuries, form and function had become parts of each other. Structure was frankly expressed; materials were used without artifice; windows and doors were punched where most convenient with little regard for visual effect. To the all but unchanging core of the house, additions were made over the years, the house adjusting to circumstances as they arose. The result was a picturesque, irregular massing of elements which could almost have grown out of the ground on which it stood.

The Renaissance principles which underlie Georgian architecture clearly are from another stage in human development. An inquiring, demanding spirit was the moving force in an age which included the Protestant Reformation, the breakdown of the feudal system, the rise of a merchant middle class, the institution of parliamentary government, the exploration of the globe, unprecedented scientific inquiry, a newly accurate historical scholarship, the philosophy of humanism—and revolution. It was known as the Age of Reason and the Age of Enlightenment. After centuries of medieval resignation, a new confidence was abroad. ''Man, the measure of all things'' sums up its overly optimistic, yet liberating stance.

The fundamental fact of the new architecture was the same spirit which moved the rest of the Renaissance world: a sense of being in command. No longer was a house something to be accepted as given—to be built as one's father and grandfather had built it. The plan, the form, the type and spacing of doors and windows, the decorative details, all could be imposed by the architect as part of a unified system under conscious control.

However, in shaking off the feudal tie, our ancestors did not substitute anarchy. Underlying the age was the assumption of a natural yet rational order; a conviction that man could discover that order and, in accord with it, become master of himself and of his universe. We have been riding on this premise ever since and it has taken us, among other places, to the moon.

In architecture and art, however, aesthetic order was believed to have been already established on timeless principles, a creation of the classical world, particularly Rome; and it was to this authority that the Renaissance turned. The aim was not simple copying but the creation of appropriate and beautiful ''modern'' buildings. Classic precedent would be followed but only as a guide in developing a new architecture for a new age.

7

Chapter 7

The Georgian Period

Even in England, Georgian is a confusing term. Encompassing the years from 1714 to 1830, it includes the reigns of four consecutive English kings, George I through George IV, and covers several changes in the style of Renaissance architecture.

In America, the time lag between England and the colonies adds to this disorder. Thirty to fifty years might elapse between an English innovation and its colonial adoption. What had been the pre-Georgian Queen Anne Style in England became our Early Georgian; England's Early Georgian (the Palladian Style) was our Mid- or Late Georgian. England's Late Georgian (the Neoclassic) reached America only after the Revolution and is known here as Federal. To make sense out of this confusing panorama, a little background information may be helpful.

When the fully developed Renaissance house reached England during the seventeenth century, it had been established in Italy for more than two hundred years. English architects and builders could therefore draw on a variety of sources, including Vitruvius, the Roman authority revived in the fifteenth century, and Andrea Palladio, his cool, formal sixteenth-century interpreter. The English were also strongly influenced by the Baroque Style, which reflected classic trends in contemporary Italy, France, and Holland.

In the early seventeenth century, the great English innovator, Inigo Jones, built the first wholly Renaissance structure in England: a symmetrical Palladian villa of pale smooth stone above, rusticated blocks below, with a second-story loggia and a flat, balustraded roof. It was a stunning departure from English brick and half-timbering. However, the Queen's House (and the similar Banqueting Hall for Whitehall Palace) would not influence English or American domestic architecture until the following century.

More to the English taste was another Inigo Jones design, the Prince's Lodging. Built of familiar red brick with stone quoins, a hipped roof, and dormer windows, it was reassuringly a house, even though a new and classically symmetrical one. It influenced the royal palaces and country houses of Sir Christopher Wren, who succeeded Jones to become England's

greatest architect. And, it was the "Queen Anne House," derived from Wren's designs, which would become the new domestic architecture of England—the prototype for America's Georgian mansions.

The Queen Anne House was not only a new style but a new kind of dwelling. In England, during the Stuart period of the late seventeenth century, trade and commerce were booming and new kinds of men were getting rich: merchants, shipowners, men in trade. This new middle class, occupying a social position between the ancient nobility and the yeoman or craftsman demanded a new type of house. The period supplied it: a "gentleman's" residence, ample and even elegant, but not grandiose in size or manner. This is what came to be known as the "Queen Anne House."

Wren had studied in both France and Holland, so the contemporary Baroque phase of the Renaissance in those countries became part of his lexicon. Of these influences, the Dutch undoubtedly was decisive. From varied sources—by way of emigrating Dutch craftsmen, out of Dutch pattern books, in the work of Wren himself—there evolved a Renaissance manner which is known as the Anglo-Dutch Style. It is one more synonym for what is variously called Late Stuart, Queen Anne, or Wren Baroque—and which provided the prototype house for our early Georgian mansions.

In addition, Wren was inadvertently responsible for the look of the American city as it grew up on the Eastern Seaboard during the eighteenth century. This prodigious architect had virtually rebuilt London after the disastrous fire of 1666. In place of the old, half-timbered row houses with their thatched roofs, jettied upper stories, and peaked gables facing the street, Wren transformed London into a city of brick. His town houses were set in neat, continuous rows with flat fronts punctuated here and there by pent roofs between stories, with small balconies above and Baroque doorway hoods below. Many of the same elements which gave the Queen Anne "gentleman's house" its Renaissance character were used to create the new urban type. The result, in both England and America, was a consistent classical architecture expressed in a variety of forms.

Both the country mansion and the city house arrived in the colonies by way of English architectural books and builder's guides. The former, including Palladio's *Four Books of Architecture,* Vignola's *Rule of the Five Orders of Architecture,* James Gibbs's *A Book of Architecture,* and Colen Campbell's *Vitruvius Brittannicus,* were expensive and somewhat theoretical, though showing many examples of existing work.

The builder's guides were practical workbooks which instructed masons and carpenters in classic proportions, the mystique of symmetry, and the proper way to carve the requisite decorative details. Among the most famous were William Salmon's *Palladio Londinensis,* Abraham Swan's *British Architect,* William Halfpenny's *The Modern Builder's Assistant,* and the various builder and style manuals by Batty Langley. Copies of doorways, windows, fireplaces, and stairways from these books can be found on houses all along the Eastern Seaboard. An early guide to bricklaying showed the townhouse type. Joseph Moxon's illustration for the Classic row house in his *Mechanick Exercises* takes concrete form before one's eyes on the streets of Philadelphia, Boston, Annapolis, Baltimore, and other colonial cities.

That the American woodworker took liberties with the doorways and chimney pieces delineated in the English books is testimony to the vitality of his craft. But it is also surprising to find how many faithful copies were made. More important is the fact that the principles of classic design, the relationship of one part to another and of each to the whole, were thoroughly understood. This is what gives our Georgian houses a grace and fitness we still recognize after 150 to 250 years.

The Georgian Period

Early Georgian:
Wren Baroque

126. The Queen Anne Mansion: *Governor's Palace, Williamsburg, Va., 1706-20.*

127. The Queen Anne House: *Wentworth-Gardner House, Portsmouth, N.H., 1760.*

126. This discreetly elegant mansion for the Royal Governor of Virginia is perhaps the finest example in America of the classic Queen Anne House. A "gentleman's residence," midway between a nobleman's palace and a commoner's cottage, it represents a happy marriage of opposites, combining the blocky form and hipped roof of the Italian Palladian villa with the warm red brick of a traditional English dwelling. The roof is high and steep, showing it to be an early type, still echoing English Gothic ancestry. The little outbuildings which flank the mansion also are from an earlier vernacular tradition.

With these exceptions, the Governor's Palace is a lesson in the basic principles of the Renaissance, lightly touched by the English Baroque, i.e., a design of classic balance, yet which has richness, change, and movement.

Most striking is the formal symmetry of the composition and the fact that it was designed to make a picture. The specifically Baroque qualities are more subtle, since these are not static but involved with movement. The progression, which starts with outbuildings at either side, travels in and up to the main house, mounting again to the composition of balustraded roof, twin chimney stacks, and two-tiered cupola which, in turn, culminates in an attenuated spire.

A separate horizontal progression acts as counterpoint to the vertical. This movement is experienced as well as seen. Starting with the broad loop of the driveway and the courtyard wall, one is led toward the focal point of the central gate with its intricate iron overthrow. Through this gate, from the open Palace green, one enters a smaller space, the formal forecourt. The focus continues to the Palace entrance, reached by a pyramidal flight of steps and emphasized by a paneled door and wrought-iron balcony. Through this doorway, one enters the third and smallest space, the reception hall of the Palace.

All effects, from large forms and spaces to small details, have been carefully calculated to produce a beginning, a middle, and an end; to focus from periphery to center, from bottom to top, and from broad to narrow. Even the space between the windows has been subtly decreased toward the center, adding one more piece of focal emphasis to the composition as a whole. The typically Baroque decorative details—gateway, balcony, cupola—provide the final focus. They are lavishly curved, molded, or interlaced, a rich conclusion to broad, simple forms.

127. Most Tidewater mansions were built of brick and most New England mansions of wood. But it was New England which used the full vocabulary of enrichment with which the Wren school in England enlivened its houses. In this superb example, quoins, doorway surround, and window lintels—ornaments which would have been done in Portland stone in England—have been translated by American carpenters into wood. The facade of the house also has been rusticated to resemble stone.

Typically Baroque is the double "swan's neck," or broken ogee, pediment above the doorway, full of curves and deeply carved. Though the house is not part of a group composition, this richly sculptured doorway draws the eye to the center of the facade in a characteristically Baroque movement.

This epitome of the Queen Anne house usually is classified by date as mid-Georgian. Conservative New England lagged behind the southern colonies and its houses often were *retardataire*, i.e., built after the period to which, stylistically, they belong.

The Georgian Period

Early Georgian:
Wren Baroque

128. The Row House: *Elfreth's Alley,
Philadelphia, Pa., early 18th c.*

129. The Small Town House: *Letitia Street House, Philadelphia, Pa., before 1713. Moved to Fairmount Park, 1883.*

130. Baroque Detailing: *Bellaire, League Island Park, Philadelphia, Pa., ca. 1720.*

131. The Queen Anne Interior: *Parlor, Rev. Jonathan Ashley House, Old Deerfield Village, Mass., ca. 1732.*

128. One of the few blocks of early-eighteenth-century houses remaining in Philadelphia, Elfreth's Alley is virtually a replica of Restoration London. These little row houses with their red brick fronts, arched gateways, and paneled shutters and doors march away into the distance like an exercise in Renaissance neatness and harmony. Sash windows are large at the bottom, smaller at the second story, with tiny dormers above—a Baroque progression not neglected even in these modest dwellings. A pent roof between the first and second story was used on both English and German houses in Pennsylvania (Figures 52 and 89). But in Philadelphia the pents were often coved, creating a depth and sculptural effect typical of the Baroque style. Eaves are similarly heavy and sculptural. These quaint little houses are unmistakably Queen Anne in a modest urban version: an echo of shopkeepers' London by Sir Christopher Wren.

129. This upright litttle dwelling is a tiny, yet near-perfect specimen of Sir Christopher Wren's London town house. In creating the English Renaissance house, Wren and his followers took any and all existing dwelling types and transformed them into classic houses. The very shape of this house has been changed from a narrow, Gothic silhouette to a compact block, its roofline lowered toward the

classic. A Baroque coved cornice gives continuity to gable and eaves. The aim: to come as close as possible to the symmetrical form of the Queen Anne mansion.

Details also are typically Queen Anne. Scrolled consoles which support the door hood are a Baroque touch, attracting the eye to the center of the composition. Paneled shutters and door add further richness to a simple facade. Though not in classic balance, the small gable window, placed off-center to light a closet beside the chimney, was a common feature of London town houses.

130. Nothing could be more Queen Anne than the deep, arched hood, set on spiral consoles, which shelters this balcony. In London, Baroque door hoods sometimes were carved in the shape of cockleshells, a type used as well for interior woodwork (Figure 131). Also copied from Wren's London was the balcony, quite common on the row houses that once lined Philadelphia streets. In the evening, after supper, the family used the balcony like a sociable Dutch stoop, talking across to near neighbors and watching passersby on the wooden sidewalks below.[11] Behind the balanced symmetry of its facade, Bellaire retains the tall, narrow silhouette of medieval tradition. However, a Baroque coved cornice ties

together eaves and gable, helping to transform an earlier type into an authentic piece of Queen Anne design.

131. This parlor, in a New England minister's house, reveals the richness of the Queen Anne interior, with its paneled woodwork and cockleshell cupboards—a typical Baroque device. Colonial cupboards based on the Roman arch became fairly common starting in the 1720s, though the elegantly carved and deeply recessed shell cupboard remained a rarity.

Paneled woodwork was a characteristic Queen Anne wall finish, replacing the plain pine sheathing and whitewashed plaster of the medieval house. It was painted in a variety of deep colors, here slate blue, with cupboard interiors of rust red. The room was symbolically conceived as a piece of Roman architecture, with columns supporting an entablature. As woodwork, these elements were transformed into decorative pilasters, cornice, and frieze. There was no mantelshelf above a Queen Anne fireplace. A paneled chimney breast and fireplace surround or a heavy bolection molding were the usual treatment. The Queen Anne wing chair, with its Baroque curves and a matching candlestand, make this a period room in furnishings as well as architecture.

The Georgian Period

Mid-Georgian:
The Palladian Style

132. The Southern Town House: *Miles Brewton House, Charleston, S.C., 1765-69. Ezra Waite, architect, builder, woodcarver.*

133. The Mid-Georgian Interior: *Drawing room, Samuel Powel House, Philadelphia, Pa., 1765.*

The early years of England's Georgian period saw a revival of interest in the Roman Palladian style which had been introduced a century earlier by Inigo Jones. Great palaces of pale chiseled stone became the fashion for country houses, their severe facades broken by porticoes, pavilions, and colonnades. In America, no houses so grand were built. But the pedimented pavilion—or even a simple pediment over the doorway—began to substitute for Baroque carving and scrollwork on colonial houses. This phase of classic architecture is England's Early Georgian. In America, because of the time lag in adopting a new style, it is called Mid-Georgian.

132. The Miles Brewton House is, at once, classic and vernacular. Its portico is a faithful and exquisitely carved wooden copy of the "Superimposed Orders," from the 1714 edition of *Palladio,* with Doric columns on the porch, Ionic on the balcony. A pediment with a delicate oval light crowns the composition.

Behind these graceful Palladian features is the basic Queen Anne house—the hip-roofed brick box—as well as glimpses of a regional idiom. A curving double stairway, typical of the southern town house, leads to the classic doorway. The *piano nobile* of the Italian Renaissance has fused with the southern "raised basement," a traditional Charleston scheme for catching the sea breeze.

The illustration shows the gate moved to the left of its actual position in the fence, in order to reveal the lower part of the house. Not shown are the *chevaux-de-frise,* guard spikes on the top of the fence, which were omitted in the source illustration.

133. This luxurious drawing room, almost overwhelming in its profusion of cream-colored woodwork, represents the height of mid-Georgian fashion. Note the pediment—that Palladian symbol—used alike over chimney breast and doorway. Though the pediment is by definition Palladian, the deeply carved, broken pediment and the heavy spiral consoles which act as supports are Baroque echoes, still part of the Georgian lexicon.

Also visible is something light and new: the French rococo which had developed from the Baroque during the reign of Louis XV. More decoration than architecture, it employed intricate traceries of flowers, fruit, scrolled leaves, and vines. It also made occasional use of Gothic or Oriental motifs, the latter known as chinoiserie. The Chinese Chippendale chair beside the harp was part of the rococo vogue. Note that the borders of the Powel drawing room match the touch of rococo on Lady Pepperell's doorway. In America, Palladian Georgian interiors might or might not be enriched with *rocaille,* as this fanciful decoration was called.

134. The Lady Pepperell Mansion shows the Palladian villa as an unmatched example of the New England woodworker's craft. Its pedimented pavilion, giant Ionic pilasters, quoins and dentils lend three dimensional character to an otherwise flat facade.

Wood also is used to create surface textures. The body of the house is finished in narrow, horizontal shiplap; the pavilion in smooth boarding. Vertical fluting in the pilasters acts as a counterpoint to both. These treatments are so delicate and finely wrought that the impression is one of exquisite femininity.

Suitably enough, this house was built by the widow of Sir William Pepperell, America's only baronet, knighted for his victory over the French at Louisburg. Even after the Revolution, Lady Pepperell kept her title, a match for the elegance of her lovely house.

134. The New England House: *Lady Pepperell*
Mansion, Kittery Point, Maine, ca. 1760.

The Georgian Period

Mid-Georgian:
The Palladian Style

135. English Palladianism: *Mathias Hammond (Hammond-Harwood) House, Annapolis, Md., 1773-74. William Buckland, architect and wood-carver.*

135. The Hammond-Harwood House is the colonial masterpiece of the Palladian Georgian Style. It was the last and best work of William Buckland, an English architect and woodcarver who came to this country as a bondsman and opened his own joinery office after working out his passage money.

Though smaller than the great houses of England and executed in the warm red brick of the colonial South, its precise edges and smooth surfaces echo the chiseled perfection of English Palladian models. Especially English are the subtle rhythms and counterrhythms of this composition, interplaying size, height, depth, form, the shapes of windows and doors, plain surfaces, and rich decoration.

In size and height, the house proper is dominant, with low curtains (the connecting passages) and dependencies of middle size. In the advance and retreat of building blocks, the dependencies come forward, the curtains retreat, and the house remains stable in middle distance. Fanlighted doorways shift from simplicity in the wings to elaboration at the center, where the formal entrance is enriched with pillars and rococo carving. The pavilion which sweeps from ground to roof lends additional emphasis to the center of the composition, repeating the pediment of the doorway at larger scale. In turn, this pavilion is repeated at small scale as a surround for side doorways. Rococo trim is centrally concentrated at the main doorway, second-story window, and attic light; rococo shape in the polygonal dependencies.

The Georgian Period

Mid-Georgian:
The Palladian Style

136. This country seat on the Schuylkill River was one of the summer retreats built by wealthy Philadelphians in Fairmount Park, not far by horse and carriage from the city.

By contrast with the subtle, understated English Palladian house (Figure 135), Mount Pleasant displays the verve and elegance of the French Renaissance. Dependencies, with their pagodalike roofs, skip a century backward to classicist François Mansart (or Mansard), inventor of the mansard roof. These little buildings are virtually identical to those which flank Mansart's seventeenth-century Château de Balleroy in Normandy—mansard roofs, quoins, flat keystone arches, dormer windows and all.

The house itself has been developed on Palladian lines from this French theme, including the elegantly pillared and pedimented doorway and the Palladian window above. Typically Gallic is the use of stucco as a smooth surfacing, combined with quoins for emphasis and textural interest. French influences were increasingly interwoven with Georgian architecture as the eighteenth century progressed.

The house also is full of the small deceptions which had become part of Georgian license in the pursuit of a classic ideal. Quoins are red brick, set to resemble stone. The stucco which covers rubblestone walls is incised to resemble ashlar. The right end wall (not shown) has no windows or doors. Yet inside the house, elegantly pedimented and enframed false doorways flank the fireplace, leading nowhere. They were placed there to create a classic balance for the real doors which lead from drawing room to hall.

This rich and elegant Georgian mansion cost its builder, Captain John MacPherson, 14,000 English pounds, such a fortune that he had to sell the house after it was completed. Benedict Arnold bought Mount Pleasant but never lived there because of his hasty retreat into the British Army.

The Georgian Period

The Queen Anne House: A Vernacular Survivor

137. Georgian: *Rufus Putnam House, Rutland, Mass., ca. 1750.*

138. Federal: *Blueford Plantation, near Pineville, Berkeley County, S.C., early 19th c.*

Throughout the history of architecture, a few basic house types have survived beyond their period, reappearing again and again in the guise of new styles as fashions changed. The gabled English house was one of these (Figures 28-35). So was the Anglo-Dutch brick dwelling, with its continuous chimney wall (Figures 46-49). The Cape Cod cottage is yet another. Each of these types survived from a relatively stable medieval past into a changing future.

During the Georgian period, a new basic type emerged, inspired by the classic Renaissance villa. It was the hip-roofed Queen Anne house of the Baroque or late Stuart period in England. In colonial America, it had remained basically the same under Palladian Georgian trim. The following illustrations show the Queen Anne house transformed into the vernacular and carried through a brief sampling of styles from the eighteenth to the twentieth century.

137. This house was a smaller, simpler wooden version of the Queen Anne mansion. It had narrow clapboards; thin, plain corner trim; delicate dentil work under the eaves; a door framed by Tuscan pilasters; and a ribbon transom, with partial entablature or simple pediment above. Doors were paneled and windows framed by architraves with inside shutters. Window panes were small, usually 12 over 12 lights.

138. To the Queen Anne house, the southern plantation owner added a raised basement and a large porch or porches, an updated version of the French *galerie*. There were louvered outside shutters to admit the breeze even when closed. Details here are a mixture of Georgian and Greek Revival, i.e., slender Tuscan columns, pyramidal Baroque entry stairs, Georgian dentils, and typical Greek Revival doorway framed with large, continuous transom and sidelights.

139. A bay window at left and a porch at right lend a touch of Italianate asymmetry to this version of the Queen Anne box. The hipped roof is classically low. Heavy bracketing under the eaves and at the portico are characteristically Italianate; so are the round-headed windows, paired on the second story and used in the projecting bay. Either elongated octagonal windows or round-headed windows might be used in double doors. Attic windows are small and

139. Italianate: *W.J. Bartlett House, Lee, Mass., ca. 1876.*

140. Georgian Revival (American Basic): *Builder's House, early 20th c.*

placed under the eaves, a substitute for dormers. Window moldings and eaves project strongly. Sheet metal roof was typical.

140. The Queen Anne house was part of the "Georgian Revival" of the late Victorian period, first built as a mansion (Figure 229), then translated into a modest builder's house. The clapboard porch enclosure, the mix of rectangular and diamond-paned windows, and the demarcation between first and second story are hangovers from the Victorian. Sometimes walls were shingled at the second story, clapboarded below. Window sash typically was 8 small panes over one large one, repeated at increased scale in the living room window.

The Georgian Period

The Row House:
A Classic Evolution

141. Typical Row Houses: *Georgian to Greek Revival, early 18th c. to mid 19th c.*

141a. Early Georgian (1700-50)

141b. Mid- or Late-Georgian (1750-the late 1820s)

141c. Federal (1790-1820)

The row house has been the usual town house and city dwelling in America ever since Jamestown built its first half-timbered row of "faire framed houses" in 1610. Shown here is a composite of houses from the classic period, illustrating changes in size and detail from early Georgian through the Greek Revival.

Houses much like this were built in early Boston, New York, Philadelphia, and other cities of the Eastern Seaboard. The New York row house usually had a raised entry, an evolution from the Dutch *stoep*. Those in Boston and Philadelphia were flush with the sidewalk. Baltimore houses were (and are) famous for their white marble steps, while Savannah and Charleston were distinguished by raised entries

with delicate ironwork railings. Door and window detailing was similar everywhere, copied from such popular handbooks as Joseph Moxon's *Mechanick Exercises* (London, 1700).

141a. The entire house and its details were at small scale. The earliest windows were topped by segmented brick arches; later, narrow wooden lintels were used. Window and door framing consisted of simple planks, called a plank-front frame. A six-paneled door, four-light transom, and sloping watershed dormers were typical.

141b. Houses might be two, but usually were three, stories in height. The scale has increased. Splayed brick lintels were the usual

treatment above windows. A variety of doorways included the round-headed brick arch, as seen here; a splayed lintel to match the windows; sometimes a simplified enframement of slender pilasters, entablature, and pediment. A pilastered and pedimented dormer window was typical.

141c. Dimensions, especially room heights and windows, have increased again. Splayed keystone lintels were the fashion for the more elegant houses, though plain splayed lintels still were used. The doorway has become larger and more important, with a characteristically intricate fanlight. The surround might be a brick arch or a pilastered enframement, sometimes with a pediment.

141d. Classic motifs were simplified and used in unorthodox ways, creating a linear character. Straight window lintels of painted, paneled wood sometimes were incised with a stylized classic design. More often, a linear block paneling was used at either end and, sometimes, in the center. This type was called a paneled lintel. If there also was a projecting molding at the top, it was called a paneled, molded lintel. Decorative lozenges might be attached to the house. Doorways were linearized and their classic elements stylized. Curved, cap-molded dormers were typical. There might or might not be a *piano nobile,* with major rooms shifted to the second story and given floor-length windows. If so, the wall was rusticated at the lower level.

141e. Treatment of details was bold, simple, realistically Greek in contrast to the delicacy and attenuation of Federal and Regency designs. Typical enframement for the doorway consisted of Greek columns, either Doric or Ionic, with a full entablature, usually flat, but occasionally with a hint of a pediment to match pointed lintels over the windows. Illustrated here are cap-molded, pointed lintels, so called because of their pointed shape and the projecting molding that caps their upper edge. Both the capped type and plain pointed lintels were common during the 1830s. Small attic windows cut into the wall were faced with a grillework typically based on the Greek anthemion, or honeysuckle.

141f. Later Greek Revival houses were essentially the same as the early ones, but the doorway grew larger and more impressive and the house might increase in width as time went on. A classic balustrade sometimes edged the roof. The flat cap-molded lintel was another of the various Greek Revival window treatments and its popularity continued into the 1860s.

The Georgian Period

The Temple-Form House

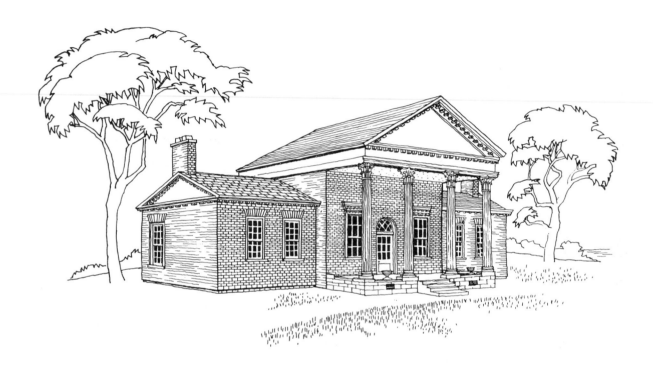

142. Like a stray from a time machine, this little temple-form house appeared in Maryland at the height of the Georgian period. Not until more than sixty years later, when the Greek Revival swept the country, would the temple-form house become a familiar American type. True to the eighteenth-century, this one is the miniature of a Roman temple, rather than Greek.

Whitehall was not the usual house, but a pavilion or "pleasure dome," built by a Maryland governor as a place for parties and balls. Guests were transported by boat from Annapolis across the Severn River. On arrival, they passed between the fluted Corinthian columns to enter a salon, 25 feet square, with a ceiling which soared 20 feet in height. Carved swags and pendants of fruits and flowers decorated its walls. The only other rooms were

in the wings, one a dining room, the other a bedroom.

Pavilions such as this were an eighteenth-century fashion on the grounds of English country houses, and their design often differed from the prevailing Georgian mode. Some were exotic Chinese pagodas, others Gothic conceits, and some Neoclassic, like Whitehall. Apparently, this elegant little pavilion pleased its owner, for he soon enlarged the house and made it his home. In that altered form, it exists today.

143. This illustration shows the Roman temple as translated into an American clapboard house. Placed gable end to street, with flanking wings, its resemblance to Whitehall (Figure 142) is striking. Such temple-form houses—though in

Greek rather than Roman trim—would be built throughout America in the nineteenth-century. Modillioned cornices, slender Roman Doric columns, and delicacy of detail throughout distinguish this one from the later Greek Revival type.

Like Whitehall, this temple-form house, the home of a judge and professor of law at the nearby College of William and Mary, was small but elegant. It was, in fact, adapted from a pavillion in Robert Morris's *Select Architecture*—presumably by Thomas Jefferson, who may have had a hand in Whitehall as well. This is larger than Whitehall by a second floor of bedrooms. But the ground floor plan is similar: a central salon opening to gardens at the rear; a dining room in one wing, a drawing room in the other.

143. The Clapboard Translation: *James Semple House, Williamsburg, Va., before 1782. Attributed to Thomas Jefferson, architect.*

8

Chapter 8

The Federal Period

The Federal period in American architecture (ca. 1790-1830) introduced the Neoclassic Style, which follows Palladian Georgian and predates the Greek Revival. The change from Georgian to Neoclassic and from Neoclassic to Greek was, in each case, gradual. Inevitably, these styles overlapped so that precise cut-off dates are impossible.

However, the size and richness of the Federal mansion sets it off from its pre-Revolutionary counterpart. The postwar years were active, exciting, and—after a difficult start—prosperous, as the nation tried out its hard-won independence. It was the day of the Yankee Clipper and the China trade, when Oriental merchants believed Salem, Massachusetts, to be a large and powerful country because so many ships under her pennant tied up at their wharves. Trade was brisk with Europe and with England, too, now that the war was over. There remained, in fact, a feeling of kinship with England which even the Revolution could not eradicate. As a result, all along the Eastern Seaboard, men of new wealth turned again to English models.

Most houses were, at first, simply larger and more elaborate versions of the pre-Revolutionary Palladian Georgian. But, gradually, a new English fashion came to prominence: the Neoclassic or "Adam Style." Robert Adam, with his brother James, had brought a fresh current into English architecture after studying the excavations at Pompeii, Herculaneum, and the Palace of Diocletian at Spalato.

The style was known as Neoclassic because it stemmed from study of actual classical houses, which were found to be far more varied than anyone had supposed. A whole new wealth of ornament appeared, along with new shapes for rooms—ovals, circles, octagons, projecting apses—sometimes separated from each other by arches or screens. This architecture evoked a sense of spatial mystery and drama in contrast to the forthright Georgian style. In decoration, deep carving gave way to delicate tracery, much of it in bas-relief, like a piece of Wedgwood china.

Though English models were followed, American divergence, in some cases, was pronounced. New, professionally trained architects like Benjamin Latrobe, and brilliant amateurs like Thomas Jefferson, consciously tried to create an original architecture for their young and optimistic nation. Latrobe would carry English Regency to a new American independence. Jefferson would go back to Rome in search of the classic dignity with which he wished to clothe the new nation. By returning to original sources, American architecture would at last achieve independence from England, finding its way to the Greek Revival, our first truly national style.

The Federal Period

The Late Georgian Style

144. A Georgian Mansion: *The President's House, Washington, D.C., 1792-1829. James Hoban, architect; North Portico, after a design by Benjamin Henry Latrobe.*

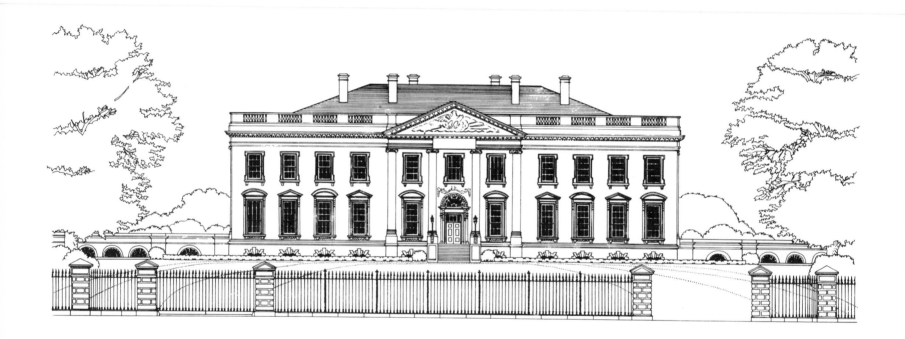

145. The Row House: *Wheat Row, Washington, D.C., early 19th c. Renovated and incorporated into Harbor Square, 1962-64. Chloethiel Woodard Smith & Associates, architects.*

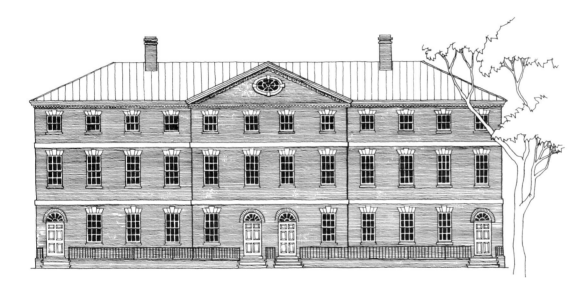

144. This late Georgian mansion, the largest and most sumptuous of the Federal period, is believed to have been modeled after the Duke of Leinster's house in Dublin, though a strikingly similar plate can be found in James Gibbs's *Book of Architecture.* It was not known as the White House until many years after its construction. The original color of the President's House, as it then was called, was a light pinkish-tan, a characteristic Georgian shade.

It was during restoration work in 1817, following its burning by the British, that the house was painted white. In 1829, the pillared portico was added, as well as a new wrought-iron fence. An earlier enclosure had been described by a caller in 1804. "The President's House," he wrote, "is encircled by a very rude pale, through which a common rustic stile introduces visitors."

The portico, the fence, and the new white paint were meant to bring a rather old-fashioned Georgian house into the Neoclassic Style of the Federal period. In addition, the imposing portico, with its large but simple pillars, framing the richly graceful doorway, projected qualities of dignity and nobility which its architect hoped would symbolize the character of the new nation.

145. This late Georgian example, also in the city of Washington, was not a mansion at all but a row of speculative builder's houses. However, it is interesting to note how much it resembles the President's House, built during the same period.

Part of English city planning in the late eighteenth and early nineteenth centuries was the organization of a number of town houses into a composition resembling a single much grander dwelling. Wheat Row gives us a minor American example of this clever Georgian pretense. There are four town houses here, each three bays in width; but the use of the pavilion, plus the centering of two of the doors, makes it appear plausible that these are separate entrances to a mansion. Wheat Row still exists, retained by history-conscious architects within the urban renewal area of southwest Washington.

The Federal Period

The Late Georgian Style

146. The Palladian House: *Colonel Alexander Field House, Longmeadow, Mass., 1794.*

147. A Palladian Mansion: *Linden Hall, Springfield, Mass., 1811. From a design by Asher Benjamin.*

146. The Federal period was marked by no sudden change in American architecture. Only gradually did the prevailing Georgian Style shift to the Neoclassic. But the post-Revolutionary years did bring new wealth to Yankee shipowners and merchants and a new enrichment to the New England clapboard box.

The Colonel Field house is a good example. A Federal version of New England Georgian, its every aperture has been decorated with a Palladian motif. Pilasters, pediments, and fanlights grace the doorways. A semipavilion repeats the pediment and fanlight at larger scale. A Palladian window illuminates the upper hall. Cornice and architrave adorn each lower window. To see how much the New England house had changed while remaining essentially the same, compare this with its predecessor of some forty years (Figure 127).

147. Like Janus, the Roman god of beginnings and endings, Linden Hall looks both forward and back. Its giant portico, with columns the height of the house, came into use during the Federal period but it repeats a Palladian Georgian theme. At the same time, it prefigures the Greek Revival and the temple-form house. Quoins are late Georgian, rarely used after 1805. Never used before that date is the combination of small side entry with a private front porch, reached only from inside the house. Also new in the Federal period are a "monitor roof" to light the stairwell and a balustrade, alternating solid with openwork panels.

This imposing design was by Asher Benjamin, a New England carpenter-architect who published the first building books specifically tailored to American conditions. He made cornices thin, columns and pilasters attenuated, in harmony with the lightness of the American wooden house. This slenderness of proportion is one of the marks of the Federal style, setting it off from the English Georgian as well as from the later Greek Revival in America.

148. With a balustrade of Chinese Chippendale fretwork atop the roof and a portico to match, the residence of Lieutenant Governor Martin was as ornamental as any New England woodcarver could make it. Despite its new richness, however, there are no new motifs in the house. The Chippendale theme, here inventively applied to the exterior, had been part of a rococo interplay with Georgian architecture since well before the Revolution.

What is remarkably new is the large size of the lower windows, reaching to the floor and flooding the interior with light. Each is composed of three separate sashes. Federal houses often had large windows, with panes as big as 12 by 14 inches, while the muntins which separated them became contrastingly slender. With the new preference for pastel walls and white woodwork, the interior achieved a clarity and freshness unprecedented in pre-Revolutionary architecture.

148. The Chippendale House: *Lieutenant Governor Simeon Martin House, Seekonk, Mass., 1810.*

The Federal Period

The Adam Style

149. The Mansion House: *First Harrison Gray Otis House, Boston, Mass., 1796. Charles Bulfinch, architect.*

149. The four preceding houses, as elegant as New England clapboard could be made, were country vernacular compared to the Boston mansion of Harrison Gray Otis. This is the work of the finest American architect of the Federal period, Charles Bulfinch, whose ideas were reflected in most New England houses of his day.

The exquisitely glassy facade of the Otis house, with second-story windows extending to the floor, illustrates the refreshingly open, airy quality of the best Federal architecture, enhanced by large rooms and high ceilings within. A subtle theme of curves is played against the plain rectangular box: vertically in the webbed fanlight, Palladian window, and lunette; horizontally in bowed wrought-iron balconies and in festoons. The Otis house as it stands today is exposed brick, but Bulfinch's drawing indicates that he may have intended to stucco or paint the house—a Federal practice giving an appearance of smoothness to the surface. Refined, delicate, and clean cut, this design is the essence of the new Adam style.

The work of Charles Bulfinch was widely copied and adapted in the pattern books of the day, most notably those of Asher Benjamin. Benjamin's popular guides are believed to have established the character of the New England town as it took shape in the late eighteenth and early nineteenth centuries.

150. There is nothing revolutionary about the Pingree House. Standard windows and a narrow, medieval silhouette make it less advanced than the examples that precede it. But Samuel McIntire, that artist among architects, did the conventional with a very special touch. Working within existing forms, he changed them through proportion, simplification, and the addition of his exquisite woodcarving into masterpieces of Federal architecture. Georgian fancywork— quoins, pilasters, pavilions, and rustication—all have been stripped away, leaving the plain brick box as a foil for delicate Adam detail.

Here, again, one sees a simplified geometry of the rectangle with superimposed curves. The counterpoint to the chaste angularity of this building is concentrated in the portico. An elliptical fanlight and sidelights form a single traceried overthrow for the door. The slender

150. The McIntire Touch: *Pingree House, Salem, Mass., 1804. Samuel McIntire, architect, housewright, and woodcarver.*

151. The Adam Interior: *Pingree House, Salem, Mass., 1804. Samuel McIntire, architect, housewright, and woodcarver.*

columns, the bowed entablature, the curves of capitals, all at the most delicate scale, form a single ornament to this subtle facade. Horizontal enrichment is provided by the balustrade atop the roof and the intricate wrought-iron fence below.

151. This Salem parlor, with its delicately carved, white woodwork and pale yellow wallpaper patterned in gray, sums up the Adam interior. Instead of paneling the entire wall surface—the Georgian ideal—the new mode called for a dado and cornice, with wallpaper or plaster between. White woodwork with pastel walls, refreshing and feminine, were innovations of the Federal period and entered our heritage with the Adam Style.

Heavy Georgian carving also gave way to delicate bas-relief. This was quite literally appliqué, usually French putty, formed in molds and glued to the surface. Samuel McIntire was among the few craftsmen sufficiently skilled to carve these fragile ornaments in wood.

For some rooms, McIntire chose a white-on-white scheme of bas-relief, woodwork, and walls to achieve the utmost subtlety in design. Other architects, including Bulfinch, used white relief on grounds of pale gray, buff, blue, or cool green, creating the effect of a piece of Wedgwood china—itself part of this period fashion.

The Federal Period

The Adam Style

152. The Adam Country House: *Gore Place, Governor Christopher Gore Mansion, Waltham, Mass., ca. 1805. Jacques Guillaume Legrand, architect, Paris, France.*

152a. Plan, Gore Place

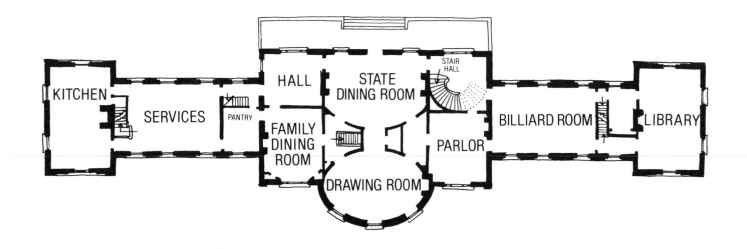

152. From Gore Place, his elegant Federal mansion, Christopher Gore rode out in splendor in an orange coach, attended by a liveried coachman, footmen, and outriders. The day after he was elected Governor, seventy-five friends dropped in for breakfast. His banqueting hall accommodated them with ease.

One of the few New England houses grand enough to have attached dependencies, Gore Place represents a Neoclassical reworking of that Georgian scheme. The curve is the new motif: in oval rooms, in the bow-front, or swell-front as it was also called, in arcaded wings, and in the fanlights of windows and French doors.

The bowed garden front of this house is its salient feature, the outward sign of radical interior change. A new idea had come into play: size, shape, height, and location of rooms should be determined by use and visibly expressed on the exterior.

Among the new shapes, the oval, or ellipse, was a favorite. This graceful enclosure was seized upon by wealthy Americans for the drawing room, the salon or "saloon," the ballroom, the music room, or the banqueting hall, one or more of which might now be included in an elegant home. Other popular shapes were the circle, the semicircle, the octagon, the square, and an elongated rectangle with or without bowed ends. Robert Adam had introduced these novel shapes after observing at first hand the unexpected variety of rooms in the remains of ancient Roman houses and the Imperial Roman Baths.

French ideas also contributed to the new Federal style, not only in this house designed by a French architect, but in others as well. Closets—a remarkable innovation two centuries earlier in the palaces of Louis XIV—now were included in some of America's best bedrooms. Dressing rooms, from the same source, might be added, too. A butler's pantry acted as a buffer between dining room and kitchen. Gore Place had, possibly, America's first billiard room.

Convenience, privacy, special rooms, and garden prospects were, of course, luxuries of the rich. But, gradually, some of the new ideas began to appear in less elaborate homes. Today, no matter how small our dwelling, each time we hang our clothes in a closet we are heirs of the Sun King, Louis XIV.

152a. In the new Neoclassic plans, a suite of rooms of varied sizes and shapes, formal and informal, might be distributed along the garden front of the house, all taking advantage of this pleasant prospect by means of large windows and French doors. With such an arrangement, lateral hallways began to supplement the entry hall, which no longer extended through the house. There was no fixed scheme but a new kind of functional and livable house was taking shape.

153. This mansion is the outstanding example of the Charleston "single house," i.e., the tall, narrow scheme of a single file of rooms with street entry at the end and a piazza overlooking the garden: the traditional medieval house reworked as a regional type.

It also has been proposed as the outstanding example of the Adam Style in America. The balconied octagonal bay shows that this mansion contains the novel room shapes of that style. At ground level, the library is an oval, decorated in Pompeiian red with buff woodwork—a scheme to match an Adam original. The oval drawing room, above, now cast as a music room, has smooth, off-white walls, enriched by carved woodwork painted pale gray, its delicate Adam ornament picked out with gilding. The typically Adam spiral staircase ascends three stories in graceful curves, seemingly without support of any kind.

153a. This mansion uses the oval, square, and rectangular rooms recommended by Robert Adam as the most felicitous combination of shapes, designed to provide continually changing pleasure for the senses.

153. The Adam Town House: *Nathaniel Russell House, Charleston, S.C., before 1809.*

153a. Plan, Nathaniel Russell House

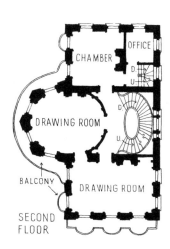

OFFICE
CHAMBER
DRAWING ROOM
BALCONY
DRAWING ROOM
SECOND FLOOR

The Federal Period

The Regency Shift

154. The Adam Style: *Grasse Mount, Captain Thaddeus Tuttle House, Burlington, Vt., built by Thaddeus Tuttle, 1804.*

The Regency in England denotes the years between 1810 and 1820, when George III was incapacitated and the future George IV ruled for his father. This small segment of time gives its name to an evanescent style of architecture that appeared in the last decade of the eighteenth century and reached its peak during the Regency years.

It is essentially a transition between the well-known Neoclassic, or Adam Style, and the even better known Greek Revival, sharing characteristics with each. The nomenclature is slippery, however, and many houses could be classified as either Adam or Regency. In America, the safe umbrella term is Federal, which shelters both.

Regency shares with some Adam work the use of recessed blind arcades, arched windows, smooth stuccoed or painted wall surfaces, large windows often reaching to the floor, door and window openings cleanly cut into the wall surface, elliptical staircases, and arched wall niches.

With the Greek Revival, at the other end of the bridge, there were fewer points of contact. But though the connection was slight, it was there. As early as 1762, Stuart and Revett had published their *Antiquities of Athens,* containing measured drawings of the Parthenon and other ancient Greek relics. Not until fifty years later would this book, like a time bomb, explode in America, scattering Greek Revival buildings across the nation. In the eighteenth century, it had very little effect. Few architects made use of it and then only as a source for decorative motifs—the usual modest beginning for any new style. But it is this use that we see in Regency work.

In its simplicity and plain surfaces, as well as ornament, the Regency corresponds to the sturdy Greek Revival Style but is unlike it in slenderness, grace, and the use of the Roman arch. The Regency Style is unusually hard to define because it cannot be codified. More than anything else, it was a trend toward a simplified and original use of classic precedent.

154. One of the aims of the Neoclassic Style, especially as developed by Robert Adam, was a

155. The Regency Style: *Owens-Thomas House, Savannah, Ga., 1816. William Jay, architect.*

sense of spatial mystery, the creation of visual retreat and advance, of spaces glimpsed through columns and arches which might sometimes be only pilasters or projections on the face of a wall. That is what is happening on the facade of this house.

A blind arcade creates the effect of a loggia; second-story pilasters, the effect of a colonnade. The balustrade alternates spindlework with solid panels, and its columns and finials are repeated at larger scale in fence posts below. The central archway is set apart by its exquisitely detailed Federal fanlight and sidelights, like a glass spiderweb spun across the doorway. But the strong focus of the Early Georgian Style, building always toward a center

and an apex, is exchanged here for continuous rhythms.

This lovely house owes its inspiration to the second Harrison Gray Otis mansion in Boston, designed by Charles Bulfinch. Its themes also connect it to the Regency example (Figure 155).

155. This Savannah mansion has been called the finest example of Regency architecture in America. In keeping with the freedom of the Regency approach, it consists of a grab-bag of themes—Queen Anne, Palladian, Adam, and a touch of Greek—all mixed together in a totally unorthodox way. Both the preceding Adam example and this one make use of blind arcades; but here they have been more cleanly cut,

creating a linear quality which is part of the style. Moreover, what seems busy in a drawing is resolved by pale stucco into a neutral composition, with barely visible uncolored enrichments on an otherwise smooth facade: the Regency look.

The curving hood which canopies the balcony is another telltale feature never present on a Georgian or a Neoclassic house. The hood is edged with anthemia, or honeysuckle, a typical Greek Revival motif; and the balcony's supports are in the shape of rolled Greek acanthus leaves. By contrast with the delicate hand-wrought ironwork which preceded it, this cast-iron balcony, made in France, is a portent of changing times and an incipient industrial age.

The Federal Period

The Regency Shift

156. The Adam Style: *President William Howard Taft House, Cincinnati, Ohio, 1819-20.*

156. This gracious house, built in the Western Reserve of Ohio, may have been designed by Benjamin Latrobe, one of America's most influential architects. Latrobe urged a direct return to classic models but, also, their free adaptation to American ways of living. The Taft House could be a demonstration of his theory. The facade is a simplified version of a classic villa, but on the opposite side, overlooking a private garden court, the house breaks open into balconies like a southern plantation house.

The Palladian entrance facade (Figure 135) has been transformed by Neoclassic styling. The separate blocks of house and dependencies have been merged together. A Palladian portico remains the focus of the composition but detail throughout is Adam: light, delicate, refined. A web of glass frames the entry under the thinnest possible Roman arch, and matching ovals serve as secondary light sources for high-ceilinged rooms within. A curving flight of stairs is railed in delicate wrought iron, black against pale walls.

157. This delightful little villa is a textbook example of what the Regency could do to a classic house. The Taft mansion showed the Palladian villa newly styled with delicate Adam detail. Swanwick Manor reduces the same elements to a hieroglyph.

Columns, pediment, and entablature have been merged into a smooth, semicircular arcade, slender and unadorned. The central block, containing hall and library, projects beyond the shallower dining rooms on either side, in a distant reference to the temple form with its balanced wings. Lest the allusion be too obvious, the kitchen has been added asymmetrically, set back a little from the dining room at left.

Walls are smooth, ornamented only by the string course in a running Greek key pattern—small pieces of iron set into the stucco with which this house is covered. At the opposite side, facing private gardens, are large, floor-length windows in all rooms, linking indoors and out. Swanwick Manor, an abstraction from the Palladian villa, is a typical Regency design and perhaps the first modern house.

157. The Regency Style: *Swanwick Manor, Farnhurst, Del., ca. 1820.*

The Federal Period

Republican Rome

158. The Palladian Villa: *Monticello, Home of President Thomas Jefferson, near Charlottesville, Va., first major building period 1768-82; second major building period 1793-1809. Thomas Jefferson, architect.*

158. Monticello, the famous home of our fourth president, Thomas Jefferson, is an American Villa Rotonda crowned by a dome, embellished with pedimented porticoes at front and rear and with arcaded loggias at either side. Its Palladian vocabulary includes a full entablature, the frieze accurately delineated down to triglyphs which form a staccato ribbon at the top of the wall.

Thomas Jefferson believed that American architecture should represent the new nation in symbolic form. He therefore rejected what he considered the mannered delicacy of the Adam and Regency styles, both linked to current fashions of the English monarchy. Instead, seeking to express qualities of strength, dignity,

and forthrightness, he turned to Republican Rome, with which the leaders of the Revolution had strongly identified.

At the same time, the most forward-looking country in the world should, he believed, make use of every possible innovation. As minister to France, Jefferson had encountered the novel room shapes which were part of Neoclassic architecture there, and he incorporated them into his plan. A semioctagonal drawing room overlooks lawns and view at the rear while, at smaller scale, octagonal side rooms open to terraces. The resulting breaks in the wall line give sculptural interest to the body of the house and express the distinctive shapes within.

Jefferson also installed a number of smaller French inventions. Not the least of these was the inside privy for inclement weather—matched by the traditional outdoor type for sunny days. So great a departure was this convenience (not yet a flushing water closet) that for years it was considered a decadent French indulgence, scarcely suitable to the sturdy American character.

Jefferson's own inventiveness and practicality virtually ensured a thorough reworking of the classic model. He developed the Palladian dome as an astronomical observatory. To Monticello's creature comforts, he contributed an array of domestic gadgetry: a dumbwaiter for

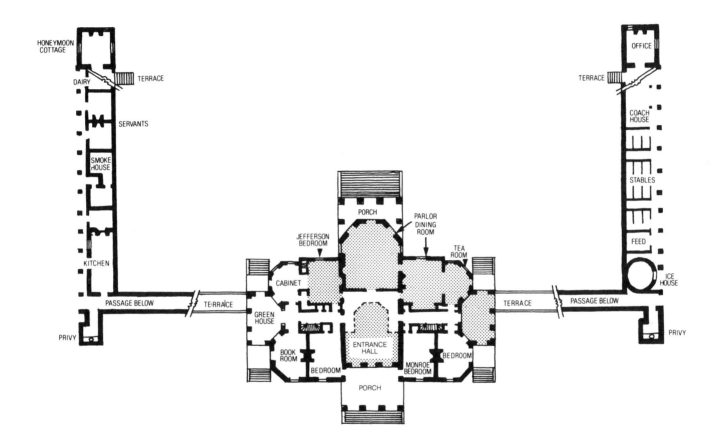

transporting wine from the cellar; a clock which records the days of the week; a weathervane on the ceiling of the entrance portico, readable in comfort from inside the house; double doors to the drawing room, so linked that each opens automatically when the other is pushed. No detail, however small, was overlooked.

At the same time, the house is the embodiment of unusually large ideas. In it, Jefferson tried to show Americans the future which he would wish for them, each independent and self-sufficient on his own acres, returning from the tasks of the farm to a templed villa to read a copy of Pliny in the candlelight. It was a classical vision

and a beautiful dream. For a time, parts of it even came true.

158a. Monticello's interior is enlivened by the shifting spaces of its varied rooms. Jefferson changed shape, size, and ceiling height to calculated effect. The shaded area on the plan indicates those rooms which rise a full two stories in height. These are the formal apartments used in entertaining, plus Jefferson's own bedroom-workroom. Together, they form a cross plan of high, open, and airy spaces. The remainder of the first floor is one story, with second-story bedrooms above. By their lowered ceilings, these other first-floor rooms are given

a feeling of coziness and enclosure. Side rooms, including a charming octagonal tea room, give directly onto terraced promenades.

Underground, beneath the promenades, passages lead from the basement of the house to service rooms—kitchen, dairy, and smokehouse on one side; stables and coach house on the other—all tucked out of sight and sound beneath raised terraces. Through these passages, undeterred by rain or snow and invisible from owner, family, and guests above, servants could bring food to the house or walk out to nearby stables when a carriage or riding horse was requested.

The Federal Period

Republican Rome

159. The Roman Villa: *Mount Vernon, Home of President George Washington, Fairfax County, Va. Original cottage, ca. 1726; additions, 1757-87.*

159. Like Monticello, Mount Vernon stands apart from the other houses of its place and period. Though basically Palladian Georgian, it is instantly recognizable by the great two-story colonnade across its river front, a unique feature which bore no relationship to the architectural currency of its day.

The appearance of this giant colonnade on an otherwise typical Virginia plantation house is one of those small mysteries which have never been solved. A central portico was the usual Palladian treatment. The only approximate match to Mount Vernon is the French colonial galleried house (Figure 96), which Washington may have seen on his far-flung travels. Trade with the West Indies, which Washington and his brother Lawrence engaged in, could have exposed them to the galleried porch. Contemporary excavations of Roman antiquities might have provided a model.

From whatever source, or as his own invention, Washington combined the pleasures of an open-air living room with the dignity of a classic colonnade, in effect recreating the ancient Roman seaside villa, paintings of which are among the remains at Pompeii.

In Monticello and Mount Vernon, the two most distinguished leaders of the young republic designed not only their own homes but what they believed were appropriate dwellings for a free people in an independent nation. In their affection for these houses, Americans perhaps have sensed the qualities of pride, accomplishment, and hope which inspired them.

Chapter 9

The Greek Revival

"The two great truths in the world are the Bible and Grecian architecture." Nicholas Biddle, 1806.

". . . every house is the whitest of the white; every Venetian blind the greenest of the green; every fine day's sky the bluest of the blue. . . . All The buildings looked as if they had been built and painted that morning." Charles Dickens, *American Notes*, 1842.

"Ovid gave me not Rome, nor himself, but a view into the enchanted gardens of the Greek mythology. . . . I loved to get away from the hum of the forum, and the mailed clang of Roman speech, to these shifting shows of nature, these Gods and Nymphs born of the sunbeam, the wave, and the shadows on the hill. . . . With these books I passed my days." *Memoirs* of Margaret Fuller Ossoli, 1852.

"It was as if man in America, around 1820, had rediscovered his five senses; had suddenly, like one breaking through from the forest to sun-drenched, sea-bordered downs, all at once become conscious of bright sun and distance and freedom; had suddenly discovered that it was better to see and hear beautiful things than ugly ones; had, in a word, waked up from a nightmare." Talbot Hamlin, *Greek Revival Architecture in America*, 1944.

The Greek Revival occurred at one of those moments in time which later generations tend to think of as golden. There was peace, prosperity, freedom—and a future which opened with all the promise of the beckoning mountains, woods, and prairie to the west. After two hundred years of Indian raids, of battles with the French, of two wars for independence from England, of the trials of forming their own government, Americans had emerged from the struggle to find that the day was sunny and the land their own.

When the Greek Revival took hold in America around the year 1820, the entire culture which welcomed it had been classically oriented for over two centuries. Latin and Greek (sometimes taught at home by clergymen fathers) were the basics of instruction beyond the three "Rs." Roman and Greek mythology, while not perhaps so thoroughly familiar as the Bible, was widely known. A contemporary novel or poem was scarcely understandable without a working knowledge of classical myth.

The vocabulary of classical architecture—column, pediment, portico, entablature, cornice, frieze, architrave, modillion, dentil, and so on and on—had thus become the common property alike of the classical scholar, the merchant, the plantation owner, and the village carpenter. The one might have this knowledge in his head and the other in his fingers, but it was there.

The Greek Revival was thus not the superficial fashion we have come to see it looking back through the subsequent revival styles of the nineteenth century. Greek architecture was a new and exciting story told, if not in the native tongue, at least in a thoroughly familiar second language, at precisely the moment when all other tales had grown stale and old.

Thomas Jefferson had proposed the Roman classic as a suitable architecture for his vision of America. But it was the Greek which proved to be the popular choice. Roman sources were indelibly associated with England. In France, Napoleon Bonaparte's fondness for Roman architecture had rubbed off what remained of its bloom. By contrast, Greek architecture symbolized the earliest democracy in the history of mankind. If further impetus were needed, in 1821, the Greek war for independence from Turkey supplied it, engaging American sympathies and making all things Greek a national fashion.

Perhaps most important of all, the Greek Revival resolved what was left of conflict between the native English medieval tradition and the imported Renaissance. In Chapters 7 and 8, we have shown almost exclusively the hipped-roof (and, later, flat-roofed) house which was the carrier of the formal Georgian style. But an engraving of Boston by Paul Revere, drawn in 1760, shows scarcely a house of that type. At the height of the Georgian period in America, prosperous Boston consisted of row after row of neat, rectangular, gable-roofed houses—the old, medieval type—Georgian only in their sash windows, balanced symmetry, and classical treatment at the doorway.

The Greek Revival fitted this house like the

glass slipper when placed on the proper foot. The temple shape was ideally suited to the traditional gable-roofed house. America's most popular dwelling need only be turned gable end to street for proper attachment of the portico. With this new orientation, and its accompanying colonnade, a modest everyday dwelling gained new dignity, quite in keeping with the changed mood of its occupants.

If a portico was beyond the owner's means, pilasters, or merely a frieze beneath the eaves, and Greek enframement at the doorways could serve the purpose. If nothing more, an existing house might become a reasonable facsimile of Greek marble by the simple expedient of painting it white. Old houses were easily brought into fashion; new houses were not beyond the ken of existing building practice.

Nor was there anything finicky or precious about the style. A Greek portico, especially in the Doric order, was bold, strong, and simple, yet far more impressive with its great two-story columns than the restrained Georgian facade. Gone were the curves and delicate traceries of the Adam fashion, its elliptical fanlights, oval attic windows, bowed rooms. Windows and doorways, even including glass transom and sidelights, were now straight, square, sturdy, and on the level—the self-image of a newly confident and independent America.

Though in style the Greek Revival was a culmination of the classical tradition, technologically it presided over the beginning of America's industrial age. The entire period was one of invention and change. The years between 1820 and the Civil War—the approximate dates of the Greek Revival—saw steamboats on the Mississippi, packet service on the Erie Canal, locomotive-powered trains whizzing by at 20 miles an hour, iron plows and mechanical reapers on the farm, and a cast-iron cookstove in at least some fortunate kitchens. If contemporary advertisements are to be believed, a few houses even had complete bathrooms with a tub, mechanical shower bath, and water closet. The Greek Revival dwelling, like no house before it, was entirely up-to-date.

At the same time, it was a pioneer homestead. As Americans pushed beyond the Allegheny Mountains, the log cabin was their first frontier

home; but as permanent settlements took shape or prosperity came to struggling plantation owners, the Greek Revival house became the fashionable choice.

In the hands of leading architects, the Greek Revival underwent a surprising "modernization" of both form and detail, resulting in stripped-down designs not unlike the English Regency. A sense of freedom is evident even in builder's handbooks. Minard Lafever entitled his most famous Greek Revival pattern book *The Beauties of Modern Architecture.* That, of course, is exactly what the Greek style was to the architects and homebuilders of the early nineteenth century. Architecture was, by definition, classic. This was modern architecture, i.e., the new Greek classic modified and made usable for a contemporary house.

The Greek Revival

The Temple-Form Mansion

160. The Doric Temple: *Andalusia, Nicholas Biddle Mansion, Bucks County, Pa., portico added to original farmhouse, 1836. Thomas Ustick Walter, architect.*

161. The Ionic Temple: *Joseph Bowers House, Northampton, Mass., 1825. Ithiel Town, architect.*

160. Like a statement of arrival, Andalusia stands on the banks of the Delaware River, a formal academic mansion in the new Greek Revival Style. It is as close a copy of the Theseum in Athens as a remodeled family farmhouse could be: a pure temple form, rare among American houses.

As striking as its giant colonnade is the shift to the Greek Doric order. Columns are thick and sturdy, especially in comparison to the slender pillars and pilasters of the Federal period just past.

The Doric is the most archaic of the Greek orders, deriving from buildings which originally were wood. Columns have no base and only a squared capital. They are slightly tapered from bottom to top like the tree trunks which were their prototypes. In the original wooden structure, the crossbeams which supported the roof and the wooden pegs which secured them were visible on the exterior. When the Greeks substituted stone for wood, what had been structural elements were retained as ornament. This is what one sees here. The repetitive triglyphs along the frieze represent the ends of beams; the spaces between them, originally voids, are called metopes; just below the triglyphs are guttae, or pegs. An American Greek Revival house was quite likely to be a wooden translation of a marble building which itself had been copied from wood.

161. This imposing home, consisting of a *cella*, or central block, and subsidiary wings, is the academic ideal of the temple-form house. With regional adjustments and simplification, dwellings of like design were built in every part of the country, the basic pattern adapted to mansion and cottage alike. Such houses have no counterpart in Europe but are an American development, perhaps the first which we can call our own.

This house was executed in the Ionic order, easily recognizable by the graceful scrolled volutes of its capitals. Behind the Ionic colonnade, anta capitals are used on piers at the corners of the house and in the wings. "Anta" means simply a subsidiary order, different from, but harmonizing with, the dominant order of the portico. A full entablature is used but there are no triglyphs, metopes, or guttae (see Figure 160).

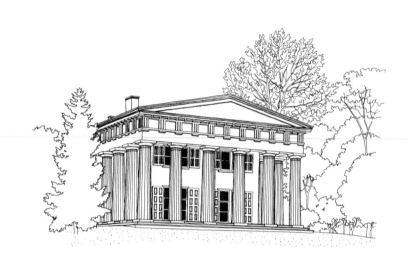

The Ionic order is later than the Doric and shows less resemblance to the archaic wooden prototypes from which both descend.

162. This double parlor is a superb example of the period room in the Greek Revival Style. Existing only as a drawing by Alexander Jackson Davis, it has never been identified, but it is a visual match for the Bowers House (Figure 161), thought to have been designed by Ithiel Town before he and Davis became partners. Note that columns and piers are identical on both interior and exterior. Together, these drawings illustrate the unity which leading Greek Revival architects tried to create in their designs.

Greek motifs are everywhere in this room. The anthemion, or honeysuckle, with its twining tendrils, and the rosette are especially prominent. Not only ornament but the forms of furniture were Greek inspired. This is English Regency, but the similar French and American Empire styles also were used in Greek Revival homes.

162. The Greek Revival Interior: *Double Parlor,*
ca. 1830. Town & Davis, architects.

The Greek Revival

The Temple-Form House

163. Carpenter's Classic: *Alonzo Olds House, Rushton, Mich., 1848.*

164. Vernacular Greek: *Alvin T. Smith House, Forest Grove, Ore., late 1850s.*

163. This tiny house shows how the academic Greek Revival was simplified and miniaturized for a modest dwelling. The portico of a mansion typically had six columns (known as hexastyle), that of a cottage only four (tetrastyle). However, in this ambitious little house, the full entablature and anta pilasters have been retained. Wings have become mere appendages, yet add much needed space to the *cella*, or central block.

In small houses like this, the doorway was pushed to one side, rather than centered, in order to leave a bit more wall space for the parlor. This one is so very small that there was no room for a parlor window, and the solitary bedroom window has been centered over the door in a brave attempt at classic balance. Nevertheless, the imposing Greek Revival portico produces a remarkable Cinderella effect, imparting the greatest possible grandeur to this little wooden house.

164. This is the temple-form house reduced to a decorative minimum. Though considerably larger than the Michigan example (Figure 163), it is a plain farmhouse rather than a miniature belle at a masquerade ball. Note, however, the subtle relationship between the two houses. The anta pilasters at the corners are similar in both; so is the wing with the hipped roof. The entablature, though not so richly worked, is nevertheless wide and heavy and obviously meant to suggest a pediment at the gable end. In the pointed lintel of both doorway and attic window, one catches another faint echo of the pediment. Transom and sidelights of simple, square panes of glass are typically Greek. Taken together with the pointed lintel, these suggest a pediment, frieze, and columns—in short, a portico—in a house which had none. Greek Revival details were never fatherless but retained classic reference points however remote.

165. A California Cottage: *House Behind the Courthouse, Downieville, Calif., mid-19th c.*

165. The transformation of the undistinguished clapboard box was the special magic of the Greek Revival. In a house too small for an academic portico, one has been suggested by means of latticed screens, interspersed with the slenderest of wooden colonnettes.

This facade can be read two ways. Colonnettes can be considered as miniature columns; but if one looks at each lattice with its framing colonnettes as a single unit, then each becomes the symbol of a wide heavy column in the academic portico. Matching latticework represents a frieze, which turns into the usual plain vernacular type at the side of the house.

In its simplified reference to classic elements, this charming temple-form cottage carries over all the grace and linear delicacy of the Regency into the following period. Few houses employed so light a touch. But this cottage is a sample of the freedom and inventiveness with which Americans made the Greek Revival their own.

The Greek Revival

The Cobblestone House

166. The Porticoed House: *Unidentified House near Rochester, N.Y., ca. 1840.*

167. The Modified Temple: *Steven Taber House, near Castile, N.Y., 1844.*

166. The glaciers that covered the Great Lakes and surrounding areas some 10,000 years ago provided the building material for one of the most interesting dwellings of the Greek Revival period: the cobblestone house. This method of building, with its surfacing of small, smooth, glacial stones over rubble masonry walls, did not originate in America. "Kidney cobbles"— the English name for these stones—have been described as "among the delights of East Anglian coastal districts," part of a building tradition dating to the Middle Ages.

The reappearance of this antique system in western New York and other Great Lakes areas was a response to the quantity of such stones accumulated when pioneer farmers cleared their fields. A few of the earliest houses were Georgian, the last Victorian. But typically, Greek detailing prevailed, as seen here in flat lintels, simplified Doric portico and broad frieze.

Windows in the frieze were a substitute for dormers in many Greek Revival houses. The glass was covered by a grillework of wood or cast iron in a Greek design. This one is the anthemion, or honeysuckle, with tendrils.

167. This cobblestone dwelling represents an elision of the distinct parts of the temple-form house. The main block and its flanking wings are so compressed that what originally was the *cella* has become, in visual effect, a glorified dormer window. The wings now flow into each other as the main floor of the house, and a pillared portico is provided by recessing the entrance. This type of entry is called a portico *in antis*, as opposed to the projecting portico known as a *prostyle*. Note also the wide, heavy entablature, a distinguishing mark of the Greek Revival.

Quoins, a Georgian feature, were retained as stabilizing for the rubblestone walls. Typically, they were a rust-red native sandstone; occasionally they were gray. Cobbles at first were mixed, but it became fashionable to select one color, usually a rusty shade, to match the quoins. Less frequently, single-color houses used cobbles of gray, brown, or shades of yellow. One striking example was limited to dark gray and black.

The Greek Revival

American Basic

168. Only a light touch of Greek detailing reveals the period of this house: a simple portico with squared pillars, rectangular sidelights at the doorway, and a wide, flat frieze broken by tiny windows. Small under-eave windows had come into occasional use as early as the 1790s, but they reached their height of popularity during the Greek Revival period as insertions in the Greek frieze. Placed so near the floor that one could look out of them only by lying flat, they were nicknamed "lie-on-your-stomach-windows" or, less genteelly, "belly windows."

Underneath the Greek detailing, this house is a regional New Jersey type, similar to the "telescope house" of the Eastern Shore of Maryland (Figure 46). The "wing" usually was built first, the larger house added with increasing prosperity. Sometimes there were three or four such attached houses, each bigger than the last, stretching out like the parts of an extended telescope.

169. Here, the Greek Revival adds its simple, bold styling to a typical Pennsylvania farmhouse. The tall, narrow dwelling, only one room deep, was a persistent nineteenth-century type in that state, owing its proportions to a lingering medieval tradition. But with the Greek Revival, the roof became much shallower and the gable end was treated with a simplified pediment and pilasters. The porch and rear lean-to act visually as "wings" in this symbolic representation of the temple-form house. At the same time, they echo the German pent roof (Figure 89) which lies behind the characteristic Pennsylvania porch. German and English traditions had merged in Pennsylvania to create a regional house, overlaid by the style of the period in which it was built.

168. A New Jersey Vernacular: *Samuel Bond House, West Caldwell, N.J., after 1822.*

169. A Pennsylvania Vernacular: *Charles Ridgeway House, Hydetown, Pa., 1830.*

The Greek Revival

Corinthian Elegance

170. The New York Town House: *Colonnade Row (originally La Grange Terrace; also called Lafayette Terrace), New York, N.Y., 1836. Alexander Jackson Davis, architect.*

171. The Mississippi Mansion: *Governor's Mansion, Jackson, Miss., 1841. William Nichols, architect.*

170. When this terrace of sumptuous marble town houses arose behind its Corinthian colonnade, skeptics predicted that there would not be millionaires enough in all of New York City to buy them. "Geer's Folly" (so called after its speculative builder) proved them wrong, becoming overnight one of the most fashionable addresses in Manhattan. Shown here are only three of the nine houses which once occupied an entire city block.

The design is a more luxurious version of the Georgian terrace (Figure 145) in which row houses were planned as a unit to give the appearance of a mansion when viewed as a whole. The effect of elegance is heightened by the *piano nobile*, with major rooms fronting on a balcony above a raised service basement. A stately colonnade ties together the upper stories, announcing that these are the master's quarters. Further unity is given by the continuous filigree of black ironwork which railed the balcony.

Alexander Jackson Davis, master of the Greek Revival and one of the most imaginative architects of his day, had planned to develop the tops of these houses as private roof gardens—an unprecedented idea at the time—but the scheme unfortunately was abandoned. Even without gardens in the sky, there had never before been anything so splendid in the city of New York as Colonnade Row.

171. This antebellum governor's mansion shows how closely allied was the Greek Revival in the North and the South. By the use of the same flat roof and the same Greek order—the elegant Corinthian—a visual kinship is established between New York City and the heart of the agrarian South. This unifying influence was one of the virtues of the Greek Revival, creating a harmonious effect within towns, regions, and the nation as a whole.

This mansion also illustrates the occasional persistence of Georgian and Federal forms into the Greek Revival period. The flat roof was a characteristic of Federal houses. The semicircular portico (Figure 150) was a Federal type. Here, however, it has been executed in giant size. There was nothing modest about a Greek Revival mansion. Note the pilasters with their anta capitals, a complement to the dominant Corinthian order.

The Greek Revival

Ornamental Ironwork

172. Greek Revival Ironwork: *House in the Vieux Carre, New Orleans, La., ca. 1845.*

173. Gothic Revival Ironwork: *Rhinelander Gardens, New York, N.Y., 1854. James Renwick, architect.*

172. This charming small house in the French Quarter of New Orleans wears the profusion of lacy ironwork for which that city is famous. Few people realize that this cast-iron filigree, so familiar to us all, was part of the flowering of the Greek Revival. But a close look reveals that this little town house is awash with Greek detail: Corinthian colonettes, anthemion and palmette cresting, rosettes on gate and door panels, and rosettes again in the openwork balcony, not to mention scrolled under-eave brackets and upside-down acanthus leaves to scallop the archway.

These Greek motifs, though impeccably classic, also were part of something entirely new. Their cast-iron lacework represents a shift from the chaste (and expensive) wrought-iron railing to a popular mass-produced commodity: an intricate, ornamental veil which could be inexpensively and lavishly applied to any house. This fusion of ancient classical ornament with our new and growing industrial technology could be taken as a symbol of the inventive and rapidly shifting scene which was America during the Greek Revival period.

173. These row houses in New York City show that cast-iron ornament was not limited to the South. With their lacy arcades and railings, they are a match for the New Orleans town house (Figure 172). However, there is one small change. Rhinelander Gardens is not a Greek Revival design. It is Gothic Revival, and technically belongs to the next chapter. It has been included here to show how one style could merge into the next, sharing so many characteristics as to be nearly indistinguishable. Greek acanthus leaves which scalloped the ironwork arches of the preceding example have here been replaced by Gothic pendants. Across the frieze, the circular figures are no longer Greek rosettes but Gothic quatrefoils. All the detail has changed periods but the effect is the same.

Moreover, the spirit of both Greek and Gothic versions is identical, and it is neither classic nor medieval. It is a love of tracery and pattern and ornament for its own sake, which was something new in architecture. For at least fifty years, it would stamp everything it touched—no matter how unlike—with the clearly recognizable effect we know as Victorian.

Part III

The Victorian Age

The Victorian era has been more maligned than any other in American architectural history. During much of the twentieth century, it has been treated as a regrettable lapse, an age of confusion and error, and its houses as a proper target for the most vitriolic epithets. "Gloomy Victorian" and "Victorian monstrosity" are but two of the descriptive phrases so widely used as to have become clichés.

This attitude began to emerge just before and after the turn of the century as new trends asserted themselves. To the restrained good taste of a more accurate "traditional" architecture as well as the radical simplicities of an emergent modern, the "incorrect" and "over-decorated" Victorian dwelling was a threat to be demolished. The old had to be destroyed to make way for the new. In addition, the new trends themselves were locked in a struggle with each other. To pioneer modernists, any kind of copying of the historic past, whether exuberant Victorian Eclectic or tasteful Colonial Revival, represented something akin to moral turpitude. The Victorian period ended in a kind of donnybrook between divergent aspects of architecture which were its own offspring.

Though both of the newer contenders survived and are still with us today, the old Victorian dragon was slain. Not content to leave it in defeat, however, American tastemakers spent the next fifty years or more applying extra whacks to the corpse.

Antiquarians taught us that this period's wooden gingerbread, its cast-iron tracery, its patterned shingling, and its intricate brickwork were awkward and vulgar substitutes for the hand craftsmanship of colonial days. Modernists explained away Victorian fancywork as a betrayal of the machine aesthetic, a copying of inappropriate handcraft models by a means which should be devoted to its own ends. Social critics also added to the general censure. They deplored these large, lavish, and comfortable dwellings as tokens of a robber baron age, behind which could be glimpsed the sweatshop and the slum. Amateur psychologists even professed to see the unconscious release of Freudian inhibition in every curve and spire. Whatever anyone disliked about the Victorians was gathered up and projected onto the Victorian house.

Today, we are far enough away from the Victorians to accept their remarkable era. The consensus of disapproval began to break apart when historians, notably Henry-Russell Hitchcock, Lewis Mumford, and Vincent Scully, extracted a few pieces and held them up for admiration: Richardson Romanesque in its large simplicities; the Stick Vernacular with its structural expressiveness; the Shingle Style, all continuous surface and free-flowing space. But true Victorian gingerbread still was dismissed as awkward, vulgar, overwrought, and distorted. Only in recent years has an appreciation of this architecture—subjected for so long to the barrage against it—begun to penetrate the national consciousness.

Surprisingly, it was a scattering of transplanted Europeans, among them John Maass in his book *The Gingerbread Age,* which helped Americans to recognize the delights of their nineteenth-century inheritance. To these fresh eyes, the American Victorian scene presented a treasure trove of design, unique to this country and quite possibly our major claim to architectural originality.

Gingerbread decoration, they pointed out, is a machine equivalent to the carved and painted peasant building of Switzerland, Germany, Scandinavia, and Russia and, on its own terms, equally a folk art. Had it been executed by handcraft methods and located in the old countries of Europe, Americans would travel across an ocean to admire these quaint and charming structures.

These observers are probably right. Certainly it could be argued that the austerities of the early colonial and the aristocratic simplicities of the classic had failed to satisfy a deep craving within Americans. Throughout the ages, as soon as the family gained leisure beyond the hard necessities of living, its members carved decorations on their home, painted magical motifs on chests and chairs and doorways, wove patterns into fabrics, embroidered their clothing. Victorian gingerbread may have been an expression of this innate love of decoration, suddenly released in a newly democratic and rapidly industrializing nation.

However, now that we are permitted to like Victorian, we should perhaps investigate what is really there behind that catch-all phrase. For gingerbread is only one aspect of the multifaceted nineteenth century. The period embraces romantic revivals by the dozen; eclectic mixtures of styles; intricate decoration and chastely plain surfaces; the sinuosities of Art Nouveau; the emergence of an original and characteristically American dwelling type; the beginnings of modern architecture; the first revival of our own colonial tradition; and, finally, an academic re-creation of the great palaces, castles, and châteaux of Europe. No other period has produced such riches.

Officially, the Victorian Age extends from 1837, when Victoria became Queen of England, to her death in 1901. Americans entered this arbitrary segment of time riding in a horse-drawn carriage. They left it behind them driving a Model T Ford. During these same years, the fireplace, the wood-burning stove, the pump, and the privy were replaced as major household aids by the furnace, the kitchen range, the water closet, and hot and cold running water. Electric lighting was not far in the future. Victorians were responsible for them all.

In addition to devising such mechanical conveniences, the Victorians broke apart and put together again in scores of new ways the plan, the form, and the decoration of the house itself. Beginning quietly with the Greek Revival in the 1830s, American architecture proliferated into an unprecedented display of fantasy and functionalism. In retrospect, the Victorian Age would seem to have been America's most versatile and creative period, exuberant and uninhibited in its expression and the originator of ideas which we are still exploring today.

10

Chapter 10

The Romantic Revivals

When James Fenimore Cooper returned from Europe to sail up his native Hudson River in 1833, he was struck by the "mushroom temples" that had sprung up along its bank. A few years later, the white columns of the Greek Revival were giving way to gray stone turrets and dun-colored wooden fretwork in castles and cottages along the same watercourse.

These two revival styles—the Greek and the Gothic—represent the double portal through which American architecture passed into a new age. Behind stretched the classic tradition that had dominated American building for more than 100 years, tying each period to its predecessor and bringing the diverse heritage of half a dozen nationalities into balance and harmony. Ahead lay an eclectic explosion unprecedented in the history of architecture.

The crucial change came in the attitude toward architecture itself. The Greek Revival, though a continuation of the classic, had appeared also as something novel: the symbol of liberty for a new nation. This use of style for its associations outside the realm of building was decisive in releasing the spirit of the age. With it, the Greek Revival made the Gothic plausible, and the Gothic, breaking through the classic seal, opened up a fountain of revival styles. From symbol, architecture passed on to stage set.

This spirit of play-acting had been hovering close to the classic since early in the eighteenth century. Chinese pagodas, miniature Doric temples, and Gothic "ruins" had served as garden houses, gazebos, and follies in otherwise formal Georgian landscapes, offering a whiff of the exotic places and periods that were being discovered and explored during these years. They were admired for the noble thoughts and/or romantic associations they were believed to evoke.

Occasionally, this theatricality alighted on the house itself. As early as 1717, John Vanbrugh, England's master of the Baroque, departed from his chosen classic to build a battlemented castle as his country seat. At the height of the Georgian period, Horace Walpole remodeled his rural hideaway, "Strawberry Hill," into a medieval fantasy, setting off an early flurry of Gothic in English country houses. Even in America there were scattered examples. Ben-jamin Latrobe, self-styled as a "bigoted Greek," relaxed his stance in 1799 to design "Sedgeley," near Philadelphia, basically a Regency villa, but with lancet windows in the Gothic style.

However, it was a writer, equally as much as any architect, who set the romantic mood for a new American architecture. The novels of Sir Walter Scott, conjuring a lost chivalry, a world of fortress castles and ringing steel, fired the collective imagination of a nation, so recently possessed by the Greek ideal.

Circa 1840, standing on the edge of their industrial age, Americans were seized by a nostalgic mood, shaking themselves free of their old, sober, and rational approach to building. In a democratic nation and a prosaic workaday world, they were ready to imagine themselves as bold knights and languishing ladies, heroes and heroines in an antique Gothic tale.

Such playing at architecture was what gave the early Victorian period its peculiar charm. Its buildings, shown in the following section, were not accurate historical recreations. They represent storybook evocations of a past that never was.

The Romantic Revivals

The Gothic Revival

174. A Villa in the Pointed Style: *Lyndhurst, Tarrytown, N.Y., 1838. Alexander Jackson Davis, architect.*

175. A Gothic Revival Interior: *John F. Singer House, Pittsburgh, Pa., 1869. Attributed to Samuel Taylor, architect.*

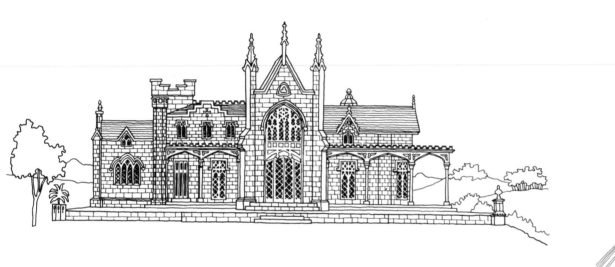

174. At the height of the Greek Revival, this fairy-tale castle of pale gray stone arose on the banks of the Hudson River, conjured up by a new spirit of romance which had overtaken America. Its turrets, pinnacles, and traceried windows show that the Victorian Age had arrived and with it a masquerade of revival styles.

Part of the mystique of those early Victorian years was the use of architecture as symbol and stage set. The Pointed Style—one of several names by which the Gothic Revival was known to Victorians—was meant to evoke an atmosphere of chivalry and romance, while offering the benison of a "Christian home."

The designer of Lyndhurst was Alexander Jackson Davis, the trend-setting architect whose Greek Revival houses were shown in Chapter 9. Equally the pioneer of the Gothic, Davis considered its picturesque asymmetries complementary to the natural landscape and thus more suitable for country residences than the temple form.

Though designing for atmosphere and effect, Davis also "modernized" his revival styles. French doors and broad verandahs open this castle to light, air, and view. The sweep of Gothic window provides a wall of filtered light—not for a chapel but for a first-floor reception room and billiard room above. Though disguised by Gothic styling, Lyndhurst was a new kind of house, attuned to nature and designed for the pleasures of nineteenth-century living.

175. Gothic Revival interiors were adrip with tracery, usually executed in dark stained wood. The pointed or lancet arch was a hallmark of the style. In keeping with its ecclesiastical character, the Gothic Revival introduced stained and etched glass to Victorian doors and windows.

176. Stone walls, rear verandah, and details in the Pointed Style give a much smaller midwestern dwelling close kinship to Lyndhurst (Figure 174). This is storybook Gothic, romanticized with lancet windows, pinnacles at the roof peaks, lacy bargeboards, and delicate pendants—an amalgam of cottage and cathedral. In his popular and influential book, *The Architecture of Country Houses*, Andrew Jackson Downing described this "picturesque" style: "It must not look all new and sunny, but show secluded shadowy corners. There must be nooks about it, where one would love to linger; windows, where one can enjoy the quiet landscape leisurely; cozy rooms, where all domestic fireside joys are invited to dwell. It must, in short, have something in its aspect which the heart can fasten upon . . . as naturally as the ivy attaches itself to the antique wall, preserving its memories from decay."

176. A Gothic Revival Cottage: *Greystone,*
Peveley, Mo., ca. 1859. David Wilbur Peat,
architect.

The Romantic Revivals

Carpenter's Gothic

177. Cottage Villa in the Pointed Style:
House in Rhinebeck, N.Y., 1844.

177. With the help of the new American scroll saw, the costly stonework which distinguished Gothic Revival mansions soon was translated into wood. The result was the Victorian gingerbread house, an airy, delicate confection.

In the twentieth century, such gingerbread typically has been painted white so that it resembles a lace-paper valentine. But when these houses were built, the Greek Revival and the white paint which went with it had become passe. Stone gray, slate blue, or fawn—muted shades which tied the house to its natural setting—were the true colors of the Gothic Revival.

Beneath the storybook styling, the understructure of this house was a remarkable technical invention: the balloon frame. A lightweight, closely spaced assembly of vertical two-by-fours, nailed to sill, plate, and rafters, it could be erected more quickly by two men than the heavy timber frame by twenty. During the nineteenth century, it became the standard construction system for the wooden house.

The exterior wall surfacing is board and batten, recommended for frame houses in the Pointed Style: an evocatively medieval system (Figure 6). At the same time, it was almost a diagram of the new supporting framework. Both were part of a nineteenth-century trend toward lightweight, articulated wood construction which historian Vincent Scully has called the Stick Style (Figures 198 and 199).

178. Because of the predominantly agricultural character of America in the 1850s, Victorian architects were not much concerned with the city house for the workingman. When presenting a country cottage for ''a mechanic or clerk,'' they recommended ''tasteful simplicity of decoration to harmonize with the character of the dwelling and its occupants.''

Andrew Jackson Downing, who wrote the words just quoted, would have disapproved of the unsuitable ''frippery'' of these Boston row houses. But speculative builders knew what the workingman wanted: the best possible imitation of the rich man's villa. These charming gingerbread houses are the result, excellent examples of poor man's Gothic Revival.

178. Vernacular Gothic: *Workers' Row Houses, Boston, Mass., ca. 1850.*

The Romantic Revivals

The Villa Styles

179. An Elizabethan Villa: *A Pattern Book House, published 1852. Samuel Sloan, architect.*

180. A Norman Villa: *Home of A.M. Eastwick, Esq., near Philadelphia, Pa., published 1852. Samuel Sloan, architect.*

181. A Villa in the Italian Style: *Edward King House, Newport, R.I., 1845. Richard Upjohn, architect.*

182. The Persian Villa: *Olana, Home of Frederick Church, near Hudson, N.Y., 1870-72; studio wing, 1888-91. Frederick Church, designer, in consultation with Calvert Vaux and Frederick Clarke Withers, architects.*

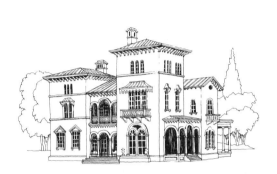

179. Andrew Jackson Downing, the arbiter of early Victorian taste, divided domestic architecture into three classes: the "Cottage" (a servantless small dwelling), the "Farm-House" (a larger but equally utilitarian homestead), and the "Villa." Cottages and farmhouses should be simple—in keeping, so Downing taught, with their owners' humble station in life. The villa, on the other hand, was a suburban house or country seat for a person of "wealth sufficient to build and maintain it with some taste and elegance . . . and requiring the care of at least three servants."

In the villa, Victorian imagination took flight, at first in Gothic Style, followed rapidly by others. Shown here is an "Elizabethan Villa," complete with Tudor arches and crenellation. Bay windows and a projecting conservatory are reminders that real Elizabethan manor houses often had "more glass than wall." Victorians used historic style to open up the house, creating an airy, verandahed dwelling soon recognized as a unique American type.

180. This mansion among villas drew on the period just preceding the Gothic, known in Europe as Romanesque and in England as Norman. A Victorian castle-turned-villa, it was built near Philadelphia of the "best Connecticut granite," with a roof of "purple Welsh slate,"

plus carved and painted wooden trim. Norman characteristics include round-headed windows with semicircular hood molds and the chevron and lozenge patterns which decorate moldings and railings. Its "embattled" bay window echoes the battlemented tower of a real Norman castle.

Despite its historical mode, this house encloses a functional plan, asymmetrically arranged and clearly revealed on the exterior. Arcades of glass and large bay windows open major rooms to sun and air. Light, openness, and functional planning introduced during the Victorian period would one day become components of twentieth-century modern architecture.

181. The classic spirit, all but submerged by the Gothic and its variants, surfaced once more in the Italian Style. However, this was classic quite unlike the formal Georgian and Greek Revival which had preceded it. Based on the irregularly massed farmhouses of Italy's Campagna, the Italian Villa was broken into towers and wings and opened up with balconies and verandahs, thus acquiring the Victorian look.

Detailing, too, was distinct from the earlier classic. Features included shallow hipped or gabled roofs with heavy bracketing under the eaves, and round-headed windows, often grouped in twos or threes. Though some houses

were built of stone, brick, or even clapboard, the ideal was a smooth stucco wall surface. This one was designed as a summer home in fashionable Newport, Rhode Island, by Richard Upjohn, one of the leading architects of the revival styles.

182. One of the last of the romantic villas, this Persian fantasy was built after the Civil War. But its irregular massing, its towers, balconies, verandah, and bay windows echo the Italian Villa of three decades earlier. These basic elements were provided by the well-known revivalist Calvert Vaux and his partner. Persian detailing, however, came from drawings and watercolors made by the owner of the house, the famous landscape painter Frederick Church. His enthusiasm for Islamic architecture had been kindled on an extended trip through the Middle East, and he put all he most admired into Olana.

Walls of quarry-faced ashlar have been decorated with polychrome brick and tile in Islamic patterns of yellow, rust, and turquoise blue with roof slates to match. Columns are like those that Church saw in the city of Isfahan. Pointed Islamic arches frame the recessed porches. Like other revival villas, Olana permitted its owner to step into an enchanted kingdom when he entered its doors.

Italianate Variations

183. The Tuscan Villa: *A Pattern Book House, published 1867. John Riddell, architect.*

184. The Italianate House: *Unidentified House, Springfield, Mass.*

185. Egyptian Revival: *Elizabeth Apthorp House, New Haven, Conn., 1837. Alexander Jackson Davis, architect.*

186. Moorish Revival: *Willis Bristol House, New Haven, Conn., 1845. Henry Austin, architect.*

183. The names Italian Villa and Tuscan Villa often were used interchangeably even in the period during which they were built. Technically, the Italian Villa was an asymmetrical house with one or more towers, while the pure Tuscan Style house was not a picturesque villa but a symmetrical cube with academic detailing.

This villa was labeled Tuscan in the pattern book from which it was taken because of its formal balance. The portico and tower are centered, flanked by identical wings, unlike the Italian Villa shown in Figure 181.

In all other features, it is typically Italianate: round-headed windows set together in groups of two or three; bay windows; small balconies; gabled wings; the tower itself. Wall surfaces are smooth. Roofs have the characteristic low pitch, and there are heavy brackets under the eaves.

This example, like the Italian Villa, also could be called "Hudson River Bracketed," after a novel of that title by Edith Wharton. The name identifies all variants of Italianate by their undereave bracketing.

184. While rich men built fanciful villas with towers and intersecting wings, the middle class made do with the simple, boxy house which had been a basic form since the late Georgian period. These smaller dwellings were Tuscan in the formal balance of their facades and in the centered belvedere, which gave them something of the height and presence of the imposingly towered Tuscan Villa. But details varied. Round-headed center windows and an asymmetrically placed porch give this example a gracefully Italianate flavor.

This type of house—easily recognized by undereave bracketing and belvedere—was widely built. The belvedere was a style element, not a regional or a useful feature like the New England widow's walk, for it was used on inland houses as often as coastal dwellings.

185. The boxlike Tuscan house rapidly became the base upon which other styles were executed, among them this rare example of the Egyptian Revival. Pillars at its entrance represent bundles of papyrus stalks, secured by a band, below a lotus capital. In Victorian America, the Egyptian Revival normally was reserved for structures of great solemnity, such as churches, courthouses, tombs, and prisons. This brownstone mansion is an unusual example of its use for a residence. The closely related Italian Villa Style, with its informal massing and round-headed openings, is an addendum in the wings.

186. The basic form of this house is symmetrically Tuscan, as are its belvedere and heavy bracketing. However, such underpinnings are little more than an armature for the exotic horseshoe arch, grillework, and window tracery which transform it into a Moorish fantasy. Detailing, particularly the cresting for the roof, echoes a "Saracenic Palace" illustrated by Viollet-le-Duc in his famous French nineteenth-century treatise on domestic architecture.

Moorish over Italianate, though rare, was an admired combination. This house is an urban counterpart to Olana, the towered and minareted Persian Villa overlooking the Hudson River (Figure 182), though each drew on different aspects of Islamic architecture.

The Romantic Revivals

The Octagon House

187. An Octagonal Villa: *Orson Squire Fowler House, Fishkill, N.Y., 1848-58.*

187. One of the intriguing mergers of the Victorian period was that of the Italianate or Tuscan Style with the octagonal plan. The octagon was promoted by an American eccentric, Orson Squire Fowler, in his book, *A Home For All . . .,* and became a fad during the 1850s. Most octagonal houses were organized around a core of hallway which cut through all floors. The Tuscan-Italianate Style, with its belvedere and porches, proved a natural partner for this new plan. The belvedere acted as both light source and ventilator for the central inner space; porches and balconies encircled the exterior, opening the house to the out-of-doors—a part of the octagon mystique.

Fowler's own house included central heating, gas lights, running water, and inside flush toilets: a veritable showcase of modern conveniences. His ingenious plumbing system collected rainwater on the roof, piped it to cisterns on the top floor, and, thence, to washstands, water closets, and a boiler heated by the kitchen range. Fowler's ''grout'' system of wall construction was equally advanced: concrete and pebbles poured into forms to make slabs, and hoisted into place.

188. Most octagons were solid, comfortable homes. This Milwaukee example was of moderate size, but still included the favorite Tuscan features of the type: belvedere, continuous verandah, and overhanging bracketed eaves. Fowler had promoted the octagon not only for its economy but also as the most healthful of plans. All rooms were open to the central hall, providing cross-ventilation throughout the house. In addition, the hall and belvedere acted together as a vertical ventilating shaft. The continuous porch provided outdoor living space while sheltering the interior from direct sun and rain. Victorian romanticism included a love affair with nature and fresh air—both, however, carefully tamed.

189. In this minimum octagon, the belvedere, while still retaining an Italianate flavor, was enlarged to become the entire upper story. To cut costs further, the usual verandah was eliminated and stock windows used throughout. Despite such economies, it is a trim and attractive little house. Eaves were decorated with a scalloped bargeboard, one of the simplest carpenter gingerbreads, known to Victorians as ''dogtooth.''

188. The Tuscan Octagon: *Dewey-Jenkins House, Milwaukee, Wisc., 1855.*

189. The Dogtooth Octagon: *Amos Merritt House, Little Genesee, N.Y., ca. 1860.*

190. The Circle House: *Martin Zezh House, Sauk City, Wisc., 1931.*

191. A Greek Revival Round House: *Enoch Robinson House, Somerville, Mass., 1854.*

This house is unusually economical, but any octagon was a cost-cutter. As Orson Fowler had pointed out, trimming the corners of the conventional square reduced by one-fifth the amount of wall necessary to enclose any given interior. Major rooms remained rectangular, while leftover triangles of space were used for closets, pantries, dressing rooms, and bathrooms.

190. A variation of the octagon was the circle house, which eliminated corners altogether. Clapboards had to be slightly bent to face it. Octagons and circles were most popular during the 1850s, but they continued to be built after the Civil War, especially in the midwestern and western states; and postwar styles were superimposed on the form. Though much modified, the combination of a main block and central "belvedere" still echoes the Italianate Style. In this stark, wooden drum of a dwelling, the belvedere was enlarged to create a usable attic room. It resembles a Norman "candle-snuffer" tower, a feature of the Romanesque Revival of the 1870s and '80s. Surprisingly, however, this very late example was built in the twentieth century.

191. This little "wedding cake" of a house reaches back to the earlier Greek Revival with its ornamental Ionic columns at the doorway and Greek honeysuckle motifs. These had become standard trim during the nineteenth century, from New England's carpenter gingerbread to the cast-iron filigree of New Orleans. Beneath the "icing," this round house is a variation of the Italianate octagon, its belvedere enlarged to serve as an upper story, encircled by a balcony. Narrow, vertical wooden strips divide the curving wall into small sections permitting the use of standard flat clapboards.

The Romantic Revivals

The Italianate Row House

192. The Italian Style: *The Brick Row House, Washington, D.C., ca. 1840-70, demolished 1968.*

193. The Tuscan Style: *The Brownstone Row House, New York City, ca. 1850-90.*

192. During the early Victorian period, the Italianate Style and its variations were adapted to row housing, taking up the classic continuum from the Georgian and the Greek. The town house shown above has the delicate arched windows, framed with hood molds, the balustraded bay window, and heavy bracketing which were typical of the style. Note also its round-headed panes of glass which give the illusion of two windows grouped under each hood. The elaborate cornice was characteristic of the Italianate row house. Visually, it helped bind together a series of narrow dwellings in the manner of the Georgian terrace.

The Italian Style traced its origin to the farmhouses of Italy. Details from that remote source have been translated here into pale ivory brick, with trim of the same color, giving an effect of understated urban elegance.

193. The classic New York brownstone[12] was designed in the Tuscan mode, sometimes referred to as Romano-Tuscan to denote its urban origin. Though closely related to the Italian Style, it was formal and academic, a translation of the Italian Renaissance palace rather than the Italian farmhouse. Its basic scheme was the *piano nobile,* with major rooms on the second story, reached by outside stairs. An elaborate entrance and the tallest windows are at this level, where rooms of state were placed in the Italian palazzo. The lower story (a basement areaway in the row house) is rusticated, like that of the palazzo, i.e., its stone blocks are larger than those above and their edges have been chamfered.

Door and window trim may be pediments (triangular or curved), flat architraves, or, occasionally, a full entablature. Like the Italian Style, the Tuscan is distinguished by wide, ornamental cornices and heavy brackets.

The Romantic Revivals

The Victorian Parlor

194. The French Taste: *Robert J. Milligan House, Saratoga Springs, N.Y., 1853.*

194. Though it had no counterpart in exterior architecture, this charming rococo period piece ''in the French taste'' was the typical parlor of the romantic revival years. All the familiar Victorian inventory is here: a matched set of brocaded furniture à la Louis XV, draperies of brocade over Venetian blinds or lace curtains, a gilded rococo mirror and matching drapery cornices, an arched marble fireplace, a rose-patterned carpet, wax flowers under glass.

The round-headed fireplace was a special favorite, used alike in plantation mansion, suburban villa, and the row house in the city. A friend of the author reports that her determined great-grandmother transported just such a marble fireplace by covered wagon into the western wilderness and that her husband installed it, along with red velvet draperies, in the log cabin which he built for her there.

Under less primitive conditions, this arched fireplace typically housed a new invention: the built-in coal stove, with a grille in front and a ''riser'' to conduct warm air to the bedroom above—an early Victorian version of central heating.

11

Chapter 11

The Mansardic and Stick Styles

The Victorian period in American architecture is divided in two by the Civil War. In both North and South, antebellum houses had been romantic revivals—the Greek, the Gothic, the Italianate, and others—evocative of a particular past and consciously used to symbolize its virtues.

Postwar houses, on the other hand, were a mixture, borrowing motifs from every period and combining them to produce something never seen before in architecture. Some of the old revival styles lingered on after the war and new ones, notably Mansardic and Eastlake, came into fashion. But again and again, the spirit of the times broke them apart, mingled and transformed them into eclectic fireworks.

To architect Alexander Jackson Davis, master of the myriad revivals and prewar leader of his profession, the new architecture was "barbarous" . . . "depraved" . . . a parade of "monstrosities." To young designers, the recent copying of historic styles now seemed "naive" and "unimaginative." The past was a source to be mined for details, then reassembled according to taste. Wrote Samuel Sloan in his *Homestead Architecture* of 1866: ". . . we pass sentence on servile imitation as being unworthy of the genius and spirit of the American people."

The dynamics of this entire era in architecture was nothing less than the industrialization of America. But unlike the earlier revival styles, the postwar response was not a retreat into romantic masquerade. Life itself was harder and more cynical. The old Jeffersonian vision of an agrarian democracy, of independent men, rooted in the security of their own land or their own handcraft skills, had become more dream than actuality. The ruptures, dislocations, and insecurities of wage work and absentee ownership were increasingly the realities of American life.

But with these miseries came also the optimism that was part of a period of phenomenal material growth. It was the opening of an age of untrammeled *laissez-faire* capitalism, of rugged individualism, of unparalleled opportunity. The period generated a unique, if sometimes brutal, confidence and *joie de vivre*. America felt herself to be the inheritor of all the riches of the historic past and scientific present, claiming furthermore an inalienable right to do with her inheritance exactly as she wished. This was true no less in architecture than in the mining, lumbering, and marketing conquest of a continent.

It was this aggressive, self-confident thrust that gave Victorian architecture its increasing vitality and originality. Not only a new approach to style, but a new type of house and a new way of building was developing. The "picturesque villa" with its free, open planning, large windows, and embracing verandahs, was unique to America, expressing living patterns totally different from those of earlier, more stringent times.

The changing structure of the wooden house provided yet another novel motif in the complicated Victorian fabric. Historian Vincent Scully has called its aesthetic the "Stick Style," a catch-all phrase for the stickwork patterning which increasingly came to be applied to the Victorian house. Because it is a technique, rather than a style per se, it cuts across the usual nomenclature. It was part of the early Gothic Revival, the post-Civil War Tudor, or Elizabethan, Revival, High Victorian Gothic, Eastlake, and other shifting fashions, structurally tying them together and acting as a link between pre- and post-Civil War periods.

The Stick Style was, in fact, a counterpart to the new structure of the house, the system of slender, repetitive studs that had replaced the heavy timber frame as this country's typical way of building. The aim was "truthfulness" between inside and out. Vertical, horizontal, and diagonal patterning, though stylistically echoing early English structural methods, also was intended as a symbol of Victorian balloon framing: light, delicate, and articulated, like the light, modern framework that supported the house.

Before the Civil War, the Stick Style employed vertical board-and-batten for this effect, as seen in the "Carpenter's Gothic" villa (Figure 177). In its final phase, shown in this chapter (along with contributing styles), it employs a "half-timber" patterning of thin boards.

In these postwar years, as in earlier times, architects believed that they were creating a truly American architecture. More than at any preceding period, they may have been right. Though the only possible starting point for High Victorian design was the vocabulary of tradition, its free usage and the innovative plans and structure that developed simultaneously created houses that were, indeed, uniquely American.

The Mansardic and Stick Styles

The Mansardic Styles

195. The French Second Empire: *Governor's Mansion, Jefferson City, Mo., 1871. George Ingham Barnett, architect.*

196. High Victorian Italianate: *William Wheeler House, New York, N.Y., ca. 1860.*

195. The French Second Empire Style ushered in a new era in Victorian architecture, offering Americans cosmopolitan elegance from the reign of Louis XIV. The seventeenth-century French version of the Baroque, with its distinctive, iron-crested mansard roof, had become the prevailing nineteenth-century revival style of the Second Empire period in France.

In America, its formal Parisian elegance was immensely appealing to the mid-nineteenth-century mind, a trifle weary of Republican Greek and rural Gothic. It became the favorite of the newly rich and powerful and was built by silver kings in Nevada, railroad tycoons in San Francisco, and by the State of Missouri for its governor, as seen here.

The Second Empire Style, also known as Mansardic, spanned the Civil War, reaching its greatest popularity in the late 1860s and '70s during the presidency of Ulysses S. Grant. Its derisive nickname, the "General Grant Style," referred to that fact, implying a heavy-handed and overly ornate attempt at elegance. Today, tastes have changed again, and this American echo of a royal palace is admired as a richly worked classic of unique Gallic charm.

196. The French Second Empire did not long remain a pure style. Americans were reluctant to give up the towers and bay windows and rambling verandahs which made life so pleasant in favor of Second Empire formality. Many therefore simply built the familiar Italian villa with a newly fashionable mansard roof.

This combination of Italianate and Mansardic would become a basic High Victorian type. Mansards of all sorts were used. Illustrated here is a modest adaptation of the graceful reverse curves seen, in France, on the new Louvre.

Fenestration was also reworked. The simple, round-headed window of the early Italianate has given way to the "stilted segmented arch" of the High Victorian. There is another new touch: the flat, angular appliqué of trim beneath the bow window and on the frieze of the porch. This motif is a harbinger of the Stick Style which would become a decorative theme on houses of all sorts in the decades following the Civil War.

197. High Victorian Gothic: *Webster Wagner House, Palatine Bridge, N.Y., 1877.*

197. This house, too, combines the Italian Villa with the mansard roof. But applied over this scaffolding is yet another style: the High Victorian Gothic. Based on the Venetian Gothic of John Ruskin, the English medievalist, this new style normally was used for large public buildings constructed of brick or stone. Dark red brick typically was decorated with stripes, diapers, and mosaics of black, yellow, or blue brick or with carved and incised stone moldings. This was known as "permanent polychrome" or "constructional coloration."

The Wagner house illustrates how American carpenters translated this masonry idiom into wood. The heavy, sculptural window enframements echo carved stone moldings. The tower and the steep, straight-sided mansard are wooden versions of typical Venetian Gothic features. In keeping with the polychrome of its brick and stone counterparts, the wooden Venetian house was painted in a variety of deep rich colors, emphasizing the difference between each element. One scarcely believable color scheme listed dark maroon walls, dark green trim, deep reddish orange window sash, and olive brown blinds.

The Mansardic and Stick Styles

The Stick Styles

198. Elizabethan: *J.N.A. Griswold House, Newport, R.I., 1862-63; Richard Morris Hunt, architect.*

199. High Victorian Eclectic: *Jacob Cram House, Middletown, R.I., 1871-72. Dudley Newton, architect.*

198. This large and comfortable dwelling is a Victorian version of the Elizabethan half-timbered house (Figure 10), at once a new revival style and a part of long-term trends in American building.

Richard Morris Hunt, its architect, had studied at L'Ecole des Beaux Arts in Paris and was one of the most highly trained historicists of his day. This house shows with what skill he was able to translate medieval simplicity into Victorian amplitude. Starting with the comparatively uncomplicated Elizabethan type, Hunt has pushed and pulled its wings out of symmetry, added verandahs and a tower. The result: a picturesque Victorian villa.

Elizabethan half-timbering also has been translated into a superb example of the Victorian Stick Style. Instead of the heavy structural timbers of the Elizabethan house, stickwork patterning creates a half-timbered effect at the same time that it suggests the new, lightweight balloon framing which actually supports the wall. Stickwork is repeated in bracketing and for braced porch posts and railings, becoming the dominant factor in the design of the house.

199. The so-called Stick Style, essentially a way of building, was part of the uniquely American development of the wooden Victorian house. It could be, and was, used in conjunction with a variety of revival styles.

As seen in the Cram House, it is part of an eclectic mix, an example of the new post-Civil War architecture in which motifs from many sources were combined in a single design. Included here are a top-heavy Venetian Gothic tower, Moorish keyhole arches, Japanese lattices with oval windows, a deeply recessed balcony a la the Swiss chalet, and a touch of Tudor half-timbering. The Japanese influence—new in the 1870s—is the most subtle, but perhaps the most pervasive. The whole feeling of airy porches, thin walls, and openwork lattices recalls the Japanese tradition, in which the house becomes a pavilion of light wooden members.

This character extends to the handling of the Stick Style itself. "Half-timbered" patterning is here abstracted into a thin, linear appliqué. In-

stead of brackets, a repetitive band of flat sticks makes a pattern beneath the eaves. Rafters project, their exposed ends creating yet another pattern at the edge of the roof. Narrow clapboards surface the upper stories; round shingles add texture to the walls below, echoing the roof shingles. In the Japanese way, and in the way similarly prescribed by Ruskin, the architect has used wood to create its own integral ornament.

The Mansardic and Stick Styles

Eastlake Gothic

200. The Original Type: *"A House in the Eastlake Style,"* ca. 1870-80.

201. Eastlake Brick: *Governor's Mansion, Raleigh, N.C., 1883-89. Samuel Sloan, architect; Gustavus Adolphus Bauer, assistant architect.*

200. During the 1860s, the English architect Charles Locke Eastlake gave his name to a third phase of Victorian Gothic. Instead of lacy gingerbread (Figure 177) or the heavily ornamented "Venetian Gothic" (Figure 197), Eastlake Gothic sought to achieve medieval character through the simple, solid forms, steep gables, and picturesque massing of the early English manor house. In fact, Eastlake Gothic was less a style than a reaction against the machine and the exaggerated "costume architecture" that it had produced. Like Ruskin and the whole Arts and Crafts movement in England, it advocated a return to the building principles of the Middle Ages: "simplicity, honesty, propriety."

This house is one of the few authentic examples of Eastlake Gothic to be built in America. The main body of the house is of stone; the squat tower which straddles the wing is half-timbered—a combination which derived from the Tudor period. The shallow mansard roof of the entry porch—characteristically Eastlake—was a Victorian addition.

201. The American touch is visible in this Eastlake mansion built for the governor of North Carolina. Balconies and verandahs have proliferated, as if forced by the southern climate or by the general American love affair with the out-of-doors. The entry has been enlarged in keeping with the official character of the house, but it retains the flattish mansard typical of Eastlake porches.

Like the preceding example, this design takes its cue from the Tudor period but from a different phase of its architecture. Brick was a Tudor innovation; its combination with stone trim, in the patterns seen here, was a feature of royal palaces and important manor houses. Such stonework was meant to suggest "battlements" in a period which had recently given them up.

In the Victorian translation, this stone "ribbonwork" is similar in effect to the wooden patterning of the Stick Style, also ultimately Tudor in derivation. Vincent Scully has pointed out the tendency of the period to "skeletonize" surfaces even when the material employed is brick or masonry.

The Mansardic and Stick Styles

Eastlake Patterning

202. Eastlake Interior: *Dining Room, Kellogg Fairbanks House, Lake Geneva, Wisc., 1875. Austin Moody, architect. Demolished 1955.*

203. Eastlake Exterior: *"Design for an Eastlake Cottage," 1881. John C. Pelton, Jr., architect.*

202. Having established a new approach to architecture, Eastlake needed a new type of furniture to go with it. In 1872, his *Hints on Household Taste* was published, causing, in the words of a contemporary, "a great awakening." In place of the voluptuous curves, carved flowers and cupids, rosewood and ebony veneers of the Rococo Revival (Figure 194), he recommended furniture cut out of solid wood, natural and unvarnished, with joints tenoned and pinned in the old medieval way.

This Eastlake dining room, from a Wisconsin millionaire's summer lodge, contains all the identifying details of the style. Integral ornament included incised linear motifs, strips of wood set in herringbone pattern, and the layering of one wood over another, a device which recalls Elizabethan strapwork. Edges and corners of the wood were, here and there, beveled or chamfered and surfaces sometimes inset with tiles in small stylized flower patterns.

Though describing the furniture as "a little stiff and seldom very graceful," a contemporary interior designer declared that "it bears the same relation to the loose and wanton *Quatorze* and *Quinze* regimes which virtue bears to vice."

203. By a strange reversal of the design process, the furniture that Charles Eastlake devised to complement his original Gothic houses inspired a new and different Eastlake Style in American architecture.

This pattern book house shows how furniture motifs were transposed into exterior ornament for a dwelling which had only the faintest connection with the Eastlake original. A half-hearted attempt has been made at asymmetrical, medieval massing. There remains also the mansarded entry, a persistent Eastlake theme. But the emphasis has shifted from solid simplicity of form to applied decoration. This patterning was part of the Stick Style which came to dominate each new fashion of its period.

Row after row of houses like this were built in San Francisco during the 1890s at a cost of around $1,000 each. With their tall, double windows and stick appliqué—picked out in green, yellow, peach, sable, Indian red, or vermilion—these minimum houses offered a gaiety and airy lightness unprecedented in workers' dwellings.

The Mansardic and Stick Styles

High Victorian Eastlake

204. Eastlake Mansardic: *Architect's Own House, Staten Island, N.Y., 1868. Henry Hobson Richardson, architect.*

205. The San Francisco Style: *Row Houses, Western Addition, San Francisco, Calif., ca. 1885. William F. Lewis, probable contractor-architect.*

204. This house, built for his own family by the great Henry Hobson Richardson at the start of his career, predates many of the Eastlake examples shown in the preceding pages. Part Stick Style, part Eastlake, and part French Mansardic, it is a typically eclectic High Victorian design. But it shows how a superior architect could extract the salient motifs of his period and use them with simplicity and dignity. Though one of Richardson's lesser works, its restraint is in sharp contrast to the vernacular houses it undoubtedly helped to inspire (Figures 205 and 206).

205. These eccentric San Francisco row houses show what happened to Eastlake Gothic in the Victorian eclectic maelstrom. Uninhibited California architects mixed pieces of American Eastlake, High Victorian Italianate, and French Mansardic with a new seasoning called Queen Anne (see the next chapter) to create a unique West Coast salad.

Such houses were the product of new steam-powered milling machinery which could carve scrolls, columns, brackets, and finials of every type and style with unprecedented speed. Decorative roofs, bay windows, porches, and other trim—prefabricated at the mill—were simply attached to the standard builder's box, providing a five-room Victorian fantasy for only $3,500.

Like the "Eastlake Cottage" (Figure 203), these houses were painted in San Francisco colors, bright and gay against an often leaden sky. Fog and chill produced the bay window. With sunlight at a premium, these "intricate prows of glass," projecting to catch every gleam, became a characteristic of San Francisco architecture.

206. Hardly ordinary architecture even by the standards of its own day, this dwelling is a parody of the way in which High Victorians bor-

rowed from a variety of styles, recombining them into something new and strange. One can pick out an Italianate tower, an exaggerated French mansard roof, Eastlake Stick Style gable ornament, an Eastlake chimney, Elizabethan diamond-paned windows, Moorish keyhole arches and parasol turret, plus a glimpse of a rather modest clapboard house which seems to have been the start of it all.

Houses like this deeply shocked Charles Eastlake, the originator of the style. "I now find [he said] that there exists on the other side of the Atlantic an 'Eastlake style' of architecture, which, judging from the specimens I have seen illustrated, may be said to burlesque such doctrines of art as I have ventured to maintain. . . . I regret that [my] name should be associated there with a phase of taste in architecture . . . with which I can have no real sympathy, and which by all accounts seems to be extravagant and bizarre."

206. Eastlake Eclectic: *"Rose Lawn," William Edgar Emery House, Flemington, N.J., ca. 1874.*

The Mansardic and Stick Styles

The Picturesque Villa

207. The Eastlake Villa: *Merriam House, Newton, N.J., ca. 1880.*

207. Whenever a new style appeared, it was rapidly adapted to America's favorite Victorian dwelling: the "picturesque villa" with its rambling verandahs and balconies, bay windows, tower, and intricate gables. The Merion house is just such a villa, wrapped about with an American version of Eastlake styling. It retains only the most tenuous connection to the original Eastlake Gothic but, in American terms, it is an Eastlake house.

Linear patterns, the layering of pieces of wood in strips, the perforated half-circle, rows of small knobs, all are motifs transferred from Eastlake furniture to the exterior of this dwelling. Its porch posts tend to resemble table legs; flat, cut-out balusters are like the backs of Eastlake chairs. Though fleetingly Eastlake in trim, this is primarily an example of the Victorian Villa, our unique invention, and an American type which remained au courant under a variety of frostings from the Gothic Revival of the 1830s to the Georgian Revival of the early twentieth century.

208. This famous Victorian, with its top-heavy Venetian Gothic tower, mansard roof, and Stick-Eastlake-Queen Anne patterning, speaks for itself as a valedictory to every style which had gone before and a harbinger of others to come.

Built entirely of redwood for a California lumber baron, the Carson house illustrates what rank exotica could be called up by the Aladdin's lamp of nineteenth-century milling machinery (sometimes combined with hand carving). Once considered almost too monstrous to contemplate, it now attracts an admiration usually reserved for great natural wonders like the Grand Canyon.

Inside its flamboyant embrace, horseshoe-arched halls, cozy wood-paneled nooks, romantic tower rooms, waterfalls of carved redwood staircases, art glass, wooden lace, and gilding reveal that life was once untrammeled and full of sensuous pleasures. At the same time, the Carson house expresses the ultimate in individualistic power, an unashamed arrogance toward nature and its materials.

208. High Victorian Eclectic Villa: *William Carson House, Eureka, Calif., 1885. Samuel and Joseph Newsom, architects.*

12

Chapter 12

The Surface Styles

During the 1870s, when the Mansardic and Stick styles were at their height, there appeared a new mode of expression which would characterize the next period in American architecture. The emphasis now was on the broad surfaces of the wall itself and the free-flowing interior planning which it expressed.

Like the patterning of the Stick Style, this continuity of wall surface cut across traditional labels, becoming part of such historic styles as Queen Anne, Romanesque, and Colonial Revival. The shingle-covered villas and cottages of the late nineteenth century were its most highly developed expression and caused it to be named (again by Vincent Scully) the Shingle Style. But because the emphasis on surface continuity is found as well in houses which are not shingled, we have called this group of related designs the Surface Styles.

The reader should be warned that the varied names for the architecture of this period are, many of them, arbitrary and confusing—like the styles themselves. The Victorian Queen Anne introduced the period and persisted as a theme in many a High Victorian mix. But it was not a pure style even in the original. In fact, the name Queen Anne normally refers to the early-eighteenth-century classic style on which much of America's Georgian colonial architecture was based (Chapter 7).

The Victorian Style called Queen Anne was entirely different. More Jacobean than Queen Anne, it employed the vocabulary of medieval building as it had survived into the Renaissance period in England.

It was this mixed architecture which inspired the Victorian Queen Anne house, an imaginative re-creation by English architect Richard Norman Shaw. Depending on the amount of its Renaissance detail, the style also was known as Free Classic. Today's historians have argued that the Victorian type labeled Queen Anne could more appropriately be called Neo-Jacobean, since it was during the Jacobean period that medieval and Renaissance forms most typically were combined. This appears to be confusing enough. But Queen Anne and the other revival styles of this period eventually became hopelessly intertwined. Their form and detail were mined and mixed by contemporary architects to create original nineteenth-century designs of infinite variety.

The Surface Styles

Victorian Queen Anne

209. The Queen Anne Original: *Watts-Sherman House, Newport, R.I., 1874. Henry Hobson Richardson, architect, with Stanford White.*

209. The earliest of the Surface Styles was the Victorian Queen Anne (not to be confused with the eighteenth-century classic Queen Anne—Figure 126). The Watts-Sherman house, first of the type in America, illustrates its horizontal emphasis, as witness the unusual second-story bay which runs almost the length of the house. Small-paned windows alternate with half-timbering there to create a single, continuous pattern, very different from the strongly accented openings of the Mansardic and Stick styles. Horizontal bands of different materials and textures were a persistent Queen Anne theme, helping to express on the exterior the spaces within.

The man who introduced Queen Anne to America was Henry Hobson Richardson, one of this country's greatest architects, whose free adaptations of historic styles helped to lay the foundation for modern architecture. Like all Richardson's work, the Sherman house appears as a small oasis of calm in the midst of Victorian fireworks.

210. This interior was the first American example of the Queen Anne "living hall" which was to become the core of the late-nineteenth-century dwelling. Based on an Elizabethan great hall, this baronial central space, with its huge fireplace and informal seating, was the most functional of rooms. It served as a family gathering place, as entry, stair hall, reception room for special occasions, and circulation center of the house. Other more specialized rooms—library, drawing room, dining room—were disposed around it. Doors in the great glass wall lead out to a terrace.

As shown in the drawing by Stanford White,[13] at the time a draftsman in Richardson's office, this wall was a transparent grid, with inserts of stained glass in heraldic designs adding color and pattern to the clear light which flooded through it. Few modern houses have produced so dramatic a conception.

210. Living Hall: *Watts-Sherman House,*
Newport, R.I., 1874. Henry Hobson Richardson,
architect, with Stanford White.

The Surface Styles

Victorian Queen Anne

211. The Queen Anne Villa: *House in Comanche, Tex.*

211. Here the familiar picturesque Victorian Villa, with its towers, balconies, and verandahs, enjoys a Queen Anne incarnation. This Texas mansion shows its derivation by the horizontal division of its wall surfaces. The lower story is of stone, the second story surfaced with shingles, and the third patterned with a hatching of sticks which suggests half-timber work: a popular translation of the Watts-Sherman house (Figure 210).

Very little has been subtracted but a great deal has been added. A squared tower, steeply spired octagonal entry, wooden lacework, ripples of cast-iron cresting, and finials erupting like fountains add up to an unsurpassed flight of Victorian fancy.

212. By the 1880s, the Victorian Villa, designed in infinite variety of plan, form, and detail, had shaken down, in the middle-class dwelling, to a fairly standard arrangement. Though smaller than the picturesque villa, it attempted to provide the amenities of that popular type at reduced scale. There was a verandah across the front, a sheltered entry, and even the ghost of a tower in the angled prow of the main portion of the house.

Dwellings like this, with every conceivable type of trim, were built in the small towns of America during the late nineteenth and early twentieth centuries. This midwestern example in the Queen Anne Style dispensed with the horizontal division of surfaces, but something of the same effect was produced by breaking the clapboard walls with shingled gables. Unusually large windows in living room and master bedroom faintly echo the glass wall of the prototype Watts-Sherman house (Figure 210). Attic fanlight, porch posts, and balusters lend credence to Queen Anne's other name, Free Classic.

The Surface Styles

The Romanesque Revival

213. Richardson Romanesque: *Franklin McVeagh House, Chicago, Ill., 1885-87. Henry Hobson Richardson, architect.*

214a. Plan: Glessner House

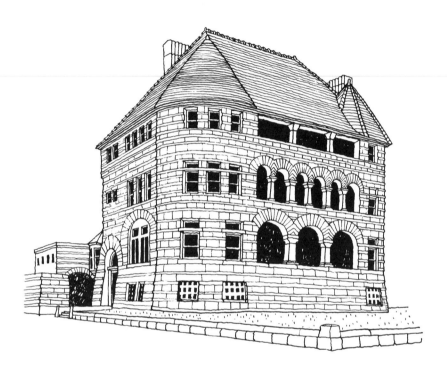

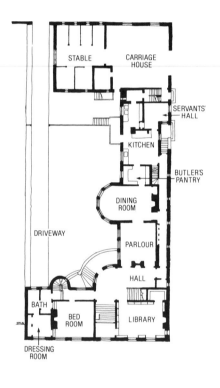

213. The Romanesque Revival, like its contemporary, the Queen Anne Style, was introduced by Henry Hobson Richardson, and the masterpieces of each style are his. The McVeagh house is typical of his strong, solid, yet simple interpretation, a widely copied type which came to be known as "Richardson Romanesque." Its conical towers and great rounded archways echo again and again through the architecture of the period. As in the Queen Anne, Richardson treats the surface of the house—in this case, stone—as a series of continuous horizontal bands, differentiated from each other by the size of blocks, arches, and windows.

Basically, this Chicago house is a bastion, a stone fortress placed on a raised basement and pierced at that level only by barred windows and a doorway suggestive of gatehouse and portcullis. But on the upper stories, Richardson has turned the dwelling into a Victorian Villa, with a spacious "verandah" and balconies recessed behind stone arcades: a safe yet delightfully livable city house.

214. The Glessner house is acknowledged to be Richardson's masterpiece of residential design. In a house of utmost simplicity, he has recreated Norman character out of rock-faced granite and a minimum of Romanesque detail. The basic form is that of a medieval manor house; the detail, especially the arched doorway, is an abstraction from the Romanesque.

At a quick glance, the Glessner house appears to have a symmetrical facade. In fact, the major rooms do balance each other on opposite sides of a central doorway. But at left, the house extends a little farther to encompass a ground-floor entrance, with small subsidiary rooms above it. This throws the entire design off center and gives it a subtle asymmetry which adds movement to an otherwise static facade.

214a. Though in the front view the Glessner house appears comparatively modest in size, it actually is a very large house, a U-shaped block which defines a private courtyard, as seen in the plan. On the inner side of this house, facing the courtyard, Richardson has broken the walls with a tower and with banks of unusually large windows set in curving bays. Unlike the flat, small-windowed public facade, these express the function of the rooms within and open the interior widely to lawns and gardens—a Victorian treatment which would become basic to modern architecture.

214. The Art of Simplicity: *John J. Glessner House, Chicago, Ill., 1885-87. Henry Hobson Richardson, architect.*

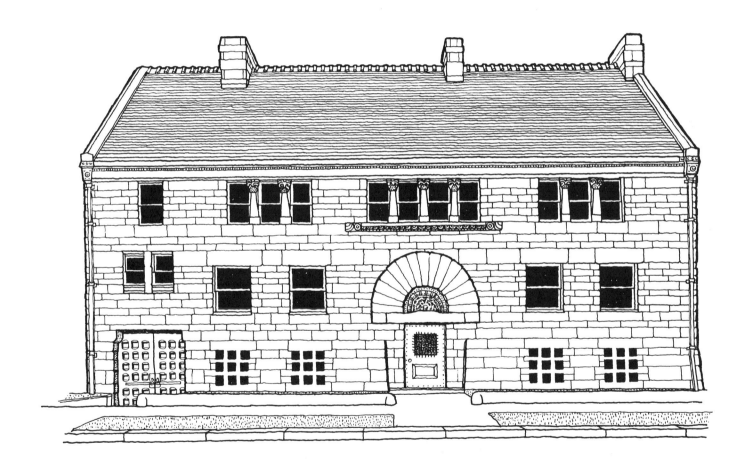

The Surface Styles

Art Nouveau

At the height of the eclectic period, in the midst of the welter of revival styles, there appeared throughout the Western world a new, strange, and evocative aesthetic. It was called by different names in different places: *Jugendstil* in Germany; *Sezession* in Austria; *Modernista* in Spain; *Lo Stile Liberty* in Italy; *Le Style Moderne* in France. In England and America it was known as Art Nouveau. By whatever name, it represented an artistic breakthrough, an authentic original, twining sinuously up between the cracks in Victorian convention.

This "new art" was a complex response to the rapidly changing world of the late nineteenth century. It grew out of the English Arts and Crafts Movement of William Morris, that ardent medievalist whose devil was the machine and all its shoddy products. Preaching a return to the craftsmanship of a preindustrial society, Morris left a legacy of hand-woven linens, sturdy oak furniture, unpretentious floral wallpapers, and chintzes as a standard to set against Victorian fancywork. This mid-nineteenth-century craft revival, borrowing its inspiration from Tudor England, was at once the initial impetus for Art Nouveau and a distinct element within the movement. Its solid, structural simplicities would emerge virtually intact in the early twentieth century as an intrinsic part of modern design.

It was another aspect of the crafts movement, however, which came to be the identifying characteristic of Art Nouveau. William Morris's deep yet conventional feeling for nature was transformed into something new and strange. Rather than simply stylizing natural forms, as Morris had, Art Nouveau re-created them, developing the coiled and twisting plant motifs, free-flowing linear patterns, and whiplash curves which were its hallmarks. The snaky continuities of this part of Art Nouveau contrasted sharply with the blocky, geometric constructions of the Arts and Crafts Movement.

Though consciously seeking a new mode of expression, Art Nouveau proved unable wholly to resist the past. But the past from which it drew was a novel and exotic one, largely outside the mainstream of Western tradition. The flat patterns found in Japanese prints, the continuous Celtic interlaces from Ireland's ancient *Book of Kells*, fluid Minoan and intricate Byzantine motifs, were plucked from their context and reworked, supplementing the forms of nature as sources for design or influencing the treatment of them.

Both new and old, an authentic original and an eclectic recombination, Art Nouveau contained complexities which made it a typical Victorian. At the same time, it reached forward into a new age which was barely under way. Though a part of the Arts and Crafts Movement, Art Nouveau did not seek to recapture a lost medieval world. It accepted the machine as an inescapable fact of nineteenth-century life; but it sought to dominate and direct it toward more artistic ends.

Indeed, the goal of this Victorian modern movement was nothing less than a design revolution. It attempted to encompass every man-made object within a new aesthetic: the arts of painting and sculpture, crafts of all sorts, and the larger art of architecture itself. Moreover, it sought to break down the division between fine and applied arts, making every artist a craftsman and every craftsman an artist at his trade.

Its vaulting ambitions were never realized. Not many houses and other structures were built in the Art Nouveau manner. It flourished primarily as a fashion in arts, crafts, and interior design and, even here, it did not entirely preempt these fields. Nevertheless, it achieved the decisive break with the past and took the daring first steps into a new world of originality in art and architecture.

Emerging in the 1880s, reaching its height at the turn of the century, and largely cut off from further development by World War I, Art Nouveau, for nearly thirty years, was part of the most advanced and innovative aspects of design in both Europe and America. The early work of America's pioneer modern architects, Louis Sullivan, Frank Lloyd Wright, Charles and Henry Greene, Bernard Maybeck, though drawing from many sources, owes such a debt to Art Nouveau that much of it can be classified only within the style. Its philosophy of total design and domination of the industrial process would surface once more in Germany's Bauhaus, though in a new machine aesthetic entirely alien to Art Nouveau. It was as if the eclectic impulses of the Victorian Age were fun-neled through this iconoclastic and short-lived style to emerge as major trends in twentieth-century European and American architecture.

215. In the immense attic space of his family's Romanesque Revival mansion on New York's Madison Avenue, Louis Comfort Tiffany created one of the most spectacular Art Nouveau interiors to be found in America. The studio's most extraordinary feature was an immense central fireplace with four great hooded hearths opening toward the four sides of the room and converging into a common chimney stack "as easy of line as the bole of a great tree" (Tiffany's words). Skylights of yellow-green Tiffany glass provided a diffuse ambience during the day and glowing color when illuminated at night. Lamps hung in clusters from the immensely high ceiling—some of them antique bronze Japanese lanterns; most spun of Tiffany's own Favrile glass, in shades of red, rose, creamy white, and yellow; a few patterned with Tiffany's stylized flower motifs. At night, these lamps were luminous against the dusk of the vast room creating, with the glowing hearth fires, a mood that made life itself a work of art.

216. This row house, designed by Louis Sullivan for his invalid mother, shows how one of the pioneers of modern architecture extrapolated from the Romanesque. Its clean-cut surfaces and intricate ornament achieve a Gallic elegance quite different from the solid powerful forms of Henry Hobson Richardson (Figures 213 and 214) but just as advanced for their day. Street-front windows were unusually large, the lower one serving as the glass front for an "interior verandah," partially screened by flowering shrubs.

The most original feature of the house was its ornament. Sullivan was unexcelled in the use of integral decoration for architectural effect. Both Sullivan's interlacing geometric motifs and Tiffany's stylized plant forms were part of Art Nouveau and their work, with that of Richardson, part of an emerging modern architecture.

215. The Tiffany Touch: *Louis Comfort Tiffany Studio-Apartment, The Tiffany Family Mansion, New York, N.Y. Louis Comfort Tiffany, designer; McKim, Mead & White, architects for the mansion.*

216. Sullivan Romanesque: *House for Mrs. Patrick Sullivan, Chicago, Ill., 1892. Louis Sullivan, architect.*

The Surface Styles

High Victorian Romanesque

217. The Romanesque Villa: *Hull-Wiehe House, Fort Wayne, Ind., ca. 1890. Wing and Mahurin, architects.*

218. High Victorian Queen Anne: *William H. Crocker House, San Francisco, Calif., 1888. Curlett & Cuthbertson, architects.*

219. High Victorian Romanesque: *P.A.B. Widener Mansion, Philadelphia, Pa., 1886. Willis Gaylord Hale, architect.*

217. While Richardson and Sullivan used Romanesque as the starting point for original designs, others simply applied the new revival style to the picturesque villa which had become a staple of Victorian architecture. Though typically of wood, the villa was easily translated into Romanesque stonework. Houses like this were built throughout the country in the wake of Henry Hobson Richardson.

218. The Romanesque Revival soon took its place as yet another ingredient in a typical Victorian pastiche. In the Crocker House, Romanesque arches and conical towers have been added to a design otherwise predominantly Queen Anne. Style has been piled upon style and the elements jumbled about into something guaranteed to appeal to the Victorian temperament.

The Queen Anne portion of this assemblage includes a distorted attempt to divide the wall horizontally. San Francisco bluestone has been used for the lower story, red brick for the upper structure, with gables surfaced in stucco and half-timbering. Upper-story windows are treated as horizontal banks, creating a continuous surface pattern, the trend of the times. What comes through most clearly, however, is the Victorian mind at work in a characteristic act of fragmentation.

219. This Philadelphia mansion, known to its contemporaries as Romanesque, includes elements of many styles: Romanesque, Queen Anne, and Mansardic as well as a sinuous hint of Art Nouveau in the rippling curves of its rhythms. The typical architect of the period worked with styles much as an artist works with paints, using them as a medium through which to create his own designs. The Widener mansion is a representative result: at once a historic patchwork, a characteristic Victorian, and a unique original.

Like house, like owner. Peter A.B. Widener could stand for a summary of the Victorian Age. Starting as a butcher's boy, he founded one of the great fortunes of America. As a testament to his arrival—and as a weapon in his conquest of Philadelphia society—he built this house with all its self-assertive splendors.

Interiors included an entrance hall of onyx and marble; a reception room paneled in ebony; a banqueting hall with a carved oak minstrels' gallery; a master bedchamber of rosewood inlaid with mother-of-pearl; chandeliers of bronze and gold; torchères of silver and ivory; mosaic-tiled bathtubs with gold-plated faucets. Against this opulent backdrop, Widener played out his lavish balls and dinners—not to mention his considerably more relaxed Saturday night

games of three-handed poker.

220. This composite of row houses in Washington, D.C., spans a half century of changing styles. Though not neighbors in reality, they have been placed together pictorially in order to illustrate the standardization of the row house. A virtually identical plan of bay-windowed living room, with bay-windowed master bedroom above, was used as a base on which to apply a succession of changing styles, all more or less Romanesque.

The first house on the left is "Norman" (the English name for Romanesque), the ornament of which is identical to that of "A Norman Villa" (Figure 180).

The next house is "Castellated," inspired by the Romanesque or Norman castle, complete to machicolation at the parapet and crenellation on the bay-windowed tower.

The third is "Richardson Romanesque," built of heavy blocks of granite with a wide, decorated arch at the entry.

Last is the "Georgian Revival," a new style applied to a house retaining the truncated Romanesque tower for bay windows, now transformed into a neoclassic "bow front."

220. The Standardized Row House: *Roman-esque Variants, Washington, D.C., ca. 1860-1900.*

1860s   1870s   1880s   1890s

The Surface Styles

The Shingle Style

221. A Victorian Shingled Villa: *Dr. John Bryant House, Cohasset, Mass., 1880. Henry Hobson Richardson, architect.*

221. A Victorian Shingled Villa: *Dr. John Bryant House, Cohasset, Mass., 1880. Henry Hobson Richardson, architect.*

221. The Bryant house shows the way in which Richardson and others created the Shingle Style out of the gabled, verandahed Victorian Villa, the Romanesque or Norman "candle-snuffer" tower, and a new addition: the shingled surfacing borrowed from our own colonial past.

Interest in America's historic dwellings had been sparked by an authentic colonial house exhibited at the Philadelphia Centennial of 1876. In addition, numbers of affluent Victorians had begun to summer in the New England seaside villages which retained the flavor—and many of the houses—of the eighteenth century. New vacation cottages logically were the first to borrow from colonial prototypes.

We see one result in the Bryant house. Though basically the picturesque Victorian Villa, its gables, shutters, and stair railings are recognizably colonial; and elements are massed in the manner of a colonial vernacular dwelling—an appropriate fusion with the similarly asymmetrical villa of nineteenth-century America.

222. The influence of Richardson's shingled houses of the 1880s was so great that their counterparts continued to be built, in sizes large and small, well into the twentieth century. This tiny bungalow is a vastly simplified descendant of the many-gabled Bryant house (Figure 221) built nearly fifty years earlier. Sturdy shingled porches with shingled pillars were a Richardson trademark which rapidly passed into the vernacular. The horizontal division of the house into shingled and clapboarded parts also illustrates the persistence of elements from his Queen Anne Style.

223. This house is a Colonial Revival saltbox, expanded to Victorian size, wrapped in the Shingle Style, and equipped with the porches, verandahs, and tower of a typical picturesque villa. There was, of course, a basic dichotomy between the colonial type and a Victorian home. The saltbox was a snug, self-contained enclosure, while the Victorian Villa shot off picturesquely in all directions. Shingleside shows how these opposites were resolved. The verandahs and balconies have been pulled deeply in under the body of the house. Sheltered outdoor spaces were retained, but the silhouette remained basically that of a colonial saltbox.

222. A Victorian Epilogue: *The Shingled Bungalow, A Pattern Book House, 1927.*

223. A Victorian Saltbox: *Shingleside, Swampscott, Mass., 1880-81. Arthur Little, architect.*

224. A Victorian-Colonial Cottage: *The Rev. Percy Brown House, Marion, Mass., 1881-82. Henry Hobson Richardson, architect.*

The structure was built into a hill, so that the main entrance (not shown) was at second-story level. The drama of entering from above the great two-storied living hall with its dazzling wall of glass overlooking the ocean must have been one of the pleasures of this remarkable house.

224. In this modest minister's cottage, said to have cost no more than $2,500, Henry Hobson Richardson did it again. Out of the hybrid style which was the contemporary Colonial Revival, he distilled the essence of colonial feeling, quietly eliminating the Norman tower and other extraneous ingredients from the design. The recessed porch carries over, in a modest way, the integration of verandah and house which had become a Victorian characteristic. The horizontal banks of windows are a Queen Anne feature as well as an echo of small-paned casements in a seventeenth- or early-eighteenth-century house. Coupled with the use of shingling to cover the walls, including porch posts (a Richardson hallmark), this treatment created a sense of continuous surfacing which was basic to the Shingle Style. This Colonial Revival within the Victorian period was rapidly absorbed into the general American scene. There were both gambrel-roofed and gable-roofed versions. Few had the long horizontal silhouette of the Brown house, but many resembled a portion excised from the middle of this design.

The Surface Styles

The Shingle Style

225. One of the monuments of the Shingle Style was Kragsyde, a seaside "cottage" of imposing dimensions, designed with a liberal helping of the Romanesque, or Norman castle, including a great, arched entry and "candle-snuffer" towers. There also are echoes of Queen Anne in the horizontal division between stone and wood, of the "Japanesque" in porch lattice-work, while many details, like the dominating gable and shingled surfaces, are colonial.

But all this eclectic dissection is beside the point. Kragsyde is yet another of those accomplished Victorians in which the language of many styles is used freely and harmoniously to create a combination of visual drama and easy livability which few modern designs can match.

Inside its rambling exterior, this is a split-level house. From the arch, a stairway leads to a vestibule before rising five more steps to the height and drama of a "living hall," floating, glass-walled, above the ocean. On opposite sides, the hall opens to living and dining rooms. The boudoir is three-quarters of a story above the hall and the bedrooms another quarter of a story beyond that. Nearly every room opens onto its own sheltered balcony. Outside, the whole complicated structure is unified by the continuous texture and silvery color of shingles weathered by the salt spray.

226. Poised on a brick base à la Queen Anne, this airy, multifaceted pavilion is yet another variation on the theme of the picturesque villa. Shingles define its style, with different types, scalloped and plain, dividing the house into horizontal bands, a subtle evocation of the Queen Anne tradition. Derivative elements have been subdued and simplified. Both colonial gables and Romanesque towers merge into the body of the house as integral parts of its smooth-flowing surface. Slender porch posts of simulated bamboo give a delicacy to the design which is quite different from the sturdy shingled pillars of Richardson.

Inside as well as out, the house is a study in the decorative uses of wood. Paneling in the living hall is solid below the chair rail but shifts to pierced work above in a repetitive pattern of medallions and rectangles, like dark lace. Spindled stair railings and woven Japanese lattices screen the stairwell, their interlacing patterns reflecting the influence of Art Nouveau. The artistic hand of Stanford White is credited with the exquisitely detailed shingle houses which the firm of McKim, Mead & White designed.

226. The Shingled Villa: *Isaac Bell House, Newport, R.I., 1882-83. McKim, Mead & White, architects.*

The Surface Styles

The Shingle Style

227. The New Art of Simplicity: *William Low House, Bristol, R.I., 1887. McKim, Mead & White, architects.*

228. A Beginning: *Architect's Own House, Oak Park, Ill., 1889. Frank Lloyd Wright, architect.*

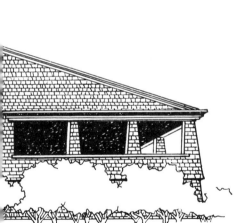

227. With a dramatic leap into simplicity, Stanford White reduced the turreted, many-gabled Victorian house into a single, abstracted shape, sweeping unbroken from apex almost to earth. The Low house, a masterpiece of the Shingle Style, contains resonances from three revivals. Of the Queen Anne, nothing remains except continuous horizontal banks of windows, the verandah, and the living hall around which the house is organized; of the Colonial Revival, only shingled walls and a peaked roof; of the Romanesque, only matched hexagonal towers which no longer look like towers without their ''candle-snuffer'' caps. One could almost describe this as a Regency house, for it has employed the same technique of abstracting from historic elements (Figure 157).

Going beyond style to the basic form hidden within it, the Low house used an approach which was now clearly leading toward modern architecture. But the formal symmetry of its design pointed in a different direction. The contradictory trends resolved here with such assurance could not hold together long. McKim, Mead & White soon would abandon simplicity and its hidden potential, turning their talents to the formal Georgian house, a new revival style but a familiar path in American architecture.

228. The young Chicago draftsman who designed and built this house for himself and his growing family obviously had been looking at the work of eastern professionals. Frank Lloyd Wright, at the time a draftsman in the office of Louis Sullivan, would, as he claimed, ''destroy the box as a building.'' But it is clear that one of his starting points was the Shingle Style.

When McKim, Mead & White shifted their allegiance from the Queen Anne-Stick-Shingle-picturesque movement, with its emphasis on functional planning and continuity of spatial flow, to the academic tradition, the search for an original architecture shifted from east to west. Frank Lloyd Wright was one of the few architects to sense the direction in which the Low house and others were pointing. His choice of this obscure path rather than the well-marked highway of the traditional styles would make him the genius of twentieth-century modern architecture.

The Surface Styles

The Georgian Revival

229. The Traditional House: *H.A.C. Taylor House, Newport, R.I., 1885-86. McKim, Mead & White, architects.*

230. A Modern Translation: *William H. Winslow House, River Forest, Ill., 1893. Frank Lloyd Wright, architect.*

229. The Taylor house set a new direction in American architecture. Rather than the shingled colonial vernacular, its prototype was the late Georgian or Federal mansion. Except for a servants' wing to the left, this house is a classic cube: balanced, formal, and elegant. Its exterior surfacing is of thin precise clapboards, painted yellow and accented with white trim in the Adam manner. However, generous Palladian windows, with balancing triple windows above, reveal a characteristic Victorian insistence on light, air, and view. Rooms are ample, high-ceilinged, and open to one another and to the terraces, which have replaced verandahs. Nostalgia aside, this was an infinitely freer and more livable house than its Georgian prototype. The design is, in fact, simply a reversal of the picturesque villa: the accommodation of open planning to the classic envelope, rather than the

merging of historic detail into an asymmetrical house.

The Taylor mansion proved to be one of the most influential houses ever built in America. Copies, exact and inexact; elegant and vernacular; in wood, brick, and occasionally even stone, went up throughout the country in the decades which followed. It remains the epitome of the elegant upper-middle-class dwelling even today.

230. The reverberations of the Georgian Revival reached the studio of Frank Lloyd Wright in the early nineties, and the Winslow house was his unique response. Built of yellow Roman brick, with harmonizing ornamental tile at the upper story and a copper roof which would weather blue-green, it revealed the sensitivity of an artist to color and pattern. It also comes through as

refreshingly "modern." The blunt, unstyled windows are Richardsonian. The interlacing pattern of the tile is Wright's version of Sullivan's Art Nouveau. The stress on the horizontal, seen in the widening and lowering of the Georgian silhouette, would become a major characteristic of Wright's work; the extended sheltering roof another.

Though eclectic echoes remain—Romanesque in the arched porte cochere; Queen Anne in the horizontal banding of the house; Georgian Colonial in its cubic form and hipped roof—these show Wright's early ability to strike through historic detail to essential form. Internally, Wright has broken up the classic plan, providing an asymmetrical room arrangement, differing levels between rooms, and a curving bay at rear.

The Surface Styles

A Victorian Epilogue

231. The Edwardian Villa: *Samuel B. Tarrant House, Manchester, N.H., ca. 1918.*

232. Georgian Revival-Romanesque: *Row Houses, North Capitol Street, Washington, D.C., early 20th c.*

231. The persistence of Victorian taste in the face of new trends was responsible for yet another hybrid: the picturesque villa with Georgian Revival detail. Americans loved the big, airy verandahs, bay windows, and tower hideaways which had made their houses so pleasant to live in, and they would not give them up.

Villas of the old Victorian type (after 1901, known as ''Edwardian'') remained a part of American domestic architecture past World War I. But, inspired by McKim, Mead & White (Figure 229), these houses were newly dressed in the latest fashion. Adam festoons at the gables, a pedimented portico, Tuscan porch posts, an occasional round-headed ''Palladian'' window, and

plain fascia boards replaced the busy gingerbread of earlier days. In the typical way by which one style glides into another, details changed first. Windows, however, retained the large sash without dividing panes, which had been a Victorian innovation: one more way in which nineteenth-century Americans had opened up their houses to the out-of-doors.

232. Row housing typically followed fashions set by leading architects of the day. Here, each house becomes a small Norman castle, a ''candle-snuffer'' tower. Those which make up the bulk of the row are squared, while a round tower sets off a larger house at each corner.

Like the villa shown in Figure 231, these

houses, too, have been brought up-to-date with Georgian Revival detailing. Note the Adam festoons which decorate the fascia, almost a facsimile of that used on the original McKim, Mead & White mansion (Figure 229).

This row was changed into rooming houses long ago. But Washington, like many other cities, has quantities of spacious, large-windowed dwellings from the Victorian and Edwardian periods which, if renovated, could supply the solid and roomy comforts impossible to build at an economic price today. Their touch of fantasy is a welcome relief from acres of subdivision colonials and ranch houses, as many buyers, moving back to the city, have discovered.

IV

Part IV

An American Renaissance

When William Kissam Vanderbilt and his family moved into their turreted Caen stone château at 680 Fifth Avenue in the year 1881, a new chapter opened in the social and architectural history of the United States—and a new career began for Richard Morris Hunt, the fifty-year old, French-trained architect who had designed the mansion. The Gilded Age had arrived, and Hunt would dominate and define it just as Henry Hobson Richardson had impressed his stamp on the picturesque eclectic period now drawing to a close. During the decade of the 1880s, the two trends—one free and experimental; the other formal, elegant, and correct—would exist side by side. In fact, the earlier impulse would never entirely be extinguished. But during the 1890s, Hunt's visions of grandeur would achieve preeminence.

The key was money. It was as if the energies which were driving America from an agricultural past to an industrial future in a blind rush for fortune had struck a gusher of wealth. As social arbiter Ward McAllister explained: ''Up to this time, for one to be worth a million of dollars was to be rated a man of fortune. . . .'' But now, 50, 100, 500 million piled up and up, money upon money. The struggling young men of a decade or two earlier awoke to the fact that they had become American Medici.

These immensely powerful men and their socially relentless wives were not light-hearted about their aspirations. Instinctively, they sought a visible announcement of their new and royal position. Picturesque informality or romantic masquerade would not do. The new requirements were grandeur, elegance, stability, order. Richard Morris Hunt, the first American to be trained at L'Ecole des Beaux Arts in Paris, the designer under Hector-Martin Lefuel of additions to the Louvre, a founder of the American Institute of Architects, and himself a Brahmin of impeccable background, was ready to instruct them. In so doing, he would make a fortune for himself.

However, like Sutter thirty-two years earlier in California, Hunt did not long remain alone with his gold mine. McKim, Mead & White, most adaptable of architects, grasped at once the significance of the first Vanderbilt mansion. They rapidly found their own metier in this new traditionalism, challenging Hunt for highest honors. These major architects were followed by a host of only slightly lesser talents, themselves honed into sensitivity and competence by Beaux Arts schooling or, later, studies at the American Academy in Rome. Some were trained in Hunt's own atelier.

In 1893, little more than a decade after the first Vanderbilt mansion had introduced Beaux Arts magnificence to America's royalty, the first Chicago world's fair introduced it to the American public.

The period's leading architects planned the fair, known as the World's Columbian Exposition. Hunt, as well as McKim, Mead & White and others of the Eastern Establishment, backed by Daniel Burnham of Chicago (Richardson was dead), presented a solid phalanx of Beaux Arts agreement. The only real oppositon came from Chicago's maverick genius, Louis Sullivan, champion of the indigenous American architecture which had been developing within the mixed Victorian scene. The Establishment won. The Exposition was planned as something new and wonderful: a ''White City'' of Imperial Roman grandeur, designed to lead America out of its wasteland of eclectic whimsy. In the oft-quoted words of Frank Lloyd Wright: ''They killed Sullivan and they very nearly killed me.''

Though this may be a typical Wrightean exaggeration, there is no doubt that the Beaux Arts school of architecture rapidly consolidated its gains. Clients rich and not quite so rich came to demand its elegant and studied traditionalism. Nor did Beaux Arts dominance end with the nineteenth century. It extended into the twentieth, giving ground only in the depression years of the 1930's. Its thrust has not spent itself even today.

13

Chapter 13

The Beaux Arts Palaces

The great era of American palace building spanned the last twenty years of the Victorian Age, the gilded ''Edwardian period'' of the early twentieth century, and the Jazz decade of the 1920s, ending only with the Wall Street crash of 1929.

During the early Beaux Arts years, New York and Newport were the magical settings—respectively operational headquarters and summer colony for the Vanderbilts, Goelets, Belmonts, and equally glittering names among America's imperially wealthy. Though individual Vanderbilts and others carved out private fiefdoms elsewhere, New York and Newport were the royal courts; and it was here that the greatest concentrations of the early palaces were built.

Not far behind, however, new rich in other parts of the country found themselves just as anxious as the original titans to announce that they had arrived. The great Beaux Arts mansions of New York inspired similar grandeurs in or near Philadelphia, Washington, Chicago, Detroit, San Francisco, and many a lesser city, as well as in the newly fashionable suburban enclaves near the cities themselves. The splendors of Newport would be re-created in watering places across the nation, but most sumptuously in those contemporary Versailles, Palm Beach, Florida, and Palm Springs, California.

Most of the twentieth-century palaces, no matter what their style, remained in the historically oriented Beaux Arts tradition. But added to the lexicon were mansions created out of American colonial themes, the English Tudor, and other precedents less formidable than the Italian and French Renaissance.

In addition, some of the new rich were rather more interested in splash than manners. When John Ringling, owner of the circus of the same name, built his pink confection in Sarasota, it was the Venetian Doges' palace as interpreted, not entirely accurately, by his wife, Mabel.

The passion for authenticity, on the other hand, brought its own extremes. International Harvester's James Deering built Viz-Caya (not shown) from fragments of real Italian palaces—columns, doors, ceilings, fountains, statues—assembled into a classical ex- travangaza on Biscayne Bay. A few perfectionists bought their castles whole (English and Scottish were preferred), had them taken apart stone by stone, shipped across the Atlantic, and re-erected in America as a properly baronial backdrop for a twentieth-century tycoon. The choice was extensive and variety within the grand manner became the order of the day.

The Beaux Arts Palaces

A Gothic Echo

233. The French Chateau: *Biltmore, The George Washington Vanderbilt Mansion, near Asheville, N.C., 1890-95. Richard Morris Hunt, architect; Frederick Law Olmsted, landscape architect.*

234. The Medieval Great Hall: *Banqueting Room, Biltmore House and Gardens, The George Washington Vanderbilt Mansion. Richard Morris Hunt, architect; Karl Bitter, sculptor.*

233. If any estate in America deserves the name feudal, Biltmore is the one. Designed in the style of a seventeenth-century French château for George Washington Vanderbilt, grandson of the founder of the Vanderbilt fortune, its foundations covered 4 acres; its grounds, gardens, farmland, and forest covered 145,000. There were 250 rooms.

At the height of its operation—with its own stables, bridle paths, greenhouses, dairy farm, school of forestry, and private railroad spur—the Biltmore estate was said to employ more men than the United States Department of Agriculture. For his workers, Vanderbilt constructed a village complete with houses, shops, schools, and a well-equipped hospital. Biltmore was the masterpiece of America's greatest Beaux Arts architect. In this château, Hunt captured the French Gothic at its moment of transition into the Renaissance. The general character of the house, with its stair towers and angle turrets, is medieval; its asymmetry picturesque. But the irregular masses are tied together with classic stringcourses. The mansard roofs are typically Renaissance in the French manner. This is not an eclectic mix but a faithful reproduction of the transitional seventeenth-century style.

234. Soaring to 75 feet at their apex, the wooden arches of this baronial banqueting room help to create its atmosphere of medieval splendor. The hall is 72 feet long by 42 feet wide, large enough to serve a castle-full of lords and ladies. Thrones, presumably for the King and Queen who held court here, were carved for the Vanderbilts in the Gothic style that echoes throughout this enormous room. Above a bas relief on the triple stone fireplace are the armorial bearings of the Vanderbilt family and above that the flags of all the great powers of the late fifteenth century.

Not seen is an organ gallery that substitutes for a medieval minstrels' gallery at the rear of the hall, completing a room fit for the most royal of America's new rich.

The Beaux Arts Palaces

The Italian Renaissance

235. An Italian Palazzo: *Henry Villard Houses, New York, N.Y., 1885. McKim, Mead & White, architects.*

236. A Modern House: *James Charnley House, Chicago, Ill., 1892. Adler & Sullivan, architects; Frank Lloyd Wright, designer.*

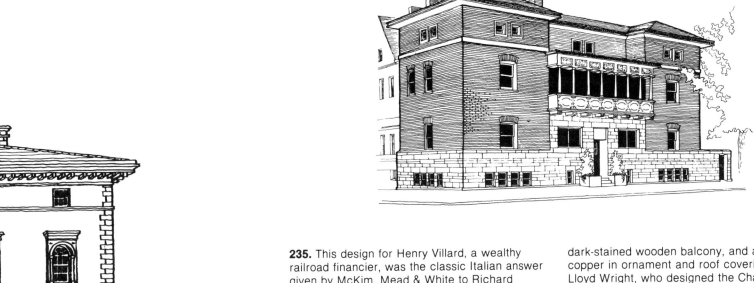

235. This design for Henry Villard, a wealthy railroad financier, was the classic Italian answer given by McKim, Mead & White to Richard Morris Hunt's first Vanderbilt mansion, which had opened the Beaux Arts era with a flourish of French.

The Villard houses were a group of six connected dwellings designed to resemble a single Italian palazzo. This practical palace was constructed of brownstone, the building material which had become almost synonymous with New York, and thus was darker and richer than Hunt's pale gray French château. Its U-shaped plan gave light, air, and the grace of a private entrance court within an urban setting.

Like Hunt's Gothic-Renaissance palaces, the style of the Villard houses was extracted from architectural history at a moment of transition. The heavy stonework of the lower story reveals descent from a fortified dwelling. But this dissolve of the medieval into the classic was typical of early Renaissance architecture everywhere. McKim, Mead & White borrowed a historically accurate sample from a style which itself had undergone many variations.

236. This landmark of modern architecture was built of yellow brick, with a limestone base,

dark-stained wooden balcony, and accents of copper in ornament and roof covering. Frank Lloyd Wright, who designed the Charnley house while employed in the office of Adler & Sullivan, called it "the first modern building."

However, as these juxtaposed drawings make clear, the Villard houses of New York, erected in 1885, and the Charnley house, which went up seven years later in Chicago, are both of classical Italian inspiration. Roman brick, first popularized by McKim, Mead & White, was used to help achieve the precise, clean-cut geometry of the latter.

In the Charnley residence, however, Wright's genius is revealed once more. Taught by Richardson's and Sullivan's examples to extract the essence from a traditional style, he produced a building which is at once modern and truly classic. It was in this house that Wright, as he himself explained, "first sensed the decorative value of the plain surface."

The Charnley house reveals an architect in transition. It is clear that modern architecture began—not once and not as a sudden inspiration but time and again—in simplified versions of the traditional styles.

The Beaux Arts Palaces

The Italian Renaissance

237. The Newport Cottage: *The Breakers, Summer Residence of Cornelius Vanderbilt II, Newport, R.I., 1892-95. Richard Morris Hunt, architect; Karl Bitter, sculptor.*

237. Colossal in size and interlaced with loggias, balconies, and terraces, this 70-room Vanderbilt palace by Richard Morris Hunt is that architect's masterpiece in the Italian Renaissance Style. Its balanced, formal composition contrasts strongly with the French Gothic asymmetries of Biltmore (Figure 233), designed by Hunt during the same years.

The Breakers takes its grand manner from the northern Italian style of Renaissance Genoa and Turin. It is flanked by formal gardens and sited upon acres of lawn, stretching away to the famous Cliff Walk above the breaking waves of the Atlantic Ocean. The epitome of the Newport "cottage," it was designed for summer living at its most sumptuous and for balls and galas of Medicean splendor.

Though he designed in many styles, The Breakers and Biltmore sum up the essence of Hunt's work. As Alan Gowans has pointed out, these two houses are a reprise, at immense scale and in academic terms, of the predominant styles of the early Victorian Age: the Gothic Revival (Figure 174) and the Italian Villa (Figure 181). Their similarities suggest why the Beaux Arts period has been called the "Revival of Revivals."

238. The Great Hall of The Breakers is a chamber of Renaissance splendors; opulently carved and gilded; enriched with onyx, white marble, and bronze; glittering in the light from its great chandeliers and torchères. It is the reception and circulation center of the house. A stairway of royal proportions leads to galleries which surround the hall, giving access to upper-story rooms. The grand entrance to the mansion is at left, oceanside loggia and terrace to the right. This loggia and a matching balcony on the second floor are designed as outdoor rooms, sumptuously decorated but taking full advantage of the sea breezes and ocean views. These great houses have so offended critics steeped in the modern, functional mystique that they failed to see how superbly they were planned for living and entertaining in the grand manner—which was, of course, their reason for being.

The Beaux Arts Palaces

The French Renaissance

239. The French Classic: *Marble House, Summer Home of Mr. and Mrs. William Kissam Vanderbilt, Newport, R.I., 1892. Richard Morris Hunt, architect; Karl Bitter, sculptor.*

239. This is the Newport "summer cottage" of the William Kissam Vanderbilts, whose New York mansion by the same architect had opened the Beaux Arts period eleven years before.

Mr. and Mrs. Vanderbilt have been described as having *le manie de batir,* a mania for building, a disease which also possessed Louis XIV of France, whom they admired extravagantly. Both the seventeenth-century Grand Trianon of Louis XIV and the Petit Trianon of Marie Antoinette, a century later, contributed to the design of this French Renaissance palace.

Its royal manner can best be summed up in the words "marble, gold, and glittering lights." Named Marble House for its lavish use of this material, it has an exterior of white marble, an entrance hall and terrace room of yellow Sienna marble, a dining room of deep pink Numidian marble, carved and picked out in gold, and mantelpieces and pedestals of *fleur de pêche* marble.

Gold is also everywhere. The ballroom, the richest salon in the house, is known as the Gold Room, from its elaborately carved wall panels, surfaced in subtly differing shades of red, green, and yellow gold. Gods, goddesses, nymphs, centaurs, satyrs, cupids, and a Numidian lion disport themselves in mythological scenes on these gilded walls. The golden mask of Apollo, the sun god, emblem of Louis XIV, the Sun King, is a ubiquitous motif, used even on door hinges. Cherubs with trumpets decorate two immense chandeliers, while bronze candelabra light the mantelpiece, and torchères upheld by sea urchins illuminate the four corners of the room. At intervals, mirrored panels substitute for bas-relief, reflecting the glint of gold and blaze of lights back and forth across the ballroom in a dazzling display. It was from this house that Consuelo Vanderbilt, only daughter of the owners, was launched to become the Duchess of Marlborough.

240. Even the Beaux Arts period had its Victorian moments. This Fifth Avenue confection, built by a copper magnate and U.S. Senator from Montana, seems a throwback to the Mansardic Style (Figure 223) that swept America after the Civil War. Though both derived from the French Second Empire, this later residence is far richer and more elaborate.

Like much late-nineteenth-century work in the Beaux Arts tradition, it is a copy of a copy, that is, an American version of a French Beaux Arts design that was, in turn, the interpretation of an earlier Renaissance period.

This one is taken most directly from mid-nineteenth-century additions to the Louvre. Its ornament is ornately Baroque and its size

palatial. One of the costliest houses ever built in New York, its choice location on Fifth Avenue at Seventy-seventh Street gave it, in effect, Central Park for a front yard. Smaller versions of this type of house, and others only somewhat simpler, were multiplied many times on Fifth and Park Avenues and on side streets as well, giving the upper East Side of New York a Beaux Arts elegance surpassed only by Paris itself.

The Beaux Arts Palaces

The Town House

241. Beaux Arts Manhattan: *A composite row; the upper East Side, New York, N.Y., early 20th c.*

241. The great mansions of America's financial giants served as inspiration for these New York town houses. Though by comparison they might be called poor man's palaces, the row houses of the Beaux Arts period were the most sumptuous and expensive ever built in New York. Those constructed in the twentieth century often had garages for the new motorcars which were becoming fashionable among the rich. Tall ones had their own elevators. Interiors included drawing rooms, reception rooms, libraries, servants' quarters—everything a gentleman would need in his house.

Most of these elegant pieds-à-terre have long since been converted into apartments or offices, and many, under pressure from developers, have been destroyed. Yet enough remain to give a Parisian elegance to the upper East Side of Manhattan, especially on the side streets just off Fifth Avenue. This is a composite row, chosen to show the variety of French Renaissance treatments. Facades were individual; but they were unified by pale stone construction accented by delicate black ironwork railings.

The Beaux Arts Palaces

The 20th Century

242. Millionaire's Colonial: *Alfred Atmore Pope Residence, Farmington, Conn., 1901. Stanford White, architect.*

243. Stockbroker's Tudor: *Summer Home for Stuart Duncan, Newport, R.I., 1912-18. John Russell Pope, architect.*

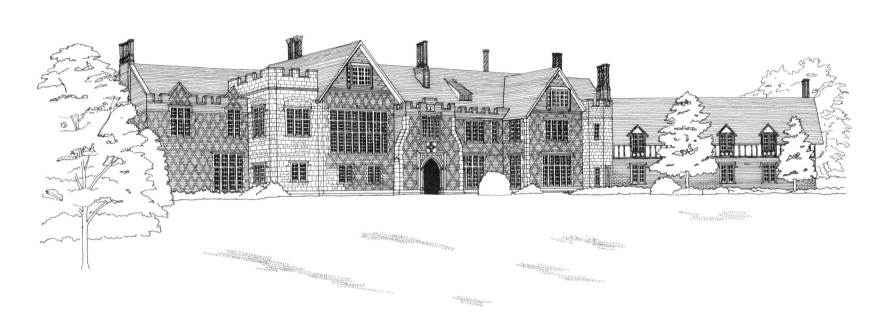

242. In 1901, Stanford White, most excellent of barometers, once again sensed the future and defined the form that it would take. The Renaissance palace, with rooms the size of railroad stations, was perhaps, after all, a bit showy. With the A.A. Pope House (aided by the owner's architect-daughter as associate), he introduced a counter to it, a new Colonial Revival, quiet and tasteful.

For lack of a more precise name, we have called this "Millionaire's Colonial": the expansion of the American farmhouse into palatial dimensions. White clapboards, dark shutters, and gabled roofs were used to recreate a colonial past fit for a king.

The required elegance was provided by an imposing pillared portico and flanking wings. Yet the house rambles to the rear in an informal series of rooms. Virtual walls of windows, some arched, some rectangular, provide a light, airy "modern" interior. Because of its familiar colonial forms and its pleasant human scale, it projected a warmth lacking in the more magnificent Beaux Arts palaces. This disarming combination of dignity and simplicity would distinguish the "era of good taste" which the Pope house ushered in.

243. Though the Colonial Revival, in infinite variety, would prove to be America's most long-lasting style, it did not travel long alone. Just before the outbreak of World War I, architect John Russell Pope, one of the most accomplished traditionalists of his day, proposed the Tudor manor as a solution to the "country house problem." His summer hideaway for Stuart Duncan, a baronial combination of diaper-patterned russet brickwork and buff stone, with inserts of half-timbering, was inspired by the renowned Compton Wynyates and others in England.

Tudor attributes included overhanging gables, turreted parapets, corkscrew chimneys, a congeries of intersecting roofs and wings, and large, many-mullioned bay windows. Inside were Elizabethan plasterwork ceilings inspired by Gothic fan vaulting, dark wood paneling, exposed beams, huge fireplaces, great halls, and cozy corners.

Though baronial in size and character, the Duncan mansion displays a quality of easy informality which gives it—like the Pope house—the twentieth-century traditional look.

14

Chapter 14

The Traditional Styles

The "American Renaissance," a creation of the Beaux Arts tradition, conjured up not only palaces for the wealthy but new types of houses for an increasingly affluent middle class. The Louvre and the Doges' Palace were scarcely adaptable to such normal residential use. Our own colonial heritage was.

As early as 1886, McKim, Mead & White had introduced the formal Georgian Revival with their H.A.C. Taylor house (Figure 229). So influential was this design that its offspring in infinite variety continued to be built at least until World War II.

But in the early twentieth century, the style took a new direction. With the Alfred Atmore Pope residence shown in Chapter 13 (Figure 242), Stanford White used a Colonial Revival vocabulary of white-painted clapboards and shuttered windows to create a palatial home of a more relaxed stance. The Pope house, with its quality of unpretentious dignity, of gracious living, of easy good taste, had created something new in traditional design: the twentieth-century look.

Once more the conviction arose that a truly American architecture was in the making, fashioned out of our own historic past. Indeed, in the long run, the so-called colonial home, in uncounted variations, proved to have tenacious staying power. But in the short run, this was not to be. Departing from the New England and Southern Colonial inspiration, architects once more ran through the period styles. Dutch Colonial was added. Half-timbered English Tudor with its beamed ceilings and leaded casement windows was redone in twentieth-century taste. Cotswold Cottage, French Provincial, and Mediterranean Villa expanded the choice. In a gush of popularity, Spanish Colonial topped the list.

This era of traditional styles started in the last years of the nineteenth century and is still with us today. However, it reached its height of architectural excellence during the first twenty-nine years of the twentieth century, when Beaux Arts schooling provided traditionally trained architects of great skill, and the stock market crash had not yet eliminated most of their clients.

The barons of industry continued to build mansions of staggering size and splendor during this period. But the houses of the merely affluent were far more visible, lending distinction and grace to better residential neighborhoods throughout America. The following chapter shows a sampling of these comfortable, tasteful, and well-proportioned dwellings. Also included are a few examples of the minimum house, as it aped the styles at the top of the heap.

The Traditional Styles

The Colonial Styles

244. Georgian Colonial: *A.W. Finlay House, Brookline, Mass. C.T. McFarland, architect.*

244a. Typical Twentieth-Century Plan: *A.W. Finlay House.*

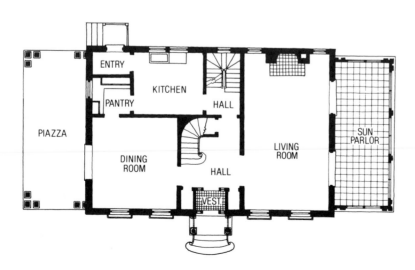

244. This brick house, with its modest Palladian portico and shuttered windows, sums up the early-twentieth-century traditional look. Porches at either end, one opening from the dining room, one from the living room, provided sheltered outdoor spaces—typically a "breakfast porch" and a "living porch" in the usage and terminology of the day. Their railed roofs were usable as decks adjoining bedrooms above. Such porches, sometimes pergolas with latticework for ivy, roses, or grapevines, sometimes (as seen here) glass-enclosed "sunrooms," were a distinctive feature of the domestic architecture of the period, attached to houses of every style and size. They predate the retreat of the American family to the patio, the barbecue, and the backyard.

Using traditional style as a starting point, these houses were designed as contemporary homes. Generous in size, soundly built, comfortable in interior arrangements, and equipped with the latest in plumbing, electric lights, central heating, refrigerators, and stoves, they were considered by far the finest houses which America had ever known. They also show the easy grace of design which was common currency during America's most professionally informed revival period.

245. The Dutch Colonial style was considered cozy and quaint, a suitable choice for the small home. Yet a remarkable amount of space was packed into what looked like modest cottages. A rear wing often contained the kitchen, with servants' quarters above. In those days, all houses except the minimum dwelling contained a separate space for servants.

The Dutch Colonial house, like the New England Colonial, usually was accompanied by the flanking porches which were a distinguishing feature of so many early-twentieth-century houses. Here, this feature has been reduced to a small wing at one end.

The architect who designed this house was one of the leading interpreters of the traditional styles, and he gave his client an accurate reflection of the Dutch Colonial type now known as the "Flemish farmhouse" (Figure 64). The graceful and distinctive gambrel roof, the side wing, the combination of stone (or sometimes brick) with a clapboarded upper story, all were authentic features of the original house.

245. Dutch Colonial: *Benjamin L. Winchell House, Fieldston, N.Y., ca. 1922. Dwight James Baum, architect.*

The Traditional Styles

The Picturesque House

246. The Elizabethan Manor: *Henry Burchard Fine House, Princeton, N.J., ca. 1900. Cope & Stewardson, architects.*

247. The Cotswold Cottage: *Duncan Harris House, South Norwalk, Conn., ca. 1923. Harrie T. Lindeberg, architect.*

248. The Norman Country House: *The French Village, Chestnut Hill, Pa., ca. 1928. Robert R. McGoodwin, architect.*

246. Tudor half-timbering had been part of American revival architecture since the Stick Style of the 1860s and 1870s. Transformed into a Victorian Villa during those years (Figure 226), it was equally a child of the times during the early twentieth century.

End porches were characteristic of this period, here drawn in under the second story to maintain the Elizabethan silhouette. The half-timbering is a structural sham: thin strips of wood set between the plastered exterior panels of a modern frame wall; but its pattern is a visual duplicate of the Elizabethan original. Double gables, edged with verge boards, clustered chimneys, and oriel windows also are faithfully Elizabethan. A lower story of gray stone, off-white plaster walls with near-black timbering, and a rust-red roof complete the picturesque effect. Though adapting historic styles to contemporary ways of living and building, Beaux-Arts architects maintained unusual accuracy of form and detail.

"One of the best examples of this type of house in the country,"[14] the Fine residence is an early specimen of a style that reached its height of popularity in the late 1920s, when "Olde English," from house to college dormitory to tea shoppe, captured the American imagination. For a real half-timbered American house, see Figure 11.

247. The Cotswold Cottage, a closely related Old English type, offered the charm of a small Tudor dwelling as seen through a golden haze. The shingles of its roof were cunningly laid and curved over at the edges to simulate thatch. In a heroic effort at verisimilitude, one such cottage in Los Angeles was given a real thatched roof.

Though consciously quaint, these were appealing houses with their informally grouped masses and broad sheltering roofs. Note the continuous brick gable end, a twentieth-century reproduction of a type which English settlers

had brought to America some three hundred years earlier (Figure 3).

248. The historically educated architects of the Beaux Arts period knew that the Cotswold Cottage was an Anglicized version of the Norman French. It was but a short step backward to borrow its historical predecessor. To distinguish the two styles, the Norman usually was given small towers and an even steeper, more pointed roofline, broken here and there by gables.

The romantic French fairy tale illustrated here is one from a stone village of Norman country houses near Philadelphia: an example of the planned residential communities which were beginning to appear in suburban areas of large cities for buyers of affluence, discernment, and taste. In a more formal version—a single symmetrical block with quoins at the corners but with the same tall, steep roofs—it was known as French Provincial.

The Traditional Styles

The Mediterranean Styles

249. The Italian Villa: *John L. Bushnell House, Springfield, Ohio, ca. 1923. Lewis Colt Albro, architect.*

249. Once the new series of revivals was launched, that old friend, the Italian Villa, was not long out of mind. It, too, was transformed into a typical child of the twenties, with French doors in the major rooms, a balconied loggiaed entrance, and porches or pergolas at either end of the house.

The low, elongated silhouette was characteristic of much work of the period, regardless of style. In this new version of the Italianate, everything was smoothed, simplified, made more graceful and delicate. It is interesting to compare this house with the Italian Villa of the 1840s (Figure 181) and the Italian Renaissance Palace of the 1890s (Figure 237) to trace the direction of architectural taste.

This middlewestern mansion was finished in a pale buff stucco, a newly popular surfacing material, used on houses of various styles during the period but particularly appropriate to a Mediterranean villa.

250. America's penchant for make-believe, suppressed into good taste by the quiet colonial revivals and carefully released once more through Old English, burst into a twentieth-century fandango with Spanish Mission. Like many styles before it, the Spanish Colonial had started innocently enough. It was simply an attempt by traditionally oriented architects in California and Florida to develop a way of building appropriate to their own states.

Touched off by Bertrand Goodhue in 1902, Spanish Colonial would become the *casa* of choice in California for the emerging royalty of movieland. Real estate magician Addison Mizner also started building a Spanish Florida at the close of World War I. But it was not until 1925 that the style slipped its regional bonds. Soon, the Wall Street broker on Long Island and the banker in Kokomo, Indiana, could indulge a newfound passion for rough stucco, red-tiled roofs, dark beamed ceilings, twisting Churrigueresque columns, black wrought iron, and hallways surfaced in blue and yellow *azujelo* tile.

Though a fever which would soon pass, the Spanish Revival left America with a new enthusiasm: the patio. Thirty years later, this feature would become an adjunct to nearly every speculative builder's house as the functions of the porch and the pergola were transferred to the backyard.

250. Spanish Mission: *W.T. Jefferson House, Pasadena, Calif., ca. 1922. Marston & Van Pelt, architects.*

The Traditional Styles

America's Dream House

251. Each period in American architecture has produced a favorite small house. During the closing years of the nineteenth century and the opening years of the twentieth, the bungalow was the achievable American dream. An inexpensive one-and-a-half-story cottage with a pleasant front porch and an easy open plan, the bungalow was a very livable house, surprisingly commodious for its size. In both name and type, it is believed to have derived from an East Indian thatched hut, though an equally logical prototype would have been the French cottage of our own American South (Figure 106). First popularized in California, it soon became a national favorite; and the *Bungalow Book,* illustrating countless variations, sold out each new edition. Our example is a mixed bag, containing a bit of Tidewater English in the chimney, of French South Carolina in the large dormer and porch, with a dash of Henry Hobson Richardson in fat brick pillars. It all adds up to a mildly Victorian-Colonial appearance which lasted through the 1920s in the face of the more accurate Beaux Arts revival styles.

252. For at least three decades, through a depression, a world war, and the immediate postwar years, America's dream house remained the Cape Cod cottage, a neat one-and-a-half-story dwelling with white clapboards and green shutters, a nostalgic and comforting symbol of home.

This quaint little house, in its twentieth-century version, spanned a period of revolutionary change in home building. Introduced by Beaux Arts architects for individual clients, it became the first "assembly line" house of the mass subdivision, its parts clicking together in programmed sequence, like the parts of an automobile.

Our example is one of the former type, designed by that master of the Colonial, Royal Barry Wills. So minutely authentic was this architect that he used progressively narrower clapboards below the windowsill—a colonial method of giving weather protection where it was most needed. He also skillfully transformed a colonial stable into a garage for that new twentieth-century necessity, the motorcar.

253. After World War II, a rival to the Cape Cod cottage appeared: the one-level "California ranch house." Remotely derived from the adobe dwellings of the Spanish colonial tradition (Figures 122 and 123), it was a favored choice for returning veterans, and could be purchased under the G.I. Bill of Rights (in a minimum two-bedroom version) for as little as $8,000 to $10,000 with no down payment. Our illustration shows this small house, typically embellished with shingles at the ends and brick veneer across the front. The use of different materials bearing no discernible relationship to one another was characteristic of these "builder's specials."

There was another change in the postwar house. The "packaged mortgage," developed in the 1940s, had now become common, allowing the inclusion of stove, refrigerator, washing machine and dryer (later, also dishwasher, garbage disposal, carpeting, and even lamps) in the original financing of the house. The consumer society had arrived and Americans were happily buying a collection of expensive machines surrounded by the smallest possible amount of living space.

254. The "builder's economic house" is a term indicating the house of size and price most in demand at any given period. Starting with the depression and continuing for nearly a decade after World War II, this marketable size was the minimum house. Gradually, as the pent-up demand of young families was satisfied and the country moved into the prosperous Eisenhower years, the builder's economic house became a larger dwelling. The split-level was born.

A creation of modern architecture, the split-level idea was taken over by the speculative builder, dressed in semicolonial or ranch trappings and presented to the customer as an expanded version of the minimum house. Rooms were small and there was no waste space; no attic, no cellar, no porch. Typically, the living area led up a few steps to the bedrooms and down a few steps to the dining, kitchen, and utility rooms at ground level. Though hardly a mansion, America's dream house had become something other than a one-and-a-half-story cottage.

254. The Split-Level: *Birchwood Model, Central Park Homes, Madison Township, N.J., 1961.*

255. The Townhouse: *Row Houses, Belair Town, Bowie, Md., 1969-70.*

255. During the late 1960s and the 1970s, America entered an unprecedented period of inflation and spiraling prices. Builders sought a new way to cut costs, and homebuyers began to abandon their love affair with the single-family dwelling.

Like their colonial and Victorian forebears, twentieth-century Americans returned to the row house, now given the more pretentious name of townhouse, or even "townhome." Using a fraction of the land, sharing party walls and sometimes master systems of heating and air conditioning, the townhouse had other advantages, especially for those tired of the paintbrush and the lawn mower. Increasingly popular was condominium ownership, by which maintenance of grounds and exterior was taken care of by a management staff—but tax benefits of home ownership were retained. Modern architects pioneered this twentieth-century type, but the speculative builder's version typically used traditional Georgian row houses (Figure 128) for inspiration.

V

Part V

The Modern House

While the traditional styles were resolving themselves from their initial period of grace into twentieth-century subdivision, a parallel development was taking place. It had begun many years before in the complicated mixture of themes which was Victorian architecture. In a sudden clumping effect, the decade between 1900 and 1910 saw the crystallization of the modern house.

This development was not merely another in the long parade of styles. New man-made materials and new structural systems had long been changing the medium through which architecture worked. But conventional architects and builders had used them merely as cheaper or more efficient substitutes for traditional methods.

By contrast, pioneers of modern domestic architecture, particularly Frank Lloyd Wright, sought to use their inherent characteristics to create radically new designs. A few examples will suffice.

Nineteenth-century experiments with reinforced and precast concrete had shown the great versatility of this material, which could be used for large, flat slabs; as small building blocks; formed into posts, beams, and arched ribs; or cast into vaults, grilles, and coffering.

Structural steel already had spawned the modern skyscraper with its skeleton framework substituting for load-bearing walls. Though steel seldom was used in domestic architecture in the early days, the reinforced concrete and wood frame could be developed in a similar way. Exterior walls and inner partitions could become lightweight screens of glass, wood, brick, or other materials, inserted at will, thus, in Wright's phrase, "breaking the box."

Plate or rolled glass could be used in sheets, permitting large windows or walls of glass without division into small panes—supplying one of the lightweight screening materials allowed by the skeleton frame.

Central heating, unlike the stove or fireplace, could provide comfort throughout rooms of any size or shape and counteract the loss of heat through glass. It made "breaking the box" practical, permitting free planning and the opening of the interior to views and greenery.

Electric lights, unlike candles, kerosene lamps, or gaslight, could be built into the fabric of the house, used to flood large rooms with soft, indirect illumination, create moods, concentrate beams on work areas, or highlight objects of art.

The gas or electric cookstove, the mechanical refrigerator, and the automatic washing machine eliminated the need to store large quantities of food and fuel. Root cellars, milk rooms, large laundry rooms, and the like could be dispensed with, shrinking the working areas of the house. Even the basement could be eliminated, if desired, or used for recreation as well as utilities.

These were some of the new materials, structural systems, and mechanical equipment the potential of which Wright and others explored to create the modern house. But, like tributaries to a main stream, other Victorian developments fed into a rapidly changing architecture.

The Arts and Crafts Movement of William Morris in England, with its emphasis on simplicity and honest craftsmanship, had surfaced time and again during the Victorian period as a counterpoint to busy gingerbread, and it would continue as a guide to the new architecture.

Art Nouveau had demonstrated that it was possible to create original decorative motifs without reliance on historic precedent.

The Stick Style, with its symbolic representation of the building system, had focused attention on the "honest expression of structure" which would become a tenet of modern architecture.

The Neoclassic introduction of novel room shapes had continued through sixty years of Victorian experiment, pointing toward the free planning made possible by technological developments.

The Shingle Style, with its emphasis on the expressive surface of a house, closely following the contours of the rooms within, foreshadowed the modern idea that "form follows function."

The picturesque villa, with its asymmetrical form, provided a precedent for "breaking the box."

The American love affair with the out-of-doors, expressed in the Victorian house by a profusion of verandahs and balconies and, occasionally, by large windows or French doors, led naturally to the decks, terraces, and walls of glass—the "indoor-outdoor living"—which would characterize the modern house.

The move from farm to city to suburb altered the way in which families lived and their requirements for shelter.

All these shifts, trends, and innovations had been moving more or less independently in the maelstrom of change which was the Victorian Age. The creative architects who bridged the nineteenth and twentieth centuries would extract the pertinent developments and put them together into modern architecture.

15

Chapter 15

The American Innovators

Both Louis Sullivan, in whose drafting room Wright learned his decisive lessons, and Wright himself were children of the nineteenth century; and their early domestic work incorporates recognizable period themes. The transformation of their designs from Victorian to modern was accomplished in a kind of historical dissolve, like the gradual shift along a color wheel which at some point (but when?) shows a discernibly new and distinct hue.

Especially in Wright's domestic work, a house in a more or less accurate revival style usually preceded a simplified, modified version which has now entered the canon as modern architecture. The mystery of contradictions in his early houses is dissipated once they are considered as historically derivative.

It is as though Wright's first "traditional" design allowed him to acquire in his hands and mind the essence of a style. Instructed by the lessons in simplification absorbed from Richardson, Sullivan, and the early work of McKim, Mead & White—as well as from his childhood experiences with Froebel kindergarten blocks and folded papers—Wright was able to abstract the basic form. Freed from distracting detail, he then proceeded to elaborate his own unique design on this essential form. But his early houses showed their antecedents.

The final step toward modern architecture, divorced from historic precedent, was taken only after many such experiments in simplification. It represents the gradual loosening of conventional modes of thought and a quickened understanding of technological potential, until the designs which emerged were entirely new.

In its own way, this process was comparable to the breaking up and recombining of many styles in the much-maligned eclectic period. Victorian architects had pulled historic detail apart and put it together again in a kaleidoscope of eclectic themes. Sullivan and Wright pulled historic form apart and put it together again as modern architecture.

The American Innovators

The Prairie House

256. A Tudor Echo: *Warren Hickox House, Kankakee, Ill., 1900. Frank Lloyd Wright, architect.*

257. Vernacular Wright: *A Pattern Book House, published 1928.*

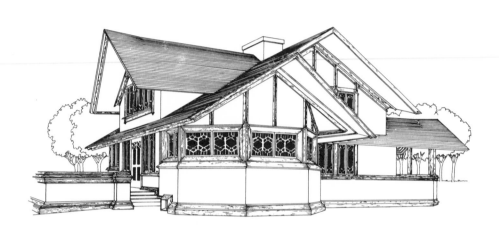

256. Just as the Charnley house (Figure 236) represents Wright's modernization of the Italian Renaissance, so the Hickox house stands as his reworking of the Tudor Revival. Gabled and intersecting roofs have been broken apart and reassembled to define new interior spaces; eaves broadened and extended to give a sense of shelter. "Half-timbering" which accents honey-colored plaster and defines windows and eaves—though clearly derivative—is handled freely as ornament and accent.

The plan is radical in its simplicity: a single, unbroken living space, terminating in octagonal bays at either end, one a dining area, the other a music room. The entry and kitchen wing extends at right, a platform terrace to the left, opening from the central living space by means of glass doors. Nothing could be simpler and nothing more unusual in terms of its times.

However, like a ghost from the past, one glimpses the freely assembled Victorian Villa, with its many gables and verandahs, as well as the specifically Queen Anne division of the house horizontally into three parts. The Stick Style, too, with its diagrammatic layering of thin wood strips—or could it be the Japanese influence?—has been merged into this design. In the Hickox house, Wright combined the essence of many styles, as had the Victorians before him.

257. Even though the Beaux Arts historical approach dominated the fashionable world of the early twentieth century, Wright's work did not go unappreciated or uncopied. The publication of his designs, both in Europe and America, rapidly established his professional reputation and profoundly affected the work of other modernists here and abroad.

This house, discovered in a builder's handbook of 1927, shows that Wright's early conceptions had been absorbed into the vernacular, influencing home building long after the architect himself had gone on to new experiments.

258. This is one of Wright's long, low "Prairie Houses," designed to relate to the flat, horizontal lines of the midwestern landscape. Here Wright has taken the classic form, pulled it apart, stretched it, and rearranged its parts according to his new concepts of interlocking

space. The result is a cross plan, anchored at the center by a massive fireplace block around which traffic flows to four wings. The living room, giving onto its own enclosed terrace, faces the viewer in this drawing; the dining room opens at left onto a walled and roofed porch. Entry and porte cochere are at right. Victorian verandahs have been transformed into outdoor rooms, making it difficult to know where the house stops and the out-of-doors begins.

259. Once again, the Wright idea is found translated into a vernacular house. Shrinkage did damage to the original design, leaving little more than the self-contained box which Wright had set out to destroy. Large banks of windows, walled terraces, and flower urns are more or less faithfully cribbed, but an inept copyist has used Wright's wood stripping like a picture frame applied to the facade. Distorted as it may be from a purist point of view, the result by ordinary standards is an attractive, livable house.

The American Innovators

The Prairie House

260. In the Robie house, after more than twenty years of experiment, Frank Lloyd Wright broke through historic precedent to create a type of dwelling never seen in America or elsewhere before the first decade of the twentieth century. There is no echo here of Georgian, Tudor, or Romanesque. This is "organic architecture," as Wright called it, the antithesis of the classic cube. The focal point is the massive chimney shaft which cuts vertically through the structure, like an anchor to earth. Shooting out from this center are the horizontal shelves of rooms, further extended by balconies and porches and sheltered by broad, sweeping roofs, all seeming to float one above the other.

The lower level contains garage, utilities, billiard room, and children's playroom. It opens onto a sunken court which is partially sheltered by the main living area projecting above. A walled court at ground level (left) leads up a few steps to the living room, down a few steps to the sunken court and recreation rooms below, providing the continuity of space, both indoors and out, which was basic to Wright's designs.

On the main floor, the central fireplace is the only separation between living and dining areas. Though the house looks deceptively solid because of its brick-walled courts and balconies, virtually all walls in the main room

are glass: French doors set back between brick piers and giving onto the balcony at front; matching windows at rear. Both ends of this long, virtually unbroken space are angled prows of glass. A smaller third floor, containing two bedrooms, each with fireplace and balcony, rides across the main story at right angles.

In a house built before air conditioning, this design created its own summer cooling out of broad, sunshade roofs, high ceilings, thick masonry, and through breezes. In winter, the same broad roofs and protective masonry helped ward off the cold. As illustrated by the Robie house, Wright revised Sullivan's "form

261. The Shingle Style: *Harold C. Bradley Bungalow, Woods Hole, Mass., 1912. Purcell & Elmslie, architects.*

262. American Basic: *A Pattern Book House, published 1928.*

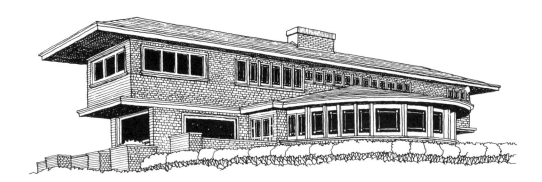

follows function'' to declare that ''form and function are one.''

261. This seaside cottage, riding a spit of land just out of reach of the breakers of the Atlantic Ocean, could almost be a part of the old Victorian Shingle Style (Figure 221), but the horizontal sweep, broad, hipped roof, and ribbons of window mark it as a midwestern newcomer from Chicago's ''Prairie School.'' Both William Gray Purcell and George Grant Elmslie had worked in the office of Louis Sullivan, and the Sullivan-Wright imprint is clear on this design. However, their interpretation is as crisply articulated as a piece of naval ar-

chitecture. A large living room cuts back to front through the center of the house, projecting toward the ocean in a semicircle of windows, like a viewing glass, but secured deep in the house by a massive brick fireplace. The long body of the house rides at right angles across this forward axis in a spacious open plan, the entire lower story (except for the service wing at rear) a single unbroken space. At center, where the two axes cross, the fireplace and angled walls create a sheltered ''hearth room,'' which nonetheless opens in three directions toward vistas of headland, ocean, and horizon. As in Wright's Robie house, this design unites the concept of central security and stability with

view, movement, and reach.

262. This house is as familiar as the city streets of residential America. It is an illustration from a builder's handbook of the late 1920's. But its origin lies earlier, on the drawing boards of Wright, Purcell and Elmslie. This design shows how the vocabulary of the Prairie School became part of the pattern of American building. Though forced back into the static, self-contained box, the new ideas opened many an American home to a modicum of air, light, and greenery which they had not known before. In modified form, the ''sunroom'' from the Bradley bungalow (Figure 261) became part of the American language.

263. Japanesque: *David B. Gamble House, Pasadena, Calif., 1908. Greene & Greene, architects.*

263. Charles Sumner Greene and Henry Mather Greene, the two brothers who designed this house, denied that their gabled, trellised, shingled dwellings could be called "modern architecture." Others have described them as "Japanesque" because of their broad latticed eaves, open porches, and expressive uses of wood. By whatever name—and no one yet has found a really suitable one—the houses which these two men designed in the early years of the twentieth century were functional, articulated, admirably adjusted to their climate, and masterpieces of craftsmanship probably never equaled in this country before or since.

These dwellings belong to the Pacific Coast just as Wright's Prairie Houses belong to the Middle West and Richardson's Shingle Style to New England. The California climate is semitropical, enjoying sunshine and beneficent breezes during the summer, alternating with a rainy season for several winter months. The Gamble house has been planned in relation to these rhythms.

Visible at right is one of three roofed sleeping porches which act as private, open-air sitting rooms. These are far more practical than decks, inviting the breeze while excluding the sun in summer and usable even in the rain. Beneath the porch—and sheltered by it—is a spacious paved terrace, an arrangement repeated at the rear of the house. Major rooms open to these outdoor spaces by means of French doors or sliding panels inset with glass. The broad overhang of porches and roofs serves a double function as sunshade and umbrella. Even in brilliant weather, this house is a cool, cavelike retreat.

The architecture of Greene & Greene developed out of a deep study of wood, its characteristics and appropriate uses. The Greenes believed that wooden members should not be forced but shaped and fitted together like interlocking puzzles. As a result, there is a lightness and "give" to this house, a "resonance" which differentiates it from the unmoving solidity of a stone or brick dwelling.

264. In their studies of Eastern architecture, the Greene Brothers had come across the small, verandahed cottage of India, sensed its appropriateness to the California climate, adapted it, and offered it to their clients. The result: a

new regional dwelling type which spread from Southern California out across the nation.

Another Greene & Greene original (not shown) was the famous "airplane bungalow," a unique California type. A second-story "conning tower," like the one atop the Gamble house, was centered above one-story wings which extended at either side like the wings of a plane. The upper room was a spacious bed-sitting room suite with views in all directions.

Yet another popular Greene & Greene house was patterned after the Spanish Colonial dwelling: a single-story, U-shaped plan, forming an interior patio to which all rooms opened through glass doors—the prototype of the one-story ranch houses so popular today. Paradoxically, by developing an indigenous California architecture, Greene & Greene influenced low-cost domestic building from coast to coast.

231

265. Poetry in Wood: *Entrance Hall, Gamble House, Pasadena, Calif., 1908. Greene & Greene, architects.*

266. Tudor Nouveau: *Leon L. Roos House, San Francisco, Calif., 1909. Bernard Maybeck, architect.*

265. This interior view of the Gamble house shows at close range how Greene & Greene worked with wood. California redwood was their structural medium, but for paneled interiors and furnishings, they used mahogany, teak, and ebony, the rarest and most beautiful they could find, shaped and polished like jewels.

Their love for wood, their study of its characteristics, and their infinite care in revealing its qualities give a house by Greene & Greene a unique personal poetry. Not even a color photograph, much less a drawing, can convey its beauty.

The woods combined in the hallway of the Gamble house were smoothed by the craftsman's tools, waxed to bring out their contrasting colors, and hand-rubbed to a satin finish. Rich, stained-glass panels in a continuous tree of life design are inset into the wooden framework of the entrance doors: a flowing, stylized piece of Art Nouveau. There is something of the flowing, curving character of Art Nouveau in the woodwork, too. But above all, it is a feat of craftsmanship.

The interlocking structural system resembles a Chinese puzzle, the result of an unusual technical understanding of the ways in which wooden members work together. Metal "straps" are used to tie several small beams into a single large one when needed for support. Joints are works of art, sculptural in form and secured with polished pegs of contrasting wood.

The men who created this perfection were graduates of the Massachusetts Institute of Technology, via the Manual Training High School of Washington University in St. Louis, where the Greenes first learned the carpentry, metalwork, and expert use of tools which allowed them to design with such technical mastery and poetic imagination.

They could not, of course, have done this entirely alone. In his acceptance speech for a special citation before the American Institute of Architects in 1952, Henry Greene explained: "In my day you could proceed to do a job and carry it out completely. We didn't need to have inspections. A craftsman's work was his reputation."

266. Bernard Maybeck's beautifully detailed shingled houses belong to the same genre as those of Greene & Greene. But the Roos house, shown here, illustrates another aspect of Maybeck's work, the exuberant interpretation of historic style.

An informal yet beautifully balanced composition of Tudor half-timbering, the Roos house blossoms with Gothic quatrefoils and flowing tracery. French doors set with tiny Elizabethan diamond panes lead onto a terrace (below) and small balcony (above). This is a derivative house, but subtle overtones of Art Nouveau unite it to the work of Greene & Greene (Figure 265) and to Maybeck's own shingled houses.

Not visible are the technical improvisations at which Maybeck excelled. He was the first to use laminated wood in a structural arch, set a single clear sheet of glass into a French door, incorporate a stove into a counter, and hang an oven on the wall. He devised a tiny chimney with twin openings to siphon up smoke, constructed walls of windows out of standard factory sash, developed cove lighting and the sliding glass door. Asbestos siding, corrugated iron roofing, prefabricated panels, and reinforced concrete were among the mundane items that turned to magic under his touch. Maybeck's work combined, in a unique way, the historic past and the technological present.

The Mayan Period

267. A Stuccoed Shell: *Hollyhock House, Aline Barnsdall Residence, Hollywood, Calif., 1920. Frank Lloyd Wright, architect.*

267. Conceived as part of a performing arts center high in the Hollywood hills, this house takes its name from the stylized frieze of hollyhocks (the client's favorite flower) which punctuates its otherwise bare white surfaces, tying together central block and wings.

Here, Wright has used forms not to be found in Western tradition. They are Mayan, recalling primitive temple buildings of pre-Columbian Chichén Itzá or Yaxchilán in Yucatán which had been published as archaeological drawings in the late nineteenth century. However, in this, his first California design, one cannot help thinking that the inspiration may have been as much Hollywood as Mayan. The original temple form, a nearly solid masonry pile, here has been hollowed out and mocked up in modern light wood frame with a stucco surfacing, like a stage set.

The plan of the house is also a theatrical con-cept. Subsidiary rooms are placed in the wings, each opening to a small private garden or reflecting pool; but the central block is a single unbroken space, reaching up to the mansard roof. It is windowless except for a pair of large French doors and flanking panels of fixed glass which open onto a formal terrace, as illustrated here. The drama of this room is enhanced by its approach. One enters either from a narrow hall and loggia or through a low-ceilinged music room, coming suddenly, after several turns, into the surprising height of this great cave that, toward the garden, breaks open into a beckoning vista.

268. Set into one side of a deep ravine, this house is entered at the rear, at street level, but faces toward the wooded cleft which has been developed with terraces and water gardens. The bedroom suite at the top of the house opens to a roof garden. At ground level, a dining room gives onto a broad terrace with steps leading down to pool and gardens. The middle floor is a balconied living room, two stories in height.

As his medium for this dramatic idea, Wright chose ordinary concrete block, which he had cast with a Mayan motif. He devised a method of webbing the blocks together by inserting steel rods into the joints both vertically and horizontally, filling the void with concrete. The finished structure combined the tensile strength of steel with the continuity of masonry. There was no supporting framework. Walls, floor, roof, and inner partitions all became part of a single, continuous web working together to stabilize the whole.

La Miniatura aptly describes this design. Including guest room and garage, which extend at top left, this is only a two-bedroom dwelling and was a comparatively inexpensive one. But Wright's imaginative conception made it a miniature Shalimar.

268. A Concrete Block House: *La Miniatura,*
Mrs. George Madison Millard House, Pasadena,
Calif., 1923. Frank Lloyd Wright, architect.

269. The Hillside House: *Interior, Taliesin, Home of Frank Lloyd Wright, Spring Green, Wisc., 1911-14; as rebuilt, 1925. Frank Lloyd Wright, architect.*

270. The Desert Camp: *Taliesin West, Paradise Valley, Ariz., 1938. Frank Lloyd Wright, architect.*

271. The A-Frame: *Gisela Bennati Cabin, Lake Arrowhead, Calif., 1934. Rudolph Schindler, architect.*

269. Taliesin, the famous home of Frank Lloyd Wright in rural Wisconsin, represents a total break with his former life as a suburban Chicago architect. It was designed as Wright's personal retreat: a home-office-workshop-farm-school for apprentices-feudal domain.

Shown here is the heart of Taliesin, a single enormous room designed for living, dining, reading, listening to music, and as a gathering place for his extended family of apprentices when work was done for the day. Its focal point is the great fireplace, around which Wright has created a room within a room. The built-in seating and the dropped ceiling define this area, setting it off as the center of otherwise free-flowing space. The ceiling starts unusually low, just above the mantel, giving a sense of protection and enclosure to this part of the room, then sweeps to great height at center and drops again to meet a lower ceiling plane near the long, horizontal band of windows on the opposite side of the house.

Contrasting with the broad, smooth lift of the main ceiling, the far end of the room is broken into irregular shapes and rough textures by ascending ledges of stone, a balcony, and a recessed ceiling decorated with strips of wood.

The entire room is tinted in shades of honey, raw sienna, and pale sand color. Through a skylight, shafts of sun play over the fireplace, emphasizing the muted gold of the limestone.

Taliesin is a demonstration of what Wright meant by the "natural house," a dwelling which was part of nature, using materials according to their intrinsic character and evolving from its site, climate, materials, and function in the same way that a shell or flower had evolved according to similar imperatives. Wright's other name for this was "organic architecture."

270. Wright's winter home, Taliesin West, as famous as the original Taliesin, is very nearly its opposite. The interplay here is with distant mountain peaks, jagged rock formations, exotically flowering cactus, as well as the simmering heat of the flat Arizona desert.

Necessity prodding invention, Wright built his great masonry blocks by making forms in which he combined poured concrete and otherwise unusable soft native stone. Out of redwood, canvas, and this "desert concrete," as he called it, Wright created a group of buildings having the primitive splendor of Mayan temples. Because the entire construction of Taliesin West stretches horizontally to such great length, only the drafting room is shown, a low masonry enclosure, dramatically overarched with a series of redwood trusses from which the canvas roof was hung. To the right are the main living quarters, a dim cave behind great masonry ramparts which shelter it from heat and dazzling sun. Steps lead down to a pool in the foreground. Wright's separate quarters may be glimpsed at left.

This spectacular desert camp was built when Wright sought winter quarters for his family and apprentices in a climate warmer than that of Wisconsin. He was sixty-nine years old at the time, and the move started a brilliant new phase of his career.

271. The A-frame has become such a familiar part of the vacation landscape that one tends to think of it as a vernacular American type. But there had to be a first one and this is it. The original A-frame was designed by Rudolph Schindler, briefly a draftsman at Taliesin under Frank Lloyd Wright, and it shows a kinship with Wright's designs.

The A-frame however, was designed as a sort of practical joke. The cabin was to be part of a tract at Lake Arrowhead which had been restricted to houses "in the Norman Style." Knowing that he could not design the type of modern house he ordinarily would have done, Schindler designed the A-frame and passed it off as Norman to a credulous building committee.

In a plan which would become virtually standard, the house was an open living area on the ground floor, bedrooms on a balconied upper story under the peaked roof. However, Schindler's original broke the roofline at one side to increase the size of the ground floor, glassed in the wall of this alcove, and opened it to a terrace.

The Regional House

272. The House in the Desert: *Rose Pauson House, near Phoenix, Ariz., 1939. Frank Lloyd Wright, architect.*

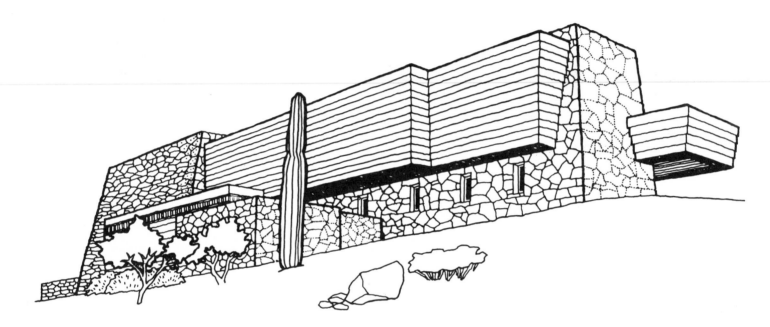

272. To Frank Lloyd Wright, the word "regional" was redundant. His "organic houses" related to their settings wherever or whatever they might be. This house and the Pew house (Figure 273) illustrate his approach. Both are built of massive masonry with a cantilevered wooden superstructure. Both contain a single large living space and segregated bedrooms. Even the treatment of the balconies is similar: horizontal boarding left to weather gray. Yet the Pauson house was a cavelike retreat against the Arizona climate, its great tapered walls of "desert concrete" designed to cut the heat and glare of the sun during the day and to release warmth after dark against cool desert nights.

The horizontal wooden baffle along the upper part of the house was glassed in at the top like an immense skylight. The baffle itself was the outer wall of a balcony which cut through without break into the height of the two-story living room, permitting the entrance of indirect light. Projecting from the opposite side of the house was an open exterior balcony from which dramatic views of the desert could be enjoyed after the heat of the day.

273. This house, designed for a wooded Wisconsin hillside overlooking Lake Mendota, reaches out to nature rather than retreating behind a protective shell. Entrance (right) is at street level, past the kitchen and around a massive fireplace into the large, airy, open living space. From its anchorage in the hillside, this room shoots out like a tree house into the landscape. Through the wall of windows, one sees a distant view of the lake, laced over by the patterning of nearby trees. Second-story bedrooms have their own balcony, usable as a sundeck. The surrounding landscape has been left in its wild state, and steps lead down by the side of the house in the direction of the lake. Nothing could be more appropriate to its setting and nothing more unlike the desert house, built of essentially the same materials.

274. The houses by Frank Lloyd Wright were brilliantly designed for their site and climate but without reference to local building tradition. This California house of native redwood, with its spacious balconies, wide overhanging pitched roofs, trellised eaves, and crisp articulation of every stick of wood, relates to the houses by Greene & Greene (Figure 263) so admirably planned for the California climate; to the Japanese tradition, strong on the Pacific Coast; and to the vernacular board and batten houses of pioneer California.

Designed by Harwell Hamilton Harris, a master of the California Style, it consists of three levels set into a hillside. Main quarters are at the top of the house, with a high-ceilinged, glass-walled living room looking out at front and giving onto a secluded patio at rear. A one-story bedroom wing extends to the right; dining room and kitchen in an ell to the left. Below the living room is a second-floor studio, opening onto a deck atop the ground-floor garage.

Among the most practical of architects, Harris designed this house for stock lumber sizes, using a module equal to three standard 12-inch boards. Exposed beams, posts, and rafters and the board and batten system itself act as integral ornament, their pattern and texture lending richness to a simple, inexpensive design.

16

Chapter 16

The International Style

During the late 1920s and early 1930s, a new kind of modern architecture arrived in America: a precise, cubistic interloper from foreign lands. Its origin lay in the period before World War I in Europe, a time of ferment and excitement, of unprecedented experiment in technology, art, and social theory. Its aim was nothing less than the harnessing of the Industrial Age for the common good through the industrialized design of architecture, furniture, and all useful objects and (with special emphasis) the mass production of inexpensive housing for the workingman.

This new movement had developed out of experiments in Holland, France, and Germany, including the early explorations of Adolf Loos in reinforced concrete; those of Walter Gropius and Adolph Meyer in steel, glass, and the standardization of building components; of the De Stijl group in the aesthetics of cubism and constructivism; of artist Piet Mondrian in linear composition; and of Le Corbusier in all of these. The publication in Berlin in 1910 and 1911 of the work of Frank Lloyd Wright also was influential, and many of his principles were absorbed in this developing idiom.

Out of these and other trends and experiments, a creative surge following World War I crystallized the International Style into a coherent pattern. Suddenly, a recognizable vocabulary emerged, cutting across national boundaries while permitting each building to retain individual character and a national accent.

Though a few houses resembling the International Style were designed and built in America long before 1932, it was in that year that the new aesthetic officially arrived and was given its name.

Two significant events were responsible. At the Museum of Modern Art in New York City, Henry-Russell Hitchcock and Philip Johnson organized the first definitive exhibit of modern architecture to be held in America. In the same year, the same two men published their immensely influential book, The International Style, drawing together the various strands of development and providing them, for the first time, with a collective name.

Though they had included the work of Frank Lloyd Wright in their exhibition, this was only as counterpoint and prelude. They omitted it from their book, labeling his buildings "half modern" and excluding him from the company of more flexible pioneers who had been "ready to learn from their juniors."

This was not something that Frank Lloyd Wright could swallow easily. It provided him with a lifelong target for hostility and introduced a schism into American architecture which was to persist long after the reverberations of the exhibit and the book had quieted.

Nevertheless, the Hitchcock-Johnson definition of modern design rapidly achieved the character of gospel among their followers. The International Style—like the Gothic Revival in the nineteenth century—was embraced as both a fashion and an imperative: a new kind of "Christian architecture."

What were its articles of faith? First and most important, its proponents believed that a new and consistent style, as fundamental as the original Greek or Gothic, was in the making. They believed that this new style would express the Machine Age in structure and appearance just as the architectures of the great ages of the past had emerged as symbols of their own times and cultures. Furthermore, they believed that they could provide a recipe for designing it, one which every architect who wished to travel the correct path into the future should now embrace.

This recipe included lightweight frame and curtain wall construction, open planning, standardized industrial materials, cubistic forms, a linear geometry of openings, asymmetrical composition, flat roofs, smooth, continuous wall surfaces, and the rejection of all applied ornament. It was almost as if these modern iconoclasts had listed the characteristics of Victorian and Beaux Arts architecture that they disliked the most and then had adopted their opposites. The break with the past was complete; the future clearly defined.

At its best, the International Style produced houses of a cool, pristine, and subtle elegance which cannot be matched by any less disciplined architecture. But the belief that a single, smooth-surfaced envelope could contain the infinite riches of the twentieth century, the multiplicity of its functions, and the variety of its regional manifestations proved to be a major error. One of its leading exponents—Le Corbusier—was at work exceeding these limitations almost before they had been set down.

Nevertheless, the International Style served a vital purpose. By establishing a pattern and a method, this movement provided the necessary backbone for the development of a new architecture which might otherwise have floundered without certain shape or purpose. Frank Lloyd Wright was a genius who could create great buildings without a formula. Most of his followers could not. The International Style consciously defined a formula by which any architect (supposedly) could design a good building. Though its rigidity has become all too evident, certain assumptions of the International Style were necessary to the broad diffusion of modern architecture and remain basic reference points even today.

The International Style

An American Prelude

275. The California Original: *Walter Luther Dodge House, West Hollywood, Calif., 1916. Irving Gill, architect.*

275. This milestone in modern architecture represents an independent American development of the International Style, predating its European counterparts. Like the Robie house in brick, Taliesin in stone, and the Gamble house in wood, its appearance expresses the nature of a material, in this case, reinforced concrete. So malleable is this man-made substance that there is no single "proper" way in which to use it. But architect Irving Gill, a former draftsman in the office of Adler & Sullivan in Chicago, found his forms in his goals: ease of building, lack of maintenance, and low cost.

His innovation was a lift-slab method of construction. Hollow tiles and reinforcing rods were laid alternately in a wall form. Steel frames for doors and windows were positioned within the same form. Concrete was poured, allowed to cure, dusted with a fine cement outer coating, and the finished wall slab hoisted into place.

It follows logically that surfaces would be plain, roofs flat, window and door openings clean-cut. But, unlike his European contemporaries, Gill never forgot the evocative character of architecture. Where appropriate, he included arched doorways, arcades, tiled roofs, and walled gardens, recalling the early Spanish tradition of California. He even devised a method by which small balconies and window boxes could be cast as integral parts of his monolithic wall slabs.

In a very American way, Gill also made the out-of-doors a part of every major room. This rear, or garden view, shows how French doors open to the terraced patio. At the front of the house, the dining room enjoys its own high-walled garden court. Bedrooms open to rooftop balconies; and, at far left, out of sight from below, is a rooftop swimming pool.

Though his houses were unornamented, Gill nevertheless achieved remarkable effects. He liked to play dark green, glossy foliage, and a sudden massing of red geraniums against white surfaces. To enhance the effect, he devised a color-reflective paint which gave trees, shrubbery, and flowers "a second blooming upon the walls." Both inside and out, his paint was a mixture of primary colors with white, the proportions of which were changed to emphasize blue, yellow, violet, red, or any desired hue, while retaining the appearance of white. The result was a luminosity which has been described as "like living in the heart of a shell."

Gill's designs also showed unusual concern for the housewife and her problems. His goal was "a perfectly sanitary, labor-saving house." To this end, he developed a special coved joining for his concrete wall and floor slabs, eliminating the crack which otherwise serves as a dirt collector. He boxed his bathtubs in magnesite and, as a base for kitchen sinks, cast magnesite into a unit with the wall "so not a particle of grease or dirt can lodge, or dampness collect to become unwholesome."

To reduce the task of dusting, he did away with projections of all sorts—picture moldings, plate and chair rails, baseboards, raised paneling and wainscoting—and replaced conventional furniture with built-in cabinets, bookcases, chests, and storage units of polished wood, let smoothly into the white walls.

Gill's labor-saving devices were endless. They included a garbage disposal which fed into an incinerator in the cellar (no grinding required); a vacuum cleaner outlet in every room to carry dust automatically to the furnace; the now-common mail slot for the front door; an inexpensive, automatic car wash for the garage. Nor were all of these devices the exclusive property of the rich. Much of Gill's innovative effort was expended designing practical and pleasant low-cost homes. The Spanish Colonial Revival cut short his innovative career. But Gill's lessons in economical building, unadorned beauty, and inventive practicality still offer themselves to any who will listen.

The International Style

The European Influence

276. The International Style: *The Health House, Lovell Residence, Los Angeles, Calif., 1927. Richard Neutra, architect.*

277. De Stijl: *Lovell Beach House, Newport Beach, Calif., 1926. Rudolph Schindler, architect.*

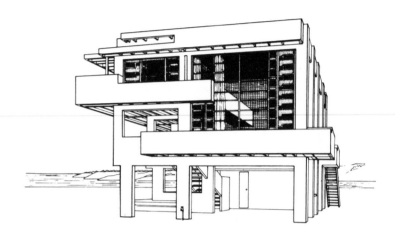

276. The Lovell house was the first authentic example of the International Style to be built in America. A cage of steel enclosed by sweeps of glass and concrete, it embodied principles which had crystallized in Europe during the 1920s, i.e., skeleton construction, transparency, a skinlike wall enclosure, standardization of building components, and elimination of applied ornament. Substituting for classic balance was the new discipline known as "regularity," by which a standardized grid system was repeated, yet the building, as a whole, was developed asymmetrically.

Viennese-born Richard Neutra was one of a long line of expatriates to bring this European version of modern architecture to America. He also was one of the first to grasp the exciting potential of industrial building parts readily available here. He simply ordered the Lovell house out of Sweet's catalogue, the supply book for the building trades.

Stock steel frame and window sash were joined into wall sections in a local machine shop, trucked to the site, and erected in forty working hours. For the balconies, forms containing reinforcing materials were attached to the framework. Ready-mixed cement was delivered through 200-foot hoses, the cement left to cure, and forms then removed. The design was a technical marvel, one of the sights of Los Angeles both during and after construction.

277. At the close of World War I, a group of architects and artists centered in Holland brought together the newest theories of painting, sculpture, and building to create a unified theory of modern architecture. Predating the International Style, it was called *De Stijl* and the Lovell beach house is an example of its approach. Basically cubist in form, its structure is brutally exposed in the constructivist manner and its windows geometrically patterned like a Neo-Plasticist painting by Piet Mondrian.

But *De Stijl* was something more than the sum of its parts. Color and pattern were no longer simply decoration but utilitarian aids in the definition of space. Conversely, structure was no longer entirely utilitarian but was designed to assume the character of sculpture so that the building itself became a work of art.

Even this cross-functioning was but the means toward an end. Rejecting the idea of a building as a static enclosure, *De Stijl* took the cube as a point of departure, breaking it and opening it out asymmetrically into what its followers referred to as the "infinite environment." The language echoes Frank Lloyd Wright who, years earlier, had also "broken the box." Wright's early buildings had contributed to half a dozen movements in European art and architecture. *De Stijl* put Wright's ideas back together again to produce a cubistic European version of the Prairie House (Figure 260).

278. This is a seldom-published view of the most famous modern house in America. Usually, it is seen in a photograph taken from below, emphasizing the dramatic fall of water beneath its cantilevered balconies. This view is less spectacular but more informative.

Fallingwater has been called Frank Lloyd Wright's personal interpretation of the International Style. It would be more accurate to call it his version of *De Stijl*.

Rudolph Schindler, the European architect who designed the Lovell beach house, had his first American job as a draftsman under Frank Lloyd Wright at Taliesin. Wright would never allow his work to be exhibited with that of his ex-draftsman. These juxtaposed drawings may show why. Yet what Wright echoed was, in fact, a European echo of his own earlier work.

Moreover, the two houses—the Lovell beach house and Fallingwater—use a similar vocabulary but speak with different voices. The first is a floating continuum of interlocking solids and voids. The second is pinned to earth by the vertical chimney mass from which forms and spaces radiate outward. The first is European, set off from nature. The second embraces nature, a uniquely American approach that began during the Victorian Age.

278. An American Response: *Fallingwater,*
Edgar J. Kaufmann House, Bear Run, Pa., 1936.
Frank Lloyd Wright, architect.

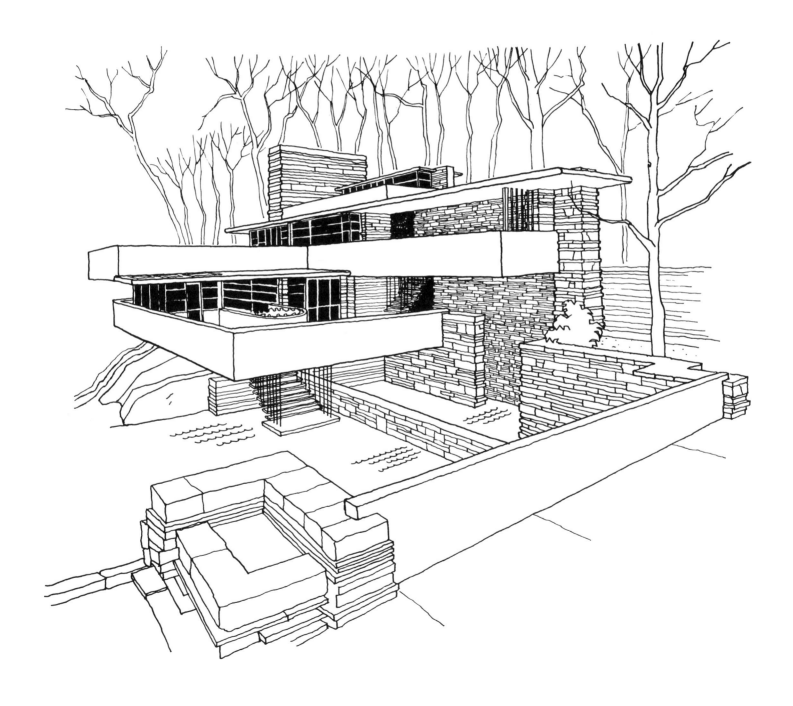

The International Style

European Imports

279. A French Accent: *Architect's Own Weekend House, Long Island, N.Y., 1932. A. Lawrence Kocher, architect; Albert Frey, associate.*

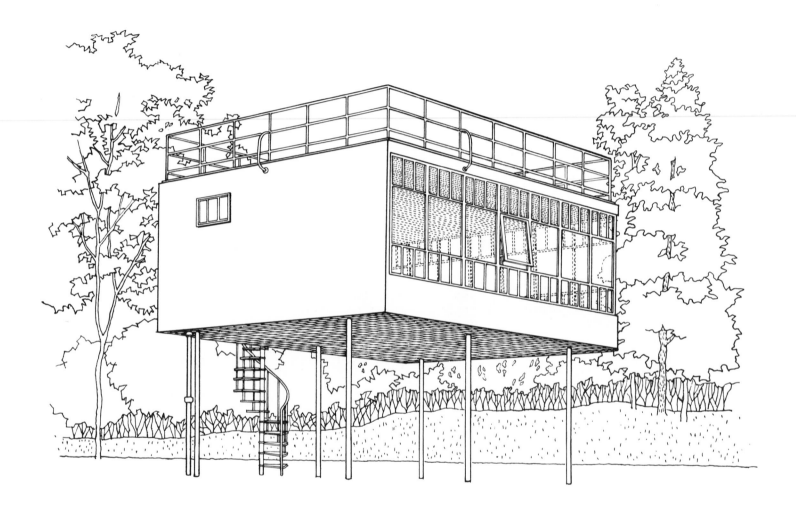

279. This precise little house, poised on its delicate *pilotis*, is the nearest that this country came to the French incarnation of the International Style. A much simplified version of Le Corbusier's Villa Savoye, it is a tiny weekend retreat in the manner of one of the most elegant modern houses in the world. In Corbusier's famous phrase, this is "a machine for living in," designed with the same functional approach as a factory or a grain elevator. The desired effect of weightlessness is achieved by "floating" the house on slender steel columns, or *pilotis*, as they were called in France. Walls were supposed to resemble not a weighty solid but a light, continuous fabric, alternately opaque and transparent. In this house, an experimental design for the Cotton Textile Institute, the solid parts of the wall really are fabric, i.e., canvas with an inner aluminum foil insulation stretched over a redwood frame.

To further accentuate its machine origin, the dwelling was set apart from natural surroundings, standing alone as a man-made artifact. Sunbathing and relaxation take place on the roof deck; the space beneath the house is used for a carport.

280. A Dutch Accent: *Ulrich Kowalski House, Mt. Kisco, N.Y., 1934. Edward Durrell Stone, architect.*

281. Art Deco: *Room for a Lady. Exhibition of Contemporary Industrial Art, Metropolitan Museum of Art, New York, N.Y., 1934. Eliel Saarinen, architect.*

280. This house and Figure 279 illustrate the variety which was possible within the discipline of the International Style. Like the Kocher house, the Kowalski house is widely opened with glass on its opposite side overlooking terrace and gardens. But the entrance front, shown here, is more opaque than transparent.

A ribbon window consciously selects a portion of exterior view, framing it like a landscape painting; hence the name "picture window." Conversely, glass brick was a means of combining illumination with privacy. The cylindrical stair tower has been placed outside the main body of the house to emphasize its separate function. But in the typical method of the International Style, all elements are unified by the taut, continuous treatment of the enclosure, shifting from solid to glass without break, like a stretched fabric.

This house echoes the curving forms, large expanses of white wall, and pronounced horizontality used by pioneer modernist J.J.P. Oud in Holland, achieving, by this association, a subtly Dutch look.

281. Art Deco is a recently invented name for the jazzy, streamlined, "modernistic" mode of design which jumped up out of the International Style into popular culture between roughly 1925 and 1935 and which became a revival fad in the late 1970s. Its name comes from parts of two words in the title of the famous 1929 Paris exhibit, the Exposition Internationale des Arts Decoratifs et Industriels Modernes. It was this world's fair of twentieth-century design which gave us chairs like overstuffed poufs; bookcases stepped like skyscrapers; circular sofas; black, white, and chrome color schemes; streamlined sunburst mirrors; cubistic teapots; blond, ebony, and white lacquered furniture; unframed round mirrors, sometimes cut in quarter circles; zigzag patterning on furniture and fabrics; and the whole 1930s Hollywood-movie-musical-kitsch.

Modern architects carefully disassociated themselves from vulgar "modernistic," yet the boundaries between "good" and "bad" modern are occasionally indistinct. Some of the best architects, notably Frank Lloyd Wright and (as seen here) Eliel Saarinen, used decorative motifs which can only be classified in retrospect as Art Deco.

The International Style

European Imports

283. The Bauhaus Interior: *Living-Dining Area, Gropius House.*

282. This house is the American home of the late Walter Gropius, one of the pioneers of modern architecture. Built in 1937, the year in which Gropius was appointed chairman of Harvard's Graduate School of Design, it reflects the principles which he had established in Germany as early as 1911 and which he had taught as founder and director of the world-famous Bauhaus.

Designed on the rule of "regularity," its guideline is the repetitive interval between members of the skeleton frame. Doors, windows, roof apertures, railings, and other details are dimensioned and placed to coincide with these structural intervals. The building as a whole is asymmetrical but the regular rhythm unifies it throughout. Projecting and receding volumes—the dining porch and open roof deck—make a three-dimensional composition. These positive and negative spaces weave in and out from the basic cube not only as expressions of function but as related parts of an abstract cubistic sculpture.

Gropius composed this superb example of the International Style out of white-painted wood siding and other stock elements which could, and still can, be purchased at any lumber or building supply center.

283. Like its exterior, the living room of the Gropius house sums up a style, a period, and a fundamental approach to design. The precise, machined look, with its smooth surfaces and large areas of glass, is indivisible inside and out. The fireplace is merely a slight projection from the continuous running fabric of the wall. The dining area, in the foreground, is entirely open to the living room, though it can be closed by a curtain hung on a ceiling track. Tubular metal chairs and side tables, a bent plywood reclining chair, a gooseneck floor lamp with baked enamel shade—all were unprecedented Bauhaus designs for factory production.

Omnipresent is the white wall, washing out the browns, russets, dark greens, and maroons of the Victorian period just past. Pattern and color were permissible only in accents.

The Prefabricated House

284. The Packaged House: *A Prefabricated System, General Panel Corporation, New York, N.Y., 1942. Konrad Wachsmann and Walter Gropius, architects.*

285. The Techbuilt House: *Concorde 400, Techbuilt, Inc., Cambridge, Mass., 1951. Carl Koch, architect and manufacturer.*

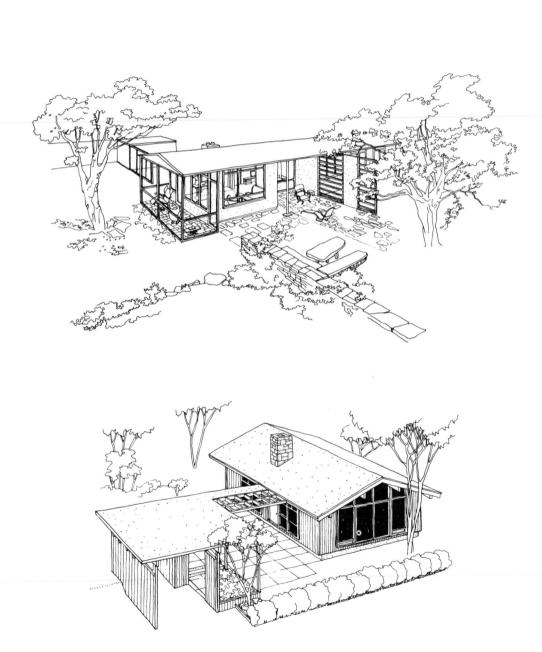

284. A fundamental goal of modern architecture, as it evolved at the Bauhaus under Walter Gropius, was the adaptation of the house to industrial production. In 1942, in America, the originator of the idea had a chance to help develop it. Shown here is one of many versions of the prefabricated "Packaged House" which could (as demonstrated) arrive by truck in a large crate and be erected in a matter of hours by unskilled labor or the homebuyer himself.

What made it so easy was an ingenious locking joint which eliminated the services of a carpenter. Everything slipped into place, locked, and held firm. Since all parts were standardized to fit every other, the house could be expanded simply by ordering another "room" or a room enlarged by adding additional panels. Various arrangements allowed the buyer, in effect, to design his own house.

It all seemed too good to be true. And indeed it was. Building unions and codes geared to hand-craft production effectively prevented national distribution. The design was too "radical" to command a mass market at a time when the Cape Cod cottage was America's favorite small house—even though its designers gave a stiff little nod toward the traditional gabled roof. The Packaged House remained only a demonstration of the handsome, livable, modestly priced home that American technology was capable of producing.

285. Techbuilt was the first prefabricated house in the modern idiom to gain acceptance in America. Designed and manufactured by Carl Koch, who had studied under Gropius at Harvard, it carried on the ideas pioneered by Gropius years earlier.

But Koch had the American eye. Its gabled roof and overhanging eaves tie this house to a traditional form which few Americans were willing to relinquish. At the same time, it obviously is modern. Its prefabrication included "sandwich panels" which combined vertical wood siding, insulation, and interior finish in a modular unit interspersed with panels of glass.

Gropius had taught that the architect must become both industrial designer and builder if he is to retain command of the product in a technological age. By establishing his own fac-

286. The Dymaxion House: *Dymaxion II, Beech Aircraft Co., Wichita, Kan., 1944. R. Buckminster Fuller, designer.*

287. The Geodesic Dome: *Peasedome Prefabricated House Kit, Designer's Own House, Carbondale, Ill., 1959. R. Buckminster Fuller, designer.*

tory, Koch was able to shepherd his houses through the technical pitfalls of mass production, the sales problems of mass distribution, and the vagaries of local building codes, without compromising quality.

286. Few American designers were as dedicated to prefabrication as Walter Gropius. A notable exception is maverick inventor R. Buckminster Fuller, who has spent a lifetime adapting the house to technology. This totally factory-fabricated dwelling was developed by Fuller for Beech Aircraft at the close of World War II. A revised version of his 1927 idea for a Dymaxion House (he combined the words "dynamic" and "maximum" to get the name), the structure was a pilot model, never put into production.

It remains, however, the most advanced house ever built in America. Poised on a central mast, its 12,000 cubic feet of living space could be quickly erected anywhere without foundations. Operating as a "closed system," it was independent of city water, electricity, and sewage. Its innovations included a stamped-out, one-piece bathroom; a mechanized kitchen and laundry; a recirculating, self-cleaning water system; and a compressed-air, automatic vacuum cleaning element (just flip the switch). Though not air conditioned, its insulating and ventilating systems were so efficient that the interior remained cool in full sun with temperature in the 90s. Shipped knocked-down in a cylindrical packing tube by truck, train, or plane it would have cost (had it been available in 1944) $6,500. Though the phrase was used to describe the International Style, it is the Dymaxion House by Fuller which really was a "machine for living in."

287. This neat little package is one of literally hundreds of variations of Buckminster Fuller's greatest triumph: the geodesic dome. Unlike his Dymaxion House, which was a fully equipped dwelling, the dome is a prefabricated structural system—merely rigid sticks, their connectors, and filler panels—which can be, and has been, used for buildings of all types and sizes from the U.S. Pavilion at Expo '67 to counterculture communes.

The geodesic dome is a realization of Fuller's life-long goal: the creation of the most from the

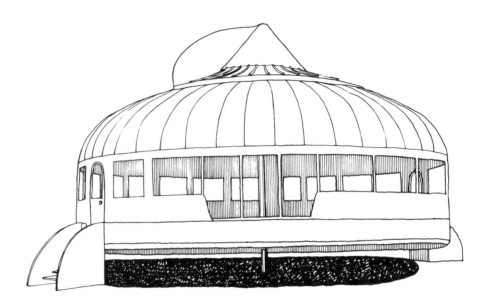

least. Classified as a "space frame," it is fundamentally different from the traditional post and lintel system in which weights and stresses are focused on supporting posts. In a geodesic dome, all members work together to diffuse stresses throughout the structure and thus combine great strength with light weight. Savings follow in materials, labor, and cost.

Filler panels can be almost anything: plexiglass, wood, aluminum, vinyl, waterproofed paperboard. An Illinois example used beer cans (with the ends cut out) between sheets of fiberglass. Totally and partially transparent domes have been built. Though unlike the cubistic International Style in appearance, both the dome and the Dymaxion used (however incidentally) the principles of continuity and regularity and the "stretched skin" enclosure which were part of the idiom.

The Glass House

288. A Universal Architecture: *Dr. Maria Farnsworth House, Plano, Ill., designed 1946; built 1950. Ludwig Mies van der Rohe, architect.*

288. This crystalline box, floating serenely above uninterrupted lawn, is the tour de force of world-famous modernist Mies van der Rohe, who spent a lifetime removing nonessentials from architecture.

His goal was an anonymous, industrialized, generalized way of building which could be used in any location for any type of structure. Mies called his system "skin and bones" architecture: simply a steel or steel-and-concrete frame with curtain walls of glass, brick, or opaque panels. This is its domestic version, a testament to the famous Mies dictum, "Less is more."

Glass walls are an example. By reducing the Farnsworth house to a transparent shell, the architect has extended its visual boundaries to the seasons themselves. To augment the effect, he also has subtracted color. The steel skeleton and plaster ceiling are painted white; the floor is travertine; curtains off-white raw silk. "When you have a white house with glass walls," Mies explained, "you see the trees and bushes and the sky framed in white—and the white emphasizes all the beautiful colors in the landscape."

Dematerialization of the walls also adds flexibility. An enclosure of wood or masonry cannot be manipulated, but glass permits a choice. With curtains open, one's habitat is nature itself. Close the curtains and one is inside a silken cocoon, a technological tent which cuts off the out-of-doors while admitting a soft, filtered light.

In plan, too, what has been subtracted changes to Miesian addition. Rooms as such have been eliminated. One large, unbroken space is divided into separate areas simply by the placement of furniture. Except for kitchen, fireplace, and bath, the interior can be shifted at will, the "living room" expanded for entertaining or contracted for coziness simply by moving lightweight tables and chairs. This is Mies's "universal space" which, he believed, bestows the ultimate freedom on its tenant.

Unfortunately, in his pursuit of the universal, Mies failed to consider the specifics of site,

289. A Classic Interpretation: *Architect's Own House, New Canaan, Conn., 1949. Philip Johnson, architect; Richard Kelly, lighting consultant.*

climate, and client. As a result, the owner sued the architect. On moving into her new house, Dr. Farnsworth discovered that the unbeautiful clutter of daily living was universally exposed to view. More vital, the house had no operable windows and only one entrance; hence, no cross-ventilation. No eaves sheltered the glass walls. Air conditioning, which would seem to be fundamental to such a design, had not been included. The house proved unbearably hot in the sizzling midwestern summer. As a last straw, the terrace, which was to have served as an outdoor living room, was made unusable by mosquitoes. To the distress of the architect, the owner screened it in, thus destroying the open, floating quality of the design. In her famous case (she lost), Dr. Farnsworth maintained that

she had paid too much for a universal perfection which had proved to be imperfect after all.

289. When architects talk about "the glass house," this is the one they mean. The famous home of architect Philip Johnson was built a year before the Farnsworth house—though designed after it and admittedly derived from it. But while taking the idea of transparency from his friend and mentor, Johnson made the glass house work.

In his design, each wall has its own center door so that one can enter or leave from any direction. On all sides, operable window sashes provide cross-ventilation. In these ways, the house has been made virtually porous, catching

every breeze.

To temper sun and wind and provide a sense of shelter, there are two lines of defense. The first is a set of separately adjustable window shades. The second is the studied grouping of trees which nearly surrounds the house. The trees shade the interior during the day, act as windbreaks, and are the visual walls of the house. Floodlighted at night, they create a brilliant horseshoe of foliage within which the house reposes. Lights are on a dimmer system so that infinitely varied effects can be achieved. The Johnson house also breaks new ground in rejecting asymmetry—a fundamental tenet of the International Style—in favor of formal balance, a "resonance" from the classic past.

The International Style

The Mies Idiom

290. The Stock Part House: *Designer's Own House, Pacific Palisades, Calif., 1950. Charles Eames, designer.*

290. In the early 1950s, the glass house was the most exciting thing in architecture. However, few besides Mies and Johnson were willing to opt for total transparency. Here, the late Charles Eames, one of America's most imaginative designers, has taken the Mies system of steel frame and curtain wall and played with it like a child's erector set.

To demonstrate how simple it all was, Eames ordered lightweight factory parts which could be bolted together on the site. Into the completed modular framework, like a series of delicate Japanese shoji screens, he set wall panels in a beautifully composed interplay of transparency, translucency, and brilliant primary color; of large surfaces and small divided panes. In our illustration, black areas are clear glass; narrow stripes are frosted glass; dotted panels are stucco, painted white, red, blue, or yellow—all strategically interwoven to control or admit sun and provide privacy or view where desired.

The larger block is the house proper, containing a two-story living room, overlooked by a bedroom balcony at right under which are a fireplace alcove, dining room, and kitchen. The smaller building is an open two-story studio plus a one-story photographic darkroom with second-floor storage above.

Though not a professional architect, Eames designed nearly everything: buildings, world's fair exhibits, movies, toys, furniture (including his first and greatest success, the Eames molded plywood chair). In this house, he used a simple system of factory-fabricated parts which, even a quarter of a century later, offers an exciting potential.

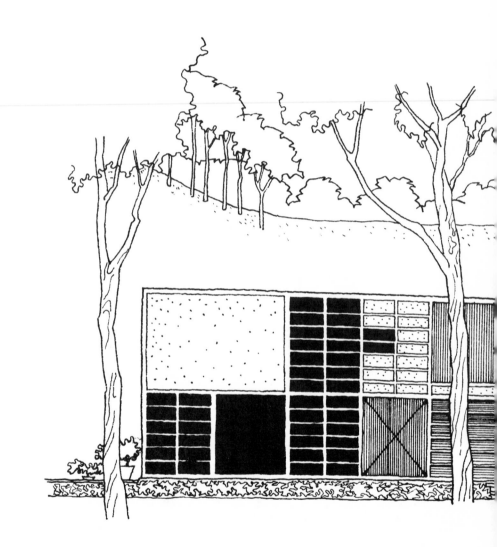

290. The Stock Part House: *Designer's Own House, Pacific Palisades, Calif., 1950. Charles Eames, designer.*

The International Style

Modifying the Glass Wall

291. The Stone Baffle: *Architect's Own House, New Canaan, Conn., 1956-57. Eliot Noyes, architect.*

291a. Plan, Noyes House

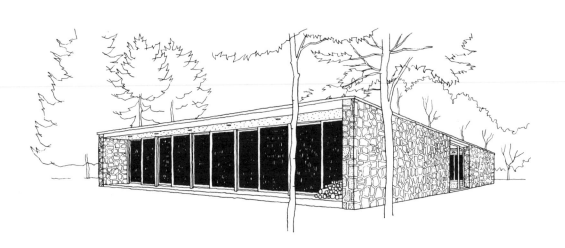

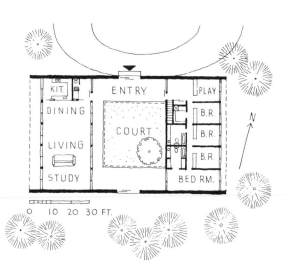

291. This design for rural New England is, in effect, two separate glass houses, sandwiched between fieldstone walls. Entrances at both sides lead to a central courtyard which separates the "houses"—one a large, open family living area; the other a bedroom wing which includes a children's playroom and snack bar.

One of many modifications of the totally transparent house which appeared during the 1950s, this design enjoys the best of two worlds: the sense of solidity and security afforded by stone walls plus the intimate enjoyment of nature which only transparency can give. Sliding glass panels are so designed that both units of the house can be thrown widely open in warm weather. The solid stone walls, extending beyond the glass, baffle house and courtyard from winter wind and act to absorb solar heat.

Designed by Eliot Noyes, a Gropius-trained graduate of Harvard, this example shows how the second generation of International Style architects were working within the rules but modifying them slightly to create their own type of American house.

292. In this Florida beach cottage, Paul Rudolph—another of the new crop of Harvard-trained architects—took the idea of the transparent house and solved its problems with a series of exterior plywood flaps, hinged at the roofline and sized to cover the wall below. Easily operated with pulleys and counterweights and fitting snugly into an exterior overhead framework, each one can be fully opened, fully closed, or adjusted to any intermediate position.

The real walls of the house are totally transparent. Each side contains one fixed glass panel; all others are filled with plastic screening. When flaps are raised, they act as awnings, shielding the interior from sun or rain but permitting a free flow of air. They also create sheltered "porches" all around the house. For privacy, cold weather, or if the house is not in use, it can be closed like a box and the flaps secured. Fashioned out of little more than a wooden frame, plywood panels, screening, and a minimum of glass, this beach house also was kind to the client's pocketbook.

293. The grille—one of the most effective methods of modifying the glass wall—was introduced to modern architecture by Edward Durrell Stone, and it soon became his hallmark. A traditional device in tropical climates, it acts to cut direct sun, reduce glare, and ensure privacy while allowing the circulation of air and permitting occupants a view from the inside out.

In this design, the second-story grille is set out from glass and masonry walls which comprise the real enclosure of the house. At rear, it continues on to enclose a large second-story terrace, open to the master bedroom. The lower story includes a dining room with a circular marble platform above a small lagoon and a living room adjoining an elliptical indoor swimming pool.

The extended roof is set several feet above the ceiling and acts as a natural breezeway to dissipate heat. A similar extension of the floor of the second story shades lower walls and terraces. Both the ornamental grillework and extended roofs represent heresies against the International Style, yet they conform to the adage of America's own early modernists that "form follows function."

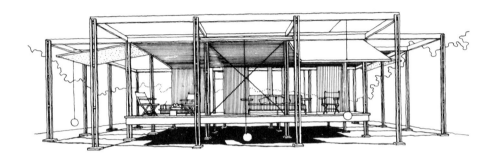

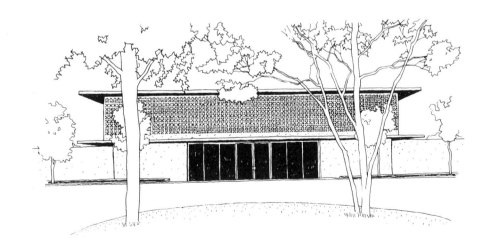

The International Style

Modifying the American House

294. The Hip-Roofed House: *Samuel Riker, Jr., House, Holmdel, N.J., 1940. Livingstone Elder and Michael Hare, architects.*

295. The Gable-Roofed House: *S. Brooks Barron House, Detroit, Mich., 1957. Yamasaki, Leinweber & Assoc., architects; Edward A. Eichstedt, landscape architect.*

296. An Oregon Vernacular: *Year-Round Vacation House, Netarts Bay, Ore., 1942. Pietro Belluschi, F.A.I.A., architect.*

297. A California Ranch House: *Albert Smith House, Stockton, Calif., 1949-50. Wurster, Bernardi & Emmons, architects.*

294. While some architects were modifying the International Style to solve the problems of the glass wall, others were modifying existing American house types, inserting glass walls into familiar houses.

Here, the durable silhouette of the classic, hip-roofed cube (Figure 127) has been used as the basis for a modern house. However, proportions have been horizontalized and classic balance abandoned. Substituted is the principle of "regularity" by which modular sizes of window and solid wall are interspersed in an asymmetrical composition. Horizontal siding, more precise than clapboards, follows another rule of the International Style, reaching for the effect of a taut, stretched "skin." The extensive use of glass, upstairs and down, fulfills the ideal of "transparency."

Broken rules are seen in the traditional overhanging hipped roof and the color of the wood walls, stained brown instead of painted white. This hybrid design represents an American domestication of the International Style, familiar, warm, and inviting.

295. The gabled roof of this house was a zoning requirement forced on one of America's leading modern architectural firms. However, within this traditional form, the architects have used the principles of the International Style—regularity, transparency, and tautness—to create a thoroughly modern design, yet one which blends with the traditional character of the neighborhood.

Facing the street is a two-story bedroom wing, joined at rear by the main living area of the house, which is only a single story. The two-story street frontage was a zoning requirement, one-story living the client's requirement—and both have been provided. With the garage at right, the house defines a courtyard, containing a reflecting pool, planting, and a wide roofed walk which connects all elements. A pierced brick wall at front gives privacy to this city house, which enjoys the trees, water, and planting of a suburban setting.

296. Pietro Belluschi's Oregon houses have been called "Belluschi's beautiful barns." Rooted in the wood building vernacular of the Pacific Northwest, they are also polished examples of modern architecture.

This one is designed around three sides of a courtyard with a sheltered walkway connecting dwelling and garage (right). Such a plan is reminiscent of the Spanish ranch house of California (Figure 123) and also of Belluschi's own Italian heritage with its use of loggias and courts. The vernacular architecture of the Pacific Northwest comes through in traditional gabled roofs, but eaves barely project beyond the building line in the taut aesthetic of the International Style. The living room at center is almost totally transparent, with walls of glass opening toward the ocean at front and to the patio at rear.

Belluschi is justly famous for his use of wood as

an intrinsic decorative element. Here, he has played vertical and horizontal siding against each other to create patterning within simple building forms. The use of various woods— rough-sawn spruce for siding, slices of cedar logs for courtyard paving, other woods in the inlaid door—juxtapose color and texture in a subtle beauty close to the Japanese.

297. William Wilson Wurster, head of the firm which designed this house, was a pioneer modernist who helped fuse California tradition and the International Style into a new kind of regional modern architecture. This example is basically a Spanish ranch house with the traditional porch across the front (Figure 122). It also is a study in the use of wood. The exposed structural system is Douglas fir; walls are vertical cedar siding; ceilings redwood, rough-sawn to create an interesting texture. The naturally contrasting colors of the woods are brought out with a clear preservative on the exterior and with wax on the interior of the house. This continuity of material inside and out is a lesson reapplied from the International Style. Also from that idiom are the flat roof, crisp, clean-cut detailing, and the wall of windows behind the sheltering porch. New in domestic architecture is the monitor roof, long used in industry to illuminate large interior spaces. Here, a deep roof overhang was necessary to shelter the glass wall from the scorching sun of the San Joaquin Valley, thus darkening the interior. The two clerestories provide gentle illumination deep inside the house.

The International Style

A New Direction

298. A Usonian Home: *Goetsch-Winkler House, Okemos, Mich., 1939. Frank Lloyd Wright, architect.*

299. The Articulated House: *Architect's Own House, New Canaan, Conn., 1947. Marcel Breuer, architect.*

This is a "Usonian Home," Wright's name for a series of low-cost houses designed to demonstrate that modest size and price (this one cost $9,500 in 1939) need not produce a crackerbox. Interior spaces are "articulated"— separately expressed on the exterior—a fundamental of Wright's work that had been absorbed by the International Style but would be neglected during its romance with the glass box. It also incorporates a remarkable reach into both the past and the future. Wright—who has been called "the last Victorian"—has divided the house into horizontal bands, a link to the nineteenth-century Queen Anne Style (Figure 209) that was a continuing element in his work. At the same time, in its breaking of the box, this house and others designed by Wright during the forties and fifties would influence the new direction of American architecture.

299. During the late 1940s and 1950s, in response to Wright and other American influences, the International Style underwent a subtle metamorphosis. One of the men who changed it was Hungarian-born Marcel Breuer, who had been Master of the Carpentry Shop at the Bauhaus during that school's exciting early years. Brought to Harvard by Walter Gropius and a partner with the elder man before establishing his own practice, Breuer was steeped in the original principles of European modernism.

His architecture, however, did not contain itself entirely within the smooth continuous envelope typical of the International Style. Increasingly, he emphasized another of its tenets: "articulation," i.e., the expression of separate elements of a building in distinct forms. In this house, for example, the white-painted concrete understructure, containing utilities, acts as the load-bearing foundation. Cantilevered out from it, the house proper is a light wooden box, inset with a ribbon of glass. Hung from this is a bedroom balcony, secured by tension cables. All are treated as separate elements, distinct from each other. The house also is distinct from its site, set down lightly, as if loath to disturb the natural environment. Above all, it has a new, tough, vigorous look which would come forward more than a decade later and dominate the 1960s, just as variations on the fragile glass box dominated the 1950s.

298. Though Frank Lloyd Wright lost few opportunities to denounce the International Style, his work was subtly influenced by it. This house displays the clean lines, flat roofs, and precise details that were intrinsic to European modernism. However, these have been expressed in a warm fabric of brick and wood, with broad eaves extending out to shelter runs of windows and, at rear, a carport (Wright invented it). Note that the brick lower wall projects as it passes under the casement windows to form a built-in flower box.

260

300. The Essential House: *Morton Weiss House, East Morristown, Pa., 1949. Louis I. Kahn, architect.*

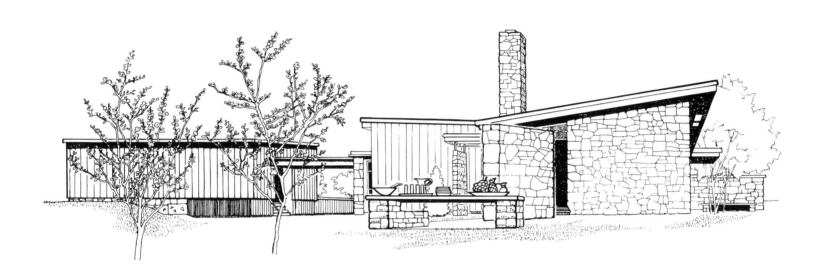

300. No less than Breuer, Louis Kahn Americanized the International Style. Here, the flat-roofed cube is gone; so is the continuous surface enclosure. Wood frame and curtain wall construction has been interspersed with bearing walls of stone. Missing also is the machine aesthetic which deliberately gave every piece of architecture the look of an industrialized product.

This is a house organized around a central fireplace, from which, under an ascending roof, it opens to distant views. This side, more or less solidly enclosed, contains the living-dining-kitchen nucleus. Beyond, a bedroom wing is physically secluded. These living and sleeping units are served by a central entrance hall which gives onto small sheltered courtyards between them. Garage and workroom are at far left, joined to the house by a roofed walk. Kahn's architecture is a blend of contradictory influences. This house combines the use of natural materials typical of Frank Lloyd Wright with the crisp, stripped-down handling which remains in tune with the International Style. His "articulation" of the distinct areas of the house à la Breuer reflects, in a new way, the Louis Sullivan dictum "form follows function."

Giving the design its special quality is Louis Kahn's own mystical philosophy summed up in his coined word, "ina," meaning the individual essence which he believed everything possesses, whether a person, a stone, a piece of wood, or a concept such as "home." In architecture, his goal was to express the intrinsic character of a building type, its parts, and its materials. In the Weiss house, stone has been built into heavy, windowless enclosures—an embodiment of strength and stability—giving a sense of protection to the living room. Wood has been made into a thin, drumlike box which floats the dining room on piers. Roof planes slant down to create a snug retreat at the central hearth, up as the living room opens to distant views. Stonework is sent skyward to create the essential chimney stack. Even though the forms are new, Kahn's elements are a summation of home.

17

Chapter 17

The Shifting Scene

During the 1950s, the International Style reached its American apogee, though the competing form of modern architecture, developed on the ''organic'' principles of Louis Sullivan and Frank Lloyd Wright, had never been entirely vanquished. Inspired by Marcel Breuer and Louis Kahn, there now occurred a rapprochement, a borrowing back and forth which resulted in something not quite like either.

Many basic principles laid down by older European modernists remained as guiding themes. But one rule after another would be broken in increasingly experimental designs. All sorts of paths were explored. New materials and new structural systems, developed during World War II for lightweight aircraft and similar necessities, now were applied to houses, producing new and startling forms. Old systems would be used in ''brutal'' ways, negating the delicacy, lightness, and smooth-flowing continuity which had been basic to the original International mystique. Eventually, the mystique itself—the ideal of beauty through technology—would be attacked by a new avant-garde, touting the jazzy and the banal. In the 1960s, the children of modern architecture—like children everywhere—were turning on their parents.

In the thirty-five years following World War II, the modern house in America has been freely experimental; pristinely pure; regionally adaptive; symbolically expressive; technologically innovative; aesthetically brutal; nostalgically Corbusian; super-graphically pop-banal; and now, facing the realities of continuing inflation and high-priced energy, experimental once more. Only one thing seems certain: the house of the future will not be what the pioneers of modern architecture had supposed.

The Shifting Scene

The New Roof

301. The Butterfly Roof: *House in the Museum Garden, Museum of Modern Art, New York, N.Y., 1949. Marcel Breuer, architect.*

302. The Airplane Roof: *Architect's Own House, Rye, N.Y., 1955. Ulrich Franzen, architect.*

303. A Different Butterfly: *Architect's Own House, Cambridge, Mass., 1958. José Luis Sert, architect.*

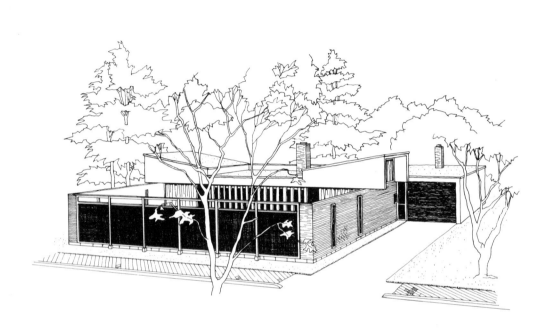

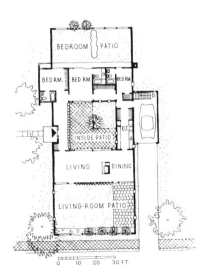

301. During the same years in which architects were experimenting with the walls of the house, they began to redesign the roof. This illustration shows the famous demonstration house erected in the garden of the Museum of Modern Art and introducing what was promptly dubbed the "butterfly roof."[15] Designed by one of the leading architects of the International Style, this mock-up broke the shibboleth of the cube. Once the roof plane was broken, so was the restraining chrysalis which had so firmly contained the style itself.

The traditional gable still was verboten; but Breuer had reversed the pitch, providing an interior downspout to carry runoff water. The major roof plane rose to two-story height at the end of the house where a balcony bedroom for parents overlooked the living room, leaving space beneath for a garage. Children's bedrooms were in the smaller one-story wing at right, with kitchen and playroom separating them from the main living quarters. The zoned house, with parents' and children's areas kept

physically apart, preserved, Breuer believed, a degree of sanity in the servantless small house.

302. Once the flat roof had proven breakable, ever more radical ideas appeared to reshape it. New lightweight structural systems and new methods of lamination, bonding, and ending had been developed by the aircraft industry during World War II. Now they were applied to the house. This roof is designed on the principle of an airplane wing: a framework of diamond-shaped light steel trusses covered by a waterproof skin. The underside, where it is exposed on the interior as a ceiling, is surfaced with fir boarding. It provides the familiar pitch of a traditional gable inside the house, coupled with an opposing skyward thrust over the terrace.

The rest of this design reverts to the by now familiar principles of European modernism. Steel frame and curtain wall construction allows the roof to be supported entirely by eight freestanding columns. Walls bear no loads; consequently, they are made of glass placed free of column supports. Brick terrace walls give a sense of enclosure. Canvas room dividers act as semipartitions within this free-flowing space.

303. Yet another master of modern architecture, Jose Sert, redesigned the butterfly roof when he built his own residence as Dean of Harvard's Graduate School of Design. Sert made use of the slant to place an unexpected slot of window at either end of a long, narrow room. Ascent occurs above the dining area (right) and part of the living area (left). The lower roof level creates a snug center by the fireplace.

With this design, Sert also demonstrated a pet theory, i.e., the practicality of walled courts carried to the building line for the small dwelling on a minimum lot. This one has a large outer courtyard, as pictured here; a secluded inner court around which rooms are organized; and a fenced bedroom patio at the opposite end of the house. Though built as a single unit, the house was designed to be deployed in groups of eight to the acre (Sert also designed two-story versions), thus freeing land for a small park, a playground, or other communal uses. With the increasing pressure on land during the 1960s, the idea was received enthusiastically by the building industry, and the "townhouse" (though scarcely resembling this one) was born.

The Shifting Scene

The New Geometry

304. The Arcaded Roof: *Unidentified House, 1958. John MacL. Johansen, Architect.*

305. The Laminated Arch: *Samuel H. Herron, Jr., House, Venice, Fla., 1956. Victor Lundy, architect.*

304. This romantic idyll, its living-dining room a glass-enclosed bridge across a woodland stream, is yet another departure from the rectilinear. Its vaulting is "restrained plywood," i.e., plywood bent and anchored into place, a spinoff from the development of high-strength plastic glues and laminates during World War II. The central bridge has been given glass walls, enveloping its occupants in shimmering water, rocky outcroppings, and the seasonal changes of a New England woods. Four solidly walled wings contain, respectively, the master bedroom, other family bedrooms, a study with its own walled court, the kitchen, and the maid's room. The severe, flat-roofed, modern idiom reappears here but only as counterpoint to the vaulted bridge. Instead of white surfaces, there are color and luster. The exterior is a soft terra-cotta stucco; the underside of the roof vaults gold leaf. Terrazzo floors and ebonized wood cabinets add to the warmth and richness of this luxurious house. At the same time, it shows how experiments of all sorts were using new technology to demonstrate the all but unlimited possibilities of modern design.

305. Victor Lundy made the sculptural potential of laminated wood the basis for his architecture. Here, he worked with plywood, which the new glues had made comparable to steel in strength and to concrete in fluidity. Columns and beams flow into each other in six, great laminated pine arches, supporting a roof of fir decking. The warm, natural color of the varnished wood contrasts with walls of glass and textured brick set inside the arches as a freestanding enclosure. A circular living-dining room is at the center, surrounded by an outer ring containing bedrooms, den, kitchen, and maid's room, with screened porches, front and rear. All spaces can be opened to each other. In normal use, however, curtains and sliding glass panels provide privacy. The lavish use of drapery gives this interior the look of a silken tent.

306. Shell construction, in which the functions of support and enclosure are amalgamated into a single, continuous curved plane, is a radical departure from frame and curtain wall construction.

In executing this revolutionary design, Eduardo Catalano used nothing more exotic than fir flooring strips, fastened together in three layers

306. The Warped Shell: *Architect's Own House, Raleigh, N.C., 1954-55. Eduardo Catalano, architect; Atilio Gallo, structural engineer.*

307. The Brise Soleil: *Arthur W. Milam House, St. John's County, Fla., 1962. Paul Rudolph, architect.*

with nails. The wood stripping was exposed on the underside as the ceiling but was protected on the exterior by a roofing of plastic-on-glass fiber. A steel fascia absorbs outward compression stresses along all edges of the roof. At its low points, hinged steel joints, imbedded in concrete buttresses, anchor the soaring structure to earth.

The resulting performance is spectacular. The shell is supported at only two points; it is but 2¼ inches thick; it spans 87 feet, 6 inches. By contrast, a 2¼-inch plank deck supported by conventional posts safely spans no more than 8 feet. Equally as astonishing is the cost: only $10,000 for the major enclosure, or $2.50 per square foot—an unusually low figure even for 1955.

307. The Milam House represents the culmination of the countertrend to Miesian frame and curtain wall construction and to the glass box. Its interior is broken into a variety of heights and depths. Its flat roof is dropped to create a sunken deck. Its facade is patterned by a system of projecting "sunbreakers," the *brise soleil,* a device pioneered by Le Corbusier to temper the glass wall, shading the spaces behind it while permitting clear views.

The theme of the Milam House is the manipulation of space, what architect Paul Rudolph calls his "cave and fishbowl" effect. The fishbowl is the high-ceilinged, glass-fronted, two-story living room, part of which is a stepped-down seating pit. Caves include a rear dining alcove tucked under a balcony; an inglenook under a dropped ceiling at left; a similar library corner to the right. This interweaving of vertical and horizontal spaces and the dramatic shift from small areas to large, was, in its own way, a return to earlier work of both Le Corbusier and Wright.

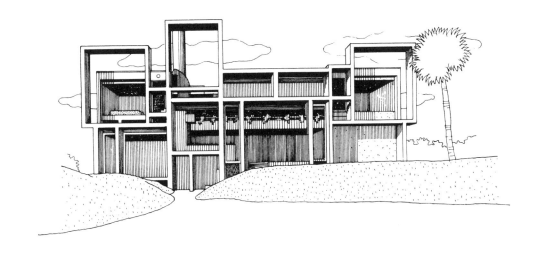

The Shifting Scene

The New Brutalism

308. The Concrete Frame: *Architect's Own House, Pittsburgh, Pa., 1963. Tasso Katselas, architect.*

309. The Continuous Wall: *Architects' Own House, Lincoln, Mass., 1965. Thomas F. McNulty and Mary Otis Stevens (McNulty), architects. After a photograph by David Plowden.*

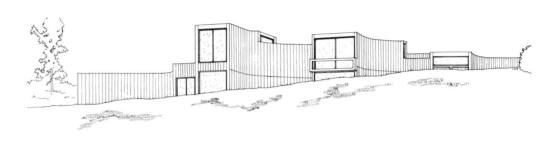

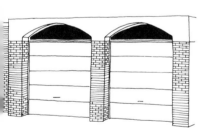

308. This house is an Americanized version of Le Corbusier's Maisons Jaoul, in which that pioneer modernist reversed the characteristics of delicacy, smoothness, and continuity which had defined the early International Style. Here, the concrete frame is heavy and blunt, brick walls solid and uncompromising, forms bold, surfaces discontinuous.

Large wall areas of brick, coupled with the set-back of glass into canopied recesses, give the interior an unusual sense of protective enclosure and shelter it against north wind and summer sun. Inside the fortress, there is, surprisingly, a feeling of freedom and aerial lightness which comes mainly from a dramatic "floating" living room at the upper level—an enlarged balcony jutting out into space on three sides. Glass panels and decks which extend the interior into the out-of-doors add to the effect. Despite the drama of interior space, it is the handling of form and materials which is novel here. This way of building has been given the satirical yet descriptive name "The New Brutalism," and it presaged a new era in architectural design.

309. Direct, primitivistic handling of materials, deliberately without grace or polish, is one of the distinguishing features of "The New Brutalism" and of this house designed by a husband and wife for their own home. Also characteristic is the rejection of nearly total transparency—the re-emphasis of solid wall over glass and the use of chunky, drumlike towers and spyglass windows which project from the long axis of the house.

Each projection contains a room, whether jutting out or up from the long axis or occupying the flaring ends of the house. Along the center, space becomes an open passage, flowing into and out of each succeeding room, vertically as well as horizontally. Except for baths and guest rooms, there are no doors and few partitions in the entire 150-foot length of the bi-level house. Yet because of the deeply curved walls, most rooms are effectively isolated from one another.

The continuity of this house, with its curves and sweeps of wall and its smooth transition into blunt-ended projections, is highly sculptural, a reflection, once more, of new work by Le Corbusier. Its intricate spatial flow set it ahead of the most advanced designs of the 1950s and vividly demonstrates that a whole new way of putting a house together had appeared on the American scene.

The Shifting Scene

The Shed/Shingle Revival

310. A House Is A House: *Cyril B. Jobson House, Palo Colorado Canyon, Calif., 1962. Charles Moore, architect.*

311. The Cluster House: *"A House Near the Harbor," Bristol, R.I., 1967. Hugh Newell Jacobsen, architect.*

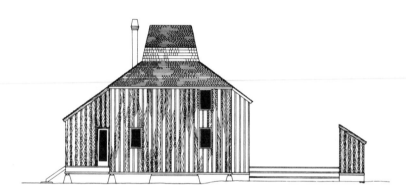

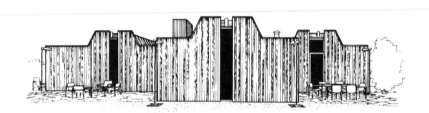

310. This design would appear to have started from a very ordinary American dwelling: the hip-roofed, boxy house which had entered the vernacular as part of the Georgian Revival of the early twentieth century (Figure 140).

However, this one is anything but ordinary. Eaves have been brought tautly in to the wall line. Small windows are punched like carefully calculated holes in the expanse of solid wall, perfectly sensible openings for what lies behind: a sleeping alcove (left), bathroom (right), sleeping loft (upper story). But their detailing is neither traditional nor modern in the accepted sense. On the opposite side of the house, the living room fronts on a spectacular canyon view, breaking open with glass walls and a deep porch, recessed, however, to keep the taut wall line and provide shelter in any weather. Most striking of all is what has happened to the hipped roof, made unfamiliar by an oversized monitor skylight which creates a silhouette like a farmer's broad-brimmed hat.

This is strikingly like Hugo Haering's design for a post-World War I hat factory, part of the search for expressive forms which appeared in Germany before the International Style came to dominance. In America, in the 1960s, it represented a deliberate rejection of the International rule book and a search for new inspiration in distortions of the vernacular, particularly shed, shingled, and cottage types. Casual and deceptively familiar in appearance, it is actually a very sophisticated piece of architecture and more functional than much so-called functional architecture. Its designer, Charles Moore, at one time head of the School of Architecture at Yale University, was enormously influential in changing the direction of American architecture.

311. The "clustering" of forms was part of the architecture of the 1960s. The famous Sea Ranch condominium (not shown) grouped houses together in an informal, shedlike massing. Here, a single house is fragmented. Each room becomes a clearly defined pavilion for a specific activity. The units are organized as a repetition of the same form, like an enlarging crystal.

Visible here are the living room (left), kitchen (right), and the dining room, which projects at center. On the opposite side, beyond a hallway, is a similar grouping: three more pavilions containing a library and two bedrooms. With this scheme, the house is divided into active and quiet areas, separated by a center hall.

Like the house by Charles Moore (Figure 310), this one echoes in its unusual roofline the slanted forms of German Expressionist Hugo Haering. The roofline also expresses interior space, shooting up from 8 feet at the periphery of each room to 11½ feet across the center. Accentuating the vertical is the slit window set in each wooden wall. Not visible are glass walls which open both sides of the projecting central dining room to the terraces pictured here. Other walls of glass open living room, library, and master bedroom to a harbor view. During the 1960s, architects had become concerned with the subtleties of space and sense and were attempting to design intangible experiences into the fabric of their houses.

312. This odd little beach house on the Jersey Shore was designed by a firm which has been stirring up the architectural establishment since the 1960s with what their critics call "Anti-

The Shifting Scene

Post-Modern Architecture: The Inclusivists

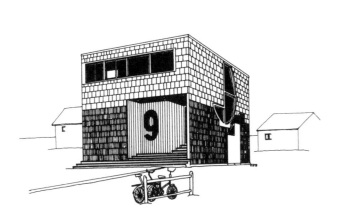

architecture'' and the ''Cult of the Ugly'' but which they prefer to label ''Inclusivist'' or ''Nonstraightforward'' architecture. Their work also has been nicknamed "Pop Architecture," after the "Pop Art" of the same period, and more recently, "Post-Modern Architecture."

The house illustrated here appears to be an ordinary, flat-roofed shed, surfaced with that anathema of modern design, wood-grained asbestos shingles. However, it is approached by a set of outsized entrance steps, decorated with a super-graphic street number and illuminated at the stairwell by a large fragmented window ''that looks like a 1930s loudspeaker'' (the words of Robert Venturi, the architect).

Where did such an array of heresies come from? As the name ''Inclusivist'' implies, the sources are many: ordinary twentieth-century tract housing; historic styles; modern architecture, especially the work of Le Corbusier, Louis Kahn, and Charles Moore (Figure 310); even the gaudy neon-land of the Las Vegas Strip (Venturi wrote a book, *Learning from Las Vegas*). Instead of creating forms which follow function, he opts for ornament, building what he calls ''decorated sheds'' as opposed to ''ducks,''[16] his name for expressive form.

This is deliberately ''banal'' and ''unbeautiful'' architecture, an ironic joke on both mass culture and the cult of the beautiful. But aesthetics aside, how do Venturi's buildings work? The answer is, very well. Those exaggeratedly broad steps are used by the Lieb children, their friends, and, on occasion, adults as a place to sit and talk, drink soda pop or eat popsicles, and watch the beach go by. The first room one enters at the downstairs level is a laundry room (washer and dryer at the ready) where bathing suits and wet towels can be dropped safely on the concrete floor. Bedrooms, opening off the laundry, double as dressing rooms. Up the stairs, one comes first to the kitchen for a snack, then into the living room where an interior wall of zigzag glass opens to a roof deck, made private by high, solid, wooden walls rather than the open railings used in nearby houses.

During this progression, the house packs a number of spatial surprises. For example, the stairway starts from a broad base, extending across the entire width of the house, shifting direction and decreasing in width as it rises to the second story. This is a small, noncurving version of a Baroque stairway, devoid of period flourishes. It gives this quite ordinary-looking

cottage a certain presence and makes entering it an experience.

313. This design and the Lieb house (Figure 312) show that the Inclusivist approach does not necessarily produce houses that look alike. Though both are Venturi's basic ''shed,'' this one has broad deep eaves, exaggerating the ''sense of shelter'' which such a roofline suggests. Picture windows after the popular subdivision type are coupled with a giant oculus, excerpted from classic tradition. The "decoration," which in this case includes the roof, is emphasized (or satirized) by a shift from normal size or context. This tough, mod architecture is repeating, in a peculiar twentieth-century way, the late Victorian period when decorative motifs were combined from many sources.

Recently, architects have gone beyond the decorated shed to include historic forms—for example, a Victorian villa with tower and turrets, otherwise bluntly and glassily modern (not shown for lack of space). Whether plaything or wave of the future, "Post-Modern" design has opened up a long-forbidden treasure house of inspiration.

The Shifting Scene

Neo-Modern Architecture:
The Exclusivists

314. Cubism Revisited: *R. Saltzman House, Long Island, N.Y., 1969. Richard Meier, architect; Carl Meinhardt, associate.*

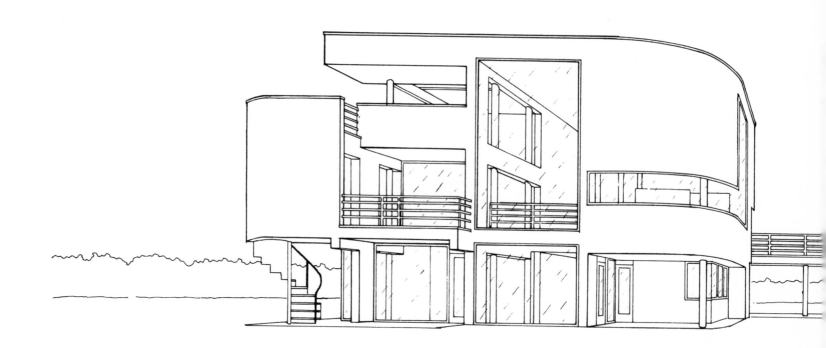

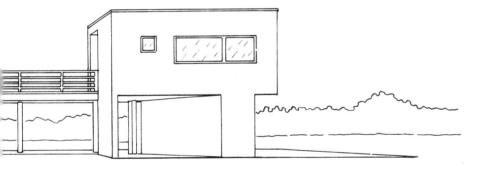

314. The Saltzman house is typical of the work of "The New York Five," a group of young New York City architects who decided to limit their designs to one source only: the pure International Style or early Le Corbusier, excluding changes which had taken place during the forty years just past. If this design were inserted next to Figures 279 and 280, it could easily be mistaken for an example of the International Style circa 1930. Here is Cubism revisited: almost, but not quite, a modern antique.

Included in its typical attributes are the flat roof; suppressed cornice; narrow strip windows set flush into the wall plane; smooth white surfaces inside and out; decks and balconies recessed inside the body of the house; precise and delicate balcony railings fashioned of metal tubing; free-standing, circular outside stairways.

This design, however, is considerably more complex than most early International Style houses in its manipulation of mass and space. It demonstrates that the work of "The Five" is more than the simple revival which it has been labeled. Believing that the pioneering thought and work of the Internationalists, especially Le Corbusier, offer a mine of ideas which has scarcely begun to be explored, they have utilized these as starting points. But within this "style," they too are innovators, using its concepts freely as a vocabulary for their own times.

The Shifting Scene

The Solar House

315. An Active Solar System: *The Solar Roof, Model 1950 Solar Cape, Saranac, N.Y., 1978. Acorn Structures Inc.*

The modern house as we know it—and also the traditional styles as they are built or have been remodeled today—are the offspring of technology and plenty. In 1974, the Arab states reminded us that both technology and plenty might some day run out of oil. Others have suggested that, if present trends in pollution continue, we might also run out of water and air.

The future, as of this writing, is unclear. On the supposition that we may have a problem, more and more alternate ways are being investigated for (among other things) building a house. Most of these are not new.

During the 1940s, James Marston Fitch, then an associate editor of *Architectural Forum* and now Professor of Architecture Emeritus at the Graduate School of Architecture and Planning, Columbia University, introduced the idea of "climatology." The enthusiasm for the un-shaded glass wall was then just reaching its height, and the air conditioning industry was gearing up for mass sales. Fitch proposed something rather different: designing the building itself and its surrounding landscape as a defense against the climate.

During those same years, Dr. Maria Telkes, a researcher at the Massachusetts Institute of Technology, designed, built, and successfully tested a solar house with the now familiar over-sized roof topped by a glass collector plate.

These two approaches—on the one hand adjusting the house to its specific region and site and on the other providing alternate sources of energy—could change the appearance of the house just as drastically as technology did during the first seventy-five years of the twentieth century. On the following pages, we show a few such experiments which already have been built.

316. A Passive Solar System: *The Trombe Wall, Vincent Polidero House, Landenberg, Pa., 1978. A Sunburst Solar Home, James Kries, designer and builder.*

316a. Diagram, Trombe Wall.

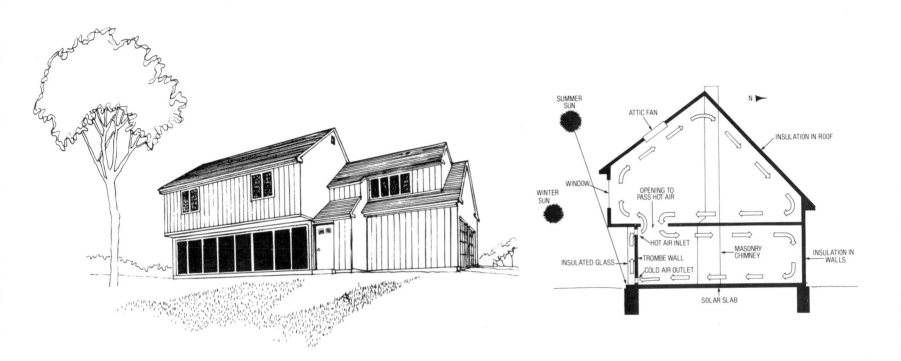

315. The south-facing rear roof of this prefabricated, updated Cape Cod cottage is angled at 47 degrees so that its flat-plate collectors can capture the maximum amount of heat from the sun. No figures are available for this New York State house, but during the severe winter of 1979, a similar Acorn solar house in Massachusetts provided 55 percent of all heating needs.

Though the house is based on familiar New England cottage forms, this is not a minimum design. Its front-facing living room opens to the deck through sliding glass doors. At rear, left to right, is the family room, dining room with bay window, a "mud-room" entrance, and a kitchen, connected by passage to the separate garage. There are four bedrooms, three baths, an upstairs dressing-sitting room, and a balconied hall that overlooks the dining room. Small

glazed roof panels are skylights.

Solar equipment, including a 2,000-gallon water storage tank in the cellar, adds approximately $8,000 to the cost of this model, partially balanced by a $2,000 Federal tax credit. Total price, exclusive of land, was $100,000 in 1978.

316. This house is one of a small development of passive solar dwellings using the "Trombe wall," named after the French physicist, Félix Trombe, who invented it. The lower story looks like the usual glass wall, but set six inches inside it is a 14-inch-thick masonry structure, painted black as it faces the glass. This Trombe wall is a passive solar collector, absorbing heat during the day and passing on excess to the 16-inch "solar slab" floor, both of which release heat at night. In addition, air between the glass and masonry walls is heated by the sun, rises

and enters the living area through vents at the top of the Trombe wall. These are equipped with one-way dampers which prevent warm air from passing out again. Cool air outlets at the base of the wall complete the loop of this self-circulating system. Rays from the high summer sun are prevented from entering by the three and a half-foot overhang of the upper story. Because there are no moving parts, no sophisticated solar hardware, no ducts, and no thermostatic controls, cost of the system is low and nothing can break or wear out. However, the Trombe wall can store heat for no more than 16 hours, so a back-up oil furnace and wood-burning stove have been installed, bringing the price of the house into the $70,000 range in 1978. During its first winter (October to May), the house used only $100 worth of oil and approximately one and a half cords of hardwood.

The Ground-Heated House

317. The Underground House: *Architect's Own House, Marston Mills, Mass., 1973. John Barnard, architect.*

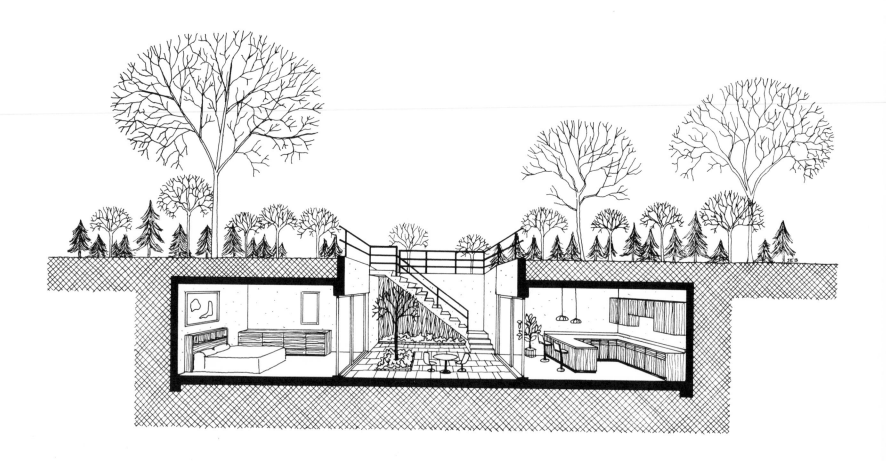

317. Like the troglodytes of Matmata in Africa, who live comfortably under the earth on the edge of the Sahara desert, architect John Barnard went underground on Cape Cod. Beneath several feet of earth, he created a sunny, airy, modern house, with sliding glass wall panels that open to a sunken atrium. Trees and sky are visible from all rooms. Illustrated here are the kitchen and bedroom with atrium between. Not seen in this cutaway drawing is the living room which extends along the near side of the house.

318. The Ground-Regulated House: *Builder's House, Colton, Calif., 1969. Passive Solar-Variant Homes; The Patented Savell System; Jesse J. Savell, Jr., designer-contractor.*

318a. Diagram, Savell System.

318b. Diagram, Wall Structure, Savell System.

As long ago as the 1950s, architect Paolo Soleri pioneered underground living in the Arizona desert, but it is equally suitable to a cold climate. Below the frostline, the earth maintains an average temperature of 54-57 degrees year-round. This becomes the constant "environment," against which mechanical heating and cooling work, rather than the extremes of temperatures above ground.

Barnard's Cape Cod house is warmed through frosty winters by a "rooftop" solar collector, plus a standard electrical resistance system, supplemented by a heat pump. It cost 25 percent less to build and costs 7 percent less to heat than a comparable above-ground house. Like all "earth-sheltered" homes, as their proponents prefer to call them, it is a noise-free, vibrationless dwelling, needing virtually no maintenance and leaving the natural environment all but undisturbed.

318. Though there are a growing number of enthusiasts for "earth-sheltered" houses, most Americans will choose to live above ground unless the price of fuel goes considerably higher.

This conventional California builder's house shows how the constant underground temperature can be tapped with another method. Searching for a system of precasting concrete walls to keep both slabs and joints from cracking, the contractor developed a sandwich of reinforced concrete, polyurethane foam insulation, and stucco exterior surfacing. To his surprise, in a hot California summer, the houses stayed pleasantly cool without air conditioning.

Savell had stumbled on the "wick-up" phenomenon. His insulation had been applied to the *outside* of the concrete wall slab. With massive concrete floors and foundations set deep into the ground, he had tapped below the constant temperature line; and the cool underground temperature of 54-57 degrees had "wicked up" to equalize the concrete structure of his house at 68 degrees. This approximate temperature is maintained both summer and winter, cutting the cost of fuel 60 percent. By contrast, houses with insulation *inside* (the usual practice) equalize at outdoor temperatures, requiring much artificial heating or cooling to make them livable.

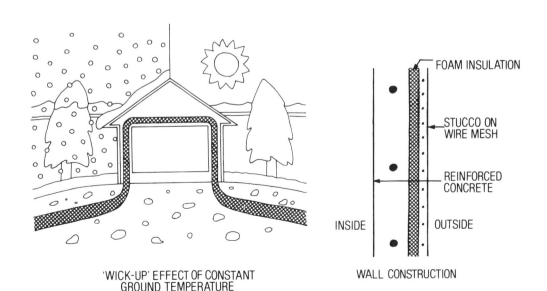

'WICK-UP' EFFECT OF CONSTANT GROUND TEMPERATURE

WALL CONSTRUCTION

FOAM INSULATION

STUCCO ON WIRE MESH

REINFORCED CONCRETE

INSIDE

OUTSIDE

The Shifting Scene

The Air-Loop House

319. The Self-Cooling House: *Prototype Farmhouse, San Joaquin Valley, Calif., A Computer-Designed Mock-Up. Department of Architecture, University of California; 1969. Project Team: Henry Sanoff, Chairman; Tyrus Porter, Amos Rapoport, Patrick Morreau.*

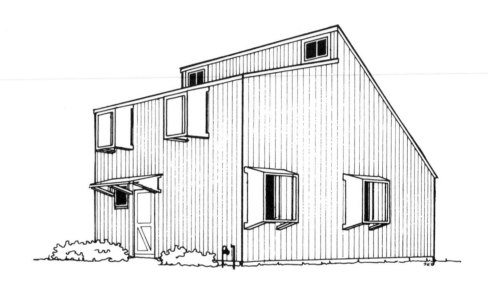

319. The goal: a minimum-cost house providing—without air conditioning—the maximum comfort in an oppressively hot climate. The astonishing result: a comparatively cool living-dining room, kitchen, three bedrooms, and bath at a cost (in 1969) of only $8,000.

The design team for this project collected data on workers' wages and living patterns; thermal properties of materials; local temperature ranges and patterns of air movement; and the impact of solar heat. They fed these into a computer and out came guidelines for a design: two stories; white walls and roof; few windows, small and shaded from direct sun; specific pitches for air movement both inside and outside the house; and low inlet windows at rear, coupled with high outlets across the center of the roof.

The computer placed second-story bedrooms in a half loft, leaving part of the living room open to the steeply slanting rear roof which directs hot air to ventilators at the top of the house. The balcony also acts as a daytime heat baffle for the living room in this uninsulated dwelling. Based on the well-known principle that hot air rises and cool air falls, the shape of the structure itself, plus low inlets and high outlets, establishes an automatic system of air circulation. Unfortunately, this inexpensive, self-cooling house—a kind of instant vernacular architecture—has remained a project.

320. This self-heating, self-cooling house represents a totally new concept of thermal regulation. Its system may mark a breakthrough in the passive use of solar energy, for it is reported to do the job of heating and cooling year round, on sunny days or gray, without expensive solar panels or a back-up furnace—even though local building codes usually require the latter.

The similarity of silhouette between this example and the preceding Figure 319 is no accident. Lee Porter Butler, who developed its heating and cooling system, once studied under Professor Sanoff, the team chairman responsible for the other house, and both designs are based on the same principles of air circulation, directed by angled roof planes. However, this one employs a far more advanced thermal system.

Its method is an envelope of continuously circulating air that extends around the house. Twelve inches of air space separate the roof from the ceiling, the north wall from a separate interior wall, and the floor from earth fill beneath. Completing the loop on the south side is an attached greenhouse, the passive "solar collector," within which heated air rises to enter the roof space, falling along the rear roof slope and wall to the under-floor passage as it cools. From beneath the dwelling, air is pulled into the greenhouse once more through one-quarter inch spaces between floor boards, and the process starts again. Excess heat stores itself in the thick layer of insulated earth beneath the house.

At night the system automatically reverses, drawing warmth from the earth fill. In summer, high clerestory windows in the south side greenhouse are opened to release warm air, and low vents on the north side opened to admit outside air. The latter is drawn through the passage above the thermal fill, which now acts as a cooling agent. By means of its continuously moving envelope of air, the house maintains a comfortable temperature winter or summer. The system works in any climate and can be adapted to modern or traditional styles, but individual calculations must be made for each design. The greenhouse, an integral part of the scheme, adds to self-sufficiency, permitting the householder to grow his own fruits and vegetables if he wishes.

In an era of rising food and fuel costs, the old ideal of an independent domain once again is exerting a strong appeal. With this new type of solar dwelling, we may have come full circle, returning, with twentieth-century comforts intact, to an independence we had all but forgotten.

320. The Envelope House: *Tom Smith House, Olympic Valley, Calif., 1978. Lee Porter Butler, inventor and architectural consultant.*

320a. Diagram, The Envelope House.

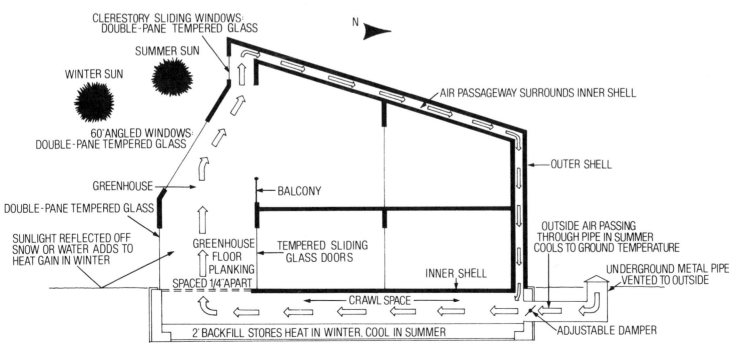

Notes

1. "Hardwick Hall, more glass than wall" refers to a stone manor house, but the comment applies equally to Elizabethan half-timbered dwellings.

2. Henry Chandlee Forman, *Architecture of the Old South*, Harvard University Press, Cambridge, Mass., 1948, p. 25.

3. Margaret Wood, *The English Medieval House*, Phoenix House, London, 1965, p. 219.

4. Ernest Allen Connally, "The Cape Cod House: An Introductory Study," *Journal of the Society of Architectural Historians*, Vol. XIX, No. 2, May 1960.

5. Henry Chandlee Forman, *The Architecture of the Old South*, Harvard University Press, Cambridge, Mass., 1948.

6. Peter Kalm, *Travels into North America*, 2nd ed., London, 1772, pp. 96-97.

7. Thomas Jefferson Wertenbaker, *The Founding of American Civilization: The Middle Colonies*, Charles Scribner's Sons, New York, 1938, pp. 67-76.

8. Thomas Paulsson, *Scandinavian Architecture*, Charles T. Branford Co., Newton, Mass., 1959, p. 22.

9. From a memoir of Judge Thomas C. Nichols, quoted by Lyle Saxon, *Old Louisiana*, The Century Company, New York, 1929, p. 108.

10. Nathaniel Cortland Curtis, *New Orleans, Its Old Houses, Shops and Public Buildings*, J.B. Lippincott Co., Philadelphia and London, 1933, p. 123.

11. Thomas Jefferson Wertenbaker, *The Founding of American Civilization: The Middle Colonies*, Charles Scribner's Sons, New York, 1938, p. 233.

12. "Brownstone" is the name given to sandstone of a special red-brown color, a regional building material of the eastern United States, used so extensively during the mid- and late nineteenth century in New York City that "New York brownstone" became a type name. Most early brownstones were Tuscan, a few Gothic Revival. Later ones were designed in a variety of Victorian styles.

13. Not precisely as constructed.

14. Aymar Embury, *One Hundred Country Houses*, The Century Company, New York, 1909, p. 128.

15. Louis Kahn used it a year later (Figure 300).

16. So called after the roadside stand in the shape of a duck.

Acknowledgments

In 1963, Brooke Alexander asked me to write a "guide to style" for *Architectural Forum*, of which he was then Assistant to the Publisher. It is this idea which, many years and changes later, is finally a book, and I am grateful to him for it. Since that beginning, Madelaine Thatcher has been the most patient and steadfast of collaborators, executing more than twice the number of drawings originally planned, and maintaining her meticulous standards on often-improvised drafting tables in New Mexico, Arizona, Florida and France. When necessary, she pictorially restored details to houses that had been remodeled over the years. She penetrated shadows, extrapolated corners hidden by trees and other obstructions and created clarity from confusion. My gratitude to her for staying with this project to its conclusion can never be adequately expressed.

During the final year of work on the book, Madelaine Thatcher was unable, because of illness, to complete some of the remaining drawings. I am therefore grateful to Steven Bauer, freelance illustrator and associate with David Gibson & Associates, preservation consultants, in New York City, who stepped into the breach, adapting his technique to create a unified style of illustration throughout the book, and working cheerfully under great pressure. Seventy-two of the illustrations were drawn by Bauer and are designated by his initials. I am also grateful to Peter Darlow, architect with the Historic American Buildings Survey in Washington, D.C., who drew the illustration of Monticello and of the "French Village", and to Janet Hochuli, architect in the same office, who drew Olana.

For each illustration, I sought a photograph, old engraving, measured drawing, other graphic material, or a combination of these from which the artist could work. The major source of this research was the Historic American Buildings Survey and other collections, in the Prints and Photographs Division, The Library of Congress, Washington, D.C. I am deeply indebted to Virginia Daiker, Specialist in American Architecture for that Division until her retirement in 1975, who apparently carried an index to its collections in her head. Since 1975, Mary Ison, Librarian, Architecture, and C. Ford Peatross, Curator, Architectural Collections, in the same Division, have given invaluable assistance.

James C. Massey, until 1972 Chief, Historic American Buildings Survey, now Executive Director, Historic House Association of America, generously gave me access to H.A.B.S. photographs not yet released to the Prints and Photographs Division.

Libraries supplied a major part of the research for illustrations and text. The Library of Congress and the New York Public Library provided definitive collections of architectural books, monographs, folios and periodicals. Adolf K. Placzek, Librarian, Avery Architectural and Fine Arts Library, Graduate School of Architecture and Planning, Columbia University, kindly permitted me to use this rich facility, including its collections of original architectural drawings. Mary Marlin-Jones, Art Librarian, Martin Luther King Public Library, Washington, D.C. gave me informed assistance over a period of many years.

For research during Massachusetts summers I am most grateful to Elizabeth Daly, formerly Librarian, The Lenox Library Association, Lenox, Massachusetts, for help in using the excellent architectural collection that exists there; for similar assistance from Jean Bousquet, Supervisor of Music and Art Services, Music and Art Department, The Berkshire Athenaeum, Pittsfield, Massachusetts; and for the helpfulness of Mrs. William Pell, Librarian, The Becket Athenaeum, Becket, Massachusetts, for obtaining books for me on Library Loan.

I also wish to thank Dorothy M. Henry, Director, Sussex County Library, Newton, N.J., for photographs she took for me of the Merion House; and William Lane, Librarian, College of Arts and Sciences at Geneseo, New York, for help in identifying houses from their Carl Schmidt collection. For her unfailing helpfulness in searching out the names of original owners of houses, their architects, current owners of museum houses, and other recalcitrant pieces of information, all in a last-minute rush against the printer's deadline, I am most grateful to Alyce Morgan, assistant Librarian, The National Trust for Historic Preservation.

Numerous museums, historical societies and preservation societies, as well as their individual members, have provided me with photographs, descriptions and valuable advice in connection with specific house types. I am grateful to them all, although space allows mention of only a few.

For Pennsylvania German houses and furnishings, special thanks go to Raymond V. Shepherd, Jr., Administrator, Clivedon, Germantown, Pennsylvania; to H. Elvin Herr, Field Representative, Hans Herr House Restoration Committee, Lancaster Mennonite Conference Historical Society; to Mrs. John A. Beard, President, The Historic Preservation Trust of Berks County; to Stephen J. Kindig, restoration architect, De Turck House; to Henry Glassie, Chairman, Department of Folklore and Folklife, Faculty of Arts and Sciences, University of Pennsylvania.

For the German houses of Old Salem, North Carolina, thanks go to Frances Griffin, Director of Information, Old Salem Inc., and to John C. Larson, Department of Restoration.

For the early Swedish log house in Pennsylvania, I am indebted to the late Amandus Johnson, Honorary President and Curator Emeritus, American Swedish Historical Foundation; to Carl Lindborg, Member of the Council, Swedish Colonial Society and Alice Lindborg, Member, American-Swedish Historical Museum, of which her husband is also a member.

For German, Norwegian and Finnish houses in Wisconsin, I am grateful to Richard W.E. Perrin, F.A.I.A., Historic Buildings Preservation Officer, The American Institute of Architects, for his generous assistance over a period of many years.

For Spanish houses in Florida, particular thanks are due Brian Bowman, Historic St. Augustine Preservation Board, for photographs of the Ribera House he took specifically for this book; to the St. Augustine Historical Society and Albert Manucy, copyright holder and author respectively of *The Houses of St. Augustine, 1565-1821*, for permission to use graphic source material from this book. For Spanish adobe houses in New Mexico, I am indebted to Bainbridge Bunting, Professor of Art History Emeritus, Department of Art, University of New Mexico; to Alan Vedder, staff member, Folk Art Museum; to the late E. Boyd and to Arthur L. Olivas, Photographic Archivist, both of the Museum of New Mexico.

For the early adobe houses of California, I wish to thank especially Robert E. Alexander, F.A.I.A., Architect and Planning Consultant, and member, California Historical Society; and Russell W. Cahill, Director, Department of Parks and Recreation, The Resources Agency, State of California.

For advice on many types of houses, as well as specific examples that should be included, I am grateful to Richard W. Howland, Special Assistant to the Secretary of The Smithsonian Institution, and to Terry Brust Morton, Vice President and Editor, Preservation Press, the National Trust for Historic Preservation.

For unusual assistance with specific houses I thank Douglas D. Boucher, The Preservation/Design Group, Albany, N.Y., for the Pieter Bronck House; Leona M. Guirard, the Acadian Museum Home, Evangeline State Park, for the "Cajun Cottage;" Susanne Brendel-Panditch, Curator, Biltmore Estate, Asheville, N.C., for Biltmore House; William R. Mitchell, Staff Historian, Georgia Historical Society, for Jarrett Manor, or "Traveler's Rest;" James Waite, architect, Colonial Williamsburg Foundation, for "The Red Lion;" Jarold Talbot, Curator, The Hill-Stead Museum, for the Alfred Atmore Pope House; and Robert Grant Irving, then a member, Department of the History of Architecture, University of Virginia, for an example of the "New Brutalism."

For supplying last-minute identification of houses I wish to thank Ted Van Dyke, Acting Director and Jane Whittlesey, Assistant, Berkshire County Historical Society; Ralph Marquardt, Treasurer, Sauk City Prairie Historical Society; Sarah McKenzie, Historic Charleston Foundation; Susan Kaup Kelley, Curator, The Somerville (Massachusetts) Historical Society; and Alice Brown, Director, the Princeton Historical Society.

Henry Jonas Magaziner, F.A.I.A., Regional Historical Architect, Mid Atlantic Regional Office, National Parks Service, and member of the Board of Directors, Society of Architectural Historians, kindly checked a number of the drawings for accuracy. If mistakes remain, they are not his.

Wherever possible, I visited the houses that are shown. The study tours of the Society of Architectural Historians gave unparalleled access to historic houses, many of them privately owned. I am also most grateful to John Poppeliers, now Chief, Historic American Buildings Survey, Division of Historic Conservation and Recreation Service, Department of the Interior; and Penelope Hartshorne Batcheler, Architect, National Parks Service, who gave both author and artist an extensive tour of Society Hill and other historic Philadelphia neighborhoods when this project first began.

Personal friends also shared my enthusiasm. Katherine Driver explored and photographed Victorian Washington with me. Rosemary Gatenby arranged a special trip to photograph the Whitfield House, Guilford, Connecticut; and her son-in-law, Jack Kenny, reporter for the Norwalk Hour, gave the book its title. Ruth Jubanyik, member, The Planning Commission, former member, The Planning Board, Borough of Merchantville, and reporter, Camden Courier Post, brought the brick houses of Salem County to my attention and arranged a memorable tour of Cape May, guided by architect A. Gregory Ogden. My sister, Margaret Kenyon Thomas, member of the faculty, Naples Art Association, joined forces with me for an extended photographic tour that took us to Williamsburg, the James River plantations, Charleston, Savannah and St. Augustine. These trips provided some of my most interesting discoveries and remain among my happiest memories.

The Virginia Center for the Creative Arts granted me three weeks of peace, quiet and release from normal duties at Wavertree Hall, then the artists' and writers' residence of the Center. I am grateful to Mrs. Churchill Newcomb, then Director of Wavertree Hall, for providing that perfect balance of seclusion and hospitality.

Without encouragement, one could hardly finish a project of such length. Warmest thanks therefore go to James Marston Fitch, Professor Emeritus of Architecture, Graduate School of Architecture and Planning, Columbia University, for his unwavering belief in the idea of this book, from inception to completion, his helpful advice and his most flattering introduction. Two other friends with books under way at the time also helped me keep my sanity: Mary Sayre Haverstock, former art critic, the Washington Post; and Margaret Mason, editor, "Style Plus," The Washington Post. I also wish to thank Mary Elizabeth O'Donnell and Nancy Craun for typing the manuscript with great skill.

I am most grateful to Ann Harris, Senior Editor, Harper & Row, and her assistant Kathy Clear, for precise guidance through the thicket of final details, and for buoying my sometimes sagging spirits.

Very special thanks go to my husband, Justin John Foley, Deputy Public Affairs Officer, D.A.R.C.O.M., U.S. Army, himself a professional writer, whose cutting of the last half of the manuscript made it possible for this book to meet its deadline.

Finally, to both my husband and to my son, Stephen Prescott Foley, my gratitude for their faith and support over a period of time almost too long to remember.

Houses Open to the Public*

1. The Half-Timbered Hall: Jamestown National Historic Site. Operated by the Jamestown Foundation.

4. The Plank-Framed Hall: Plimoth Plantation, Plymouth, Mass.

5. Peak House: Operated by the Medfield Historical Society. Medfield, Mass.

7. Jabez Howland House: Operated by the Pilgrim John Howland Society. Plymouth, Mass.

8. Parson Capen House: Operated by the Topsfield Historical Society. Topsfield, Mass.

11. "The Witch House:" Operated by the town of Salem. Salem, Mass.

12. Rev. Henry Whitfield House: Operated by the State of Connecticut. Guilford, Conn.

15. Thomas Clemence House: Operated by the Society for the Preservation of New England Antiquities. Manton, R.I.

20. Adam Thoroughgood House: Owned by the City of Norfolk. Princess Anne County, Va.

21. The Red Lion: Operated by Colonial Williamsburg Foundation. Williamsburg, Va.

25. Lord Mayor William Ramsay House: Headquarters, The Alexandria Tourist Council. Probable original site, Dumfries, Va., 1724; enlarged and moved to Alexandria, Va., ca. 1749-51.

26. Dep. Gov. Jonathan Nichols (Nichols-Wanton-Hunter) House: Operated by the Preservation Society of Newport County. Newport, R.I.

29. Mission House: Operated by the Trustees of Reservations. Stockbridge, Mass.

39. Maria Mitchell House: Operated by the Nantucket Maria Mitchell Association. Nantucket, Mass.

45. Ferry House Kitchen: Part of Van Cortlandt Manor, Sleepy Hollow Restorations. Croton-on-Hudson, N.Y.

48. Archibald Macphaedris House: Operated by the Warner House Association. Portsmouth, N.H.

*This list was compiled at the time research on The American House was completed. Readers may want to confirm information about a particular house they wish to visit beforehand.

50. Nicholas Vechte-Jacques Cortelyou House: Reconstructed to its 19th-c. appearance. Gowanus, N.Y.

52. William and Sarah Hancock House: Operated by New Jersey Department of Environmental Protection. Salem County, N.J.

55. Bad Shot Gulch: Bodie Historic District. Administered by the California State Division of Beaches and Parks. Bodie, Calif.

58. Pieter Bronck House: Headquarters, Greene County Historical Society. West Coxsackie, N.Y.

59. Jean Hasbrouck House: Part of the Huguenot Street Historic District. Operated by the Huguenot Historical Society. New Paltz, N.Y.

60. Van Cortlandt Manor House: Operated by Sleepy Hollow Restorations. Croton-on-Hudson, N.Y.

61. Jan Martense Schenck House: Installed as an exhibit at the Brooklyn Museum. Brooklyn, N.Y.

70. Fridolin Ketola (or Getto) Cabin: Part of the Finnish Farmstead, Old World Wisconsin. Operated by The State Historical Society of Wisconsin in cooperation with The Department of Natural Resources. Near Eagle, Waukesha County, Wisc.

74. Cade's Cove: Operated by the National Park Service, U.S. Department of the Interior.

79. Hans Herr House: Operated by the Lancaster Mennonite Conference Historical Society. Lancaster County, Pa.

80. Johan and Debora De Turck House: Operated by the Historic Preservation Trust of Berks County. Oley Valley, Pa.

82. Winkler Bakery: Operated by Old Salem, Inc. as part of the Old Salem Historic District. Salem, N.C.

85. Squire Boone House: Administered by the Pennsylvania Historical and Museum Commission. Baumstown, Pa.

88. Christian Turck House: Part of the German Farmstead, Old World Wisconsin. Operated by The State Historical Society of Wisconsin in cooperation with The Department of Natural Resources. Near Eagle, Waukesha County, Wisc.

90. Jonathan Hager House: Restored and operated by the Washington County Historical Society. Hagerstown, Md.

94. Jean Baptiste Saucier House: Operated by the State of Illinois. Cahokia, Ill.

98. Bon Sejour or Oak Alley: Privately owned. Open daily. St. James Parish, La.

101. "The Cajun Cottage": A reconstruction. Evangeline State Park, St. Martinsville, La.

103. Shadows-on-the-Teche: Owned and operated by the National Trust for Historic Preservation. New Iberia, La.

105. Louis Bolduc House: Operated by the Society of Colonial Dames. St. Genevieve, Mo.

107. Jarrett Manor or Traveler's Rest: Restored and operated by the Georgia Historical Commission. Toccoa, Ga.

113. Ribera House, San Augustin Antigue: Maintained and operated by the Historic St. Augustine Preservation Board. St. Augustine, Fla.

116. "The Oldest House": Owned and operated by the St. Augustine Historical Society. St. Augustine, Fla.

118. Palace of the Governors: Restored to its appearance in the early 19th c. Santa Fe, N.M.

124. Thomas Larkin House: Operated by the California Department of Parks and Recreation. Monterey, Calif.

125. Gen. Mariano Guadalupe Vallejo Adobe: The Petaluma Adobe State Historical Monument. Petaluma, Calif.

126. The Governor's Palace: Operated by the Colonial Williamsburg Foundation. Williamsburg, Va.

127. Wentworth-Gardner House: Operated by the Wentworth-Gardner and Tobias Lear House Assoc. Portsmouth, N.H.

129. Letitia Street House: Operated by the Philadelphia Museum of Art. Fairmount Park, Pa.

131. Rev. Jonathan Ashley House: Restored as part of Old Deerfield Village, Mass.

133. Samuel Powel House: Original paneling in the Philadelphia Museum of Art. Copy in the Powel House, operated by The Philadelphia

Society for the Preservation of Landmarks. Philadelphia, Pa.

134. Lady Pepperell Mansion: Operated by the Society for the Preservation of New England Antiquities. Kittery Point, Maine.

135. Mathias Hammond (Hammond-Harwood) House: Operated by the Hammond-Harwood House Assoc. Annapolis, Md.

136. Mount Pleasant: Owned and operated by the City of Philadelphia as part of Fairmount Park. Fairmount Park, Pa.

144. The President's House (The White House): Operated by the National Park Service. Washington, D.C.

147. Linden Hall: Owned by the Society for the Preservation of New England Antiquities. Springfield, Mass.

149. First Harrison Gray Otis House: Headquarters, The Society for the Preservation of New England Antiquities. Boston, Mass.

150. Pingree House: Operated by the Essex Institute. Salem, Mass.

152. Gore Place: Operated by the Gore Place Society. Waltham, Mass.

153. Nathaniel Russell House: Operated by the Historic Charleston Foundation. Charleston, South Carolina.

155. Owens-Thomas House: Operated by the Telfair Academy. Savannah, Ga.

156. Pres. William Howard Taft House: The Taft Museum. Cincinnati, Ohio.

158. Monticello: Operated by the Thomas Jefferson Memorial Foundation. Charlottesville, Va.

159. Mount Vernon: Operated by the Mount Vernon Ladies Association of the Union. Fairfax County, Va.

160. Andalusia: Visiting program conducted by the National Trust for Historic Preservation (Clivedon). Advance reservations only. Bucks County, Pa.

174. Lyndhurst: Owned and operated by the National Trust for Historic Preservation. Tarrytown, N.Y.

181. Edward King House: Operated by the Senior Citizens' Center. Newport, R.I.

182. Olana: Operated by the New York State Historic Trust. Near Hudson, N.Y.

194. Parlor, Col. Robert J. Milligan House: Installed as a period room in the Brooklyn Museum. Brooklyn, N.Y.

198. J. N. A. Griswold House: Operated by the Art Association of Newport. Newport, R.I.

208. William Carson House: Owned and operated by the Ingomar Club. Open by appointment. Eureka, Calif.

214. John J. Glessner House: Operated by the Chicago School of Architecture Foundation. Chicago, Ill.

228. Frank Lloyd Wright's Home and Studio: Owned by the National Trust for Historic Preservation. Leased to and operated by the Frank Lloyd Wright Home and Studio Foundation.

233. Biltmore: Owned and operated by the Biltmore Trust. Near Asheville, N.C.

237. The Breakers: Operated by the Preservation Society of Newport County. Newport, R.I.

239. Marble House: Operated by the Preservation Society of Newport County. Newport, R.I.

242. Alfred Atmore Pope Residence: The Hill-Stead Museum. Farmington, Conn.

260. F. C. Robie House: Owned by the University of Chicago. Operated by the Office of Special Events, University of Chicago. Open by appointment. Chicago, Ill.

263. David B. Gamble House: Owned and operated by the University of Southern California School of Architecture and Fine Arts. Pasadena, Calif.

267. Hollyhock House: Owned, restored and operated by the City of Los Angeles. Open for special events. Hollywood, Calif.

278. Fallingwater: Entrusted to the Western Pennsylvania Conservancy by Edgar Kaufmann, Bear Run, Pa.

Sources of the Drawings

1. After a drawing by Robert Henninger, courtesy of the Jamestown Foundation.

2. *Colonial Living* by Edwin Tunis. Cleveland, World Publishing Co., 1957, by permission of Harper & Row, Publishers, Inc.

3. Based on H.A.B.S. photographs by Thomas Tileston Waterman, Prints and Photographs Div., Library of Congress.

4. Freely based on a house from the reconstructed Plimoth Plantation, *Old Time New England*, Vol. XL, No. 3, January 1950; and a drawing by Samuel Chamberlain, *The Log Cabin Myth* by Harold Shurtleff. Cambridge, Mass., Harvard University Press, 1938, by permission of Harvard University Press.

5. After a H.A.B.S. photograph by Arthur C. Haskell, Prints and Photographs Div., Library of Congress.

6. Based on a restoration drawing by Henry Chandlee Forman, *Tidewater Maryland Architecture and Gardens* by Henry Chandlee Forman. New York, Architectural Book Publishing Co., Inc., 1956.

6a. After a drawing, *American Georgian Architecture,* by Harold Donaldson Eberlein and Cortlandt van Dyke Hubbard. Bloomington, Indiana University Press, 1962.

7. Based on a photograph, courtesy The Pilgrim John Howland Society.

8. Based on H.A.B.S. photographs by Thomas Tileston Waterman and C. E. Peterson, Prints and Photographs Div., Library of Congress. Pictorial restoration of typical 17th-c. casement windows as described in *American Buildings and Their Architects,* Vol. I by William H. Pierson, Jr., p. 53. New York, Doubleday and Co., Inc., 1970.

9. Based on photographs by the author and a restoration drawing by Henry Chandlee Forman, *The Architecture of the Old South* by Henry Chandlee Forman. Cambridge, Mass., Harvard University Press, 1948, by permission of Harvard University Press.

9a. After a drawing, *The Homes of America* by Ernest Pickering. New York, Bramhall House, 1951, by permission of Thomas Y. Crowell.

10. After a reconstruction drawing by Wallace E. Dibble, *The Log Cabin Myth* by Harold Shurtleff. Cambridge, Mass., Harvard University Press, 1939, courtesy, Mr. Henry A. Wright.

11. After a photograph by Samuel Chamberlain, *Open House in New England* by Samuel Chamberlain. New York, Hastings House, Publishers, 1937.

12. After a photograph by Rosemary Gatenby.

13. After a H.A.B.S. photograph by Arthur C. Haskell, Prints and Photographs Div., Library of Congress.

14. A composite drawing.

15. After a H.A.B.S. photograph by Wilfred Anderton, Prints and Photographs Div., Library of Congress.

16. A composite drawing.

17. After a drawing, *Architecture in Early New England* by Abbott Lowell Cummings. Old Sturbridge Village Booklet Series 7. Sturbridge, Mass., 1958.

18. Based on a photograph and restoration drawing (wooden chimney) by Henry Chandlee Forman, *Early Nantucket and Its Whale Houses* by Henry Chandlee Forman. New York, Hastings House, Publishers, 1966.

19. After a H.A.B.S. photograph by Arthur C. Haskell, Prints and Photographs Div., Library of Congress.

20. A composite drawing based on a photograph by Frances Benjamin Johnston, Prints and Photographs Div., Library of Congress and a photograph by Phil Morrison, *American Houses in History* by Arnold Nicholson, New York, Viking Press, 1965.

21. After a photograph, courtesy Colonial Williamsburg Foundation.

22. After a drawing by John B. Lear, Jr., *American Georgian Architecture* by Harold Donaldson Eberlein and Cortlandt Van Dyke Hubbard. Bloomington, Indiana University Press, 1962.

23. After a H.A.B.S. photograph by Thomas Tileston Waterman, Prints and Photographs Div., Library of Congress.

24. After a H.A.B.S. photograph by Arthur C. Haskell, Prints and Photographs Div., Library of Congress.

25. After a photograph by the author.

26. After a photograph by John Hopf, courtesy the Preservation Society of Newport County.

27. After a H.A.B.S. photograph by Arthur C. Haskell, Prints and Photographs Div., Library of Congress.

28. After a drawing, *Early Connecticut Houses* by Norman M. Isham and Albert F. Brown. New York, Dover Publications, Inc., 1965.

29. After a photograph, *Stockbridge 1739-1939* by Sarah Cabot Sedgwick and Christina Sedgwick Marquand. Great Barrington, *The Berkshire Courier*, 1939, Bicentennial Limited Edition, No. 42.

30. A composite drawing.

31. After a H.A.B.S. photograph by Herbert Wheaton Congdon, Prints and Photographs Div., Library of Congress.

32. Based on a H.A.B.S. photograph by Carl Waite, Prints and Photographs Div., Library of Congress.

33. After a photograph by the author.

34. After a photograph by John Maass, *The Gingerbread Age* by John Maass. New York, Bramhall House, 1957.

35. After a photograph, courtesy, Levitt & Sons, Inc.

36. After a photograph, collection of the author.

37. After a photograph, collection of the author.

38. After a photograph by Samuel Chamberlain, collection of the author.

39. After a photograph, *Old Houses of Nantucket* by Kenneth Duprey. New York, Architectural Book Publishing Co., Inc., 1959.

40. After a photograph by Flournoy, *Houses Virginians Have Loved* by Agnes Rothery. New York, Rinehart, 1954.

41. After a photograph by Penelope Hartshorne Batcheler.

42. Based on the Dewitt View of Nieuw Amsterdam, 1653. Conjectural restoration of details from contemporary Dutch paintings by Henrick Avercamp, Cornelisz Gerrits Decker, Adriaen van Ostade, Isack van Ostade, Adriaen de Venn, and Jan Vermeer, The picture collection, the Art Division, Martin Luther King Public Library; and a photograph, Hordur Agustson, *European Folk Art in Europe and The Americas,* edited by Hans Jurgen Hansen, New York, McGraw-Hill, Inc., 1968.

43. *Colonial Living* by Edwin Tunis. Cleveland, World Publishing Co., 1957, by permission of Harper & Row, Publishers, Inc.

44. After the Burgis View of New York, 1717, courtesy The New-York Historical Society.

45. After a photograph, courtesy Sleepy Hollow Restorations.

46. After a H.A.B.S. photograph by E. H. Pickering, Prints and Photographs Div., Library of Congress.

47. After a H.A.B.S. photograph by E. H. Pickering, Prints and Photographs Div., Library of Congress.

48. After a photograph, plus details from a drawing by Philip Sanfilippo, *Great Georgian Houses of America,* Vol. I, Architects' Emergency Committee. New York, Dover Publications, Inc., 1970.

49. After a photograph, courtesy Missouri Historical Society.

50. Based on an illustration, *Valentine's Manual,* 1858, courtesy The New-York Historical Society; 17th-c. details from an illustration, *Cassell's History of the United States* by Edmound Ollier. London, Paris, New York, Cassell, Petter & Galpin, 1874-77.

51. After a H.A.B.S. photograph by George Neuschafer, Prints and Photographs Div., Library of Congress, and a photograph, *The Old Houses of Salem County* by Joseph S. Sickler, Salem, N.J., Sunbeam Publishing Co., 1934.

52. After a H.A.B.S. photograph by Nathaniel R. Ewan, Prints and Photographs Div., Library of Congress.

53. A composite drawing based on a H.A.B.S. photographs by W. Harry Bagby, Prints and Photographs Div., Library of Congress; and drawings by Henry Chandlee Forman, *The Architecture of the Old South* by Henry Chandlee Forman. Cambridge, Mass., Harvard University Press, 1948, by permission of Harvard University Press.

54. After a sketch by Augustus Pruyn, as reproduced in *Dutch Houses in the Hudson Valley Before 1776* by Helen Wilkinson Reynolds. The Holland Society of New York. New York, Dover Publications, Inc., 1965.

55. After H.A.B.S. photographs by Ronald Partridge, Prints and Photographs Div., Library of Congress.

56. After a photograph, *Worth Saving,* Charleston, The Historic Charleston Foundation; 1957.

57. After a photograph, *Gaslights and Gingerbread* by Sandra Dallas Atchison. Denver, Sage Books, 1965.

58. After photographs and drawings, Greene County Historical Society and the Preservation/Design Group, Albany, N.Y.

59. After a photograph by Margaret De Motte Brown, *Dutch Houses in the Hudson Valley Before 1776* by Helen Wilkinson Reynolds. The Holland Society of New York. New York, Dover Publications, Inc., 1965.

60. After a photograph, Sleepy Hollow Restorations.

61. Freely based on the restored Jan Martense Schenck House, Brooklyn, N.Y., originally built ca. 1675.

62. Based on a H.A.B.S. photograph by E. P. McFarland, Prints and Photographs Div., Library of Congress.

63. After a photograph, *Dutch Houses in the Hudson Valley Before 1776* by Helen Wilkinson Reynolds. The Holland Society of New York. New York, Dover Publications, Inc., 1965.

64. After a H.A.B.S. photograph by R. Merritt Lacey, Prints and Photographs Div., Library of Congress. Wing restored according to John T. Boyd, Jr., "Some Early Dutch Houses in New Jersey," *Architectural Record,* July-Aug.-Sept., 1914, p. 39.

65. After a H.A.B.S. photograph by R. Merritt Lacey, Prints and Photographs Div., Library of Congress.

66. Based on H.A.B.S. photographs by Stanley P. Mixon and measured drawings, Prints and Photographs Div., Library of Congress. Pictorial restoration of 17th-c. roof, windows and appearance of logs on the advice of Carl and Alice Lindborg, based on consultation with the late Amandus Johnson. Split logs at gable end substituted for existing planking as in the restored Swedish granary, Greenwich, New Jersey, ca. 1650.

66a. *The Dwellings of Colonial America* by Thomas Tileston Waterman. Chapel Hill, © 1950, The University of North Carolina Press.

67. Based on a H.A.B.S. drawing, Prints and Photographs Div., Library of Congress. Window restored to early Swedish type after a drawing, *The Swedish Settlements on the Delaware 1638-1664,* Vol. I, by Amandus Johnson. Philadelphia, University of Pennsylvania; New York, D. Appleton & Co., Agents, 1911.

68. A composite drawing based on photographs, Prints and Photograph Div., Library of Congress, and illustrations, *The Log Cabin: Homes of the North American Wilderness* by Alex W. Bealer and John O. Ellis, New York, Barre Publ. Co., 1978.

69. After a photograph, collection of Richard W. E. Perrin, F.A.I.A.

70. After a photograph, collection of Richard W. E. Perrin, F.A.I.A. Finnish original, "Ketola House."

71. After a drawing, "Louisiana House Types" by Fred B. Kniffen, *Annals of the Association of American Geographers,* XXVI, 1936.

72. A conjectural restoration drawing based on a H.A.B.S. photograph by Allen L. Hubbard and measured drawings, Prints and Photographs Div., Library of Congress.

73. After a H.A.B.S. photograph by Cervin Robinson, Prints and Photographs Div., Library of Congress. Pictorial restoration of typical early 18th-c. German casement windows after H.A.B.S. photographs, Fort Zeller, Newmanstown, Pa., by Stanley P. Mixon, Prints and Photographs Div., Library of Congress.

74. After a photograph, courtesy Cade's Cove, Great Smoky Mountains National Park.

75. After a photograph by Arthur Rothstein, F.S.A./O.W.I Collection, Prints and Photographs Div., Library of Congress.

76. After a photograph by S. D. Butcher. Collection No. 3026, Prints and Photographs Division, Library of Congress.

77. After a photograph by Fynmore Photos, Boonville, N.Y.

78. After a H.A.B.S. photograph by Stanley P. Mixon, Prints and Photographs Div., Library of Congress.

79. After a photograph, Lancaster County Historical Society.

80. Based on a H.A.B.S. photograph by Cervin Robinson, Prints and Photographs Div., Library of Congress. Pictorial restoration of decorated shutters after a rubbing from the originals, Historical Society of Berks County, made by Theresa R. Beard, Executive Director, The Historic Preservation Trust of Berks County, Pa. Other details, Stephen J. Kindig, restoration architect.

81. After a photograph, courtesy Old Salem, Inc.

82. After a photograph, courtesy Old Salem, Inc.

83. Based on the Georg Mueller House, Milbach, Pa., 1752.

83a. After a plan, Georg Mueller House, courtesy of Donald McDonald-Millar, from *The Dwellings of Colonial America* by Thomas Tileston Waterman. Chapel Hill, © 1950, The University of North Carolina Press.

84. Used by permission of Charles Scribner's Sons from *The Founding of American Civilization: The Middle Colonies,* by Thomas Jefferson Wertenbaker. © 1966, Thomas Jefferson Wertenbaker.

85. After a H.A.B.S. photograph by Cervin Robinson, Prints and Photographs Div., Library of Congress.

86. After a drawing, courtesy Joane R. Smith and Richard Flanders Smith.

87. After a H.A.B.S. photograph by Cervin Robinson, Prints and Photographs Div., Library of Congress.

88. After a photograph, collection of Richard W. E. Perrin, F.A.I.A.

89. A composite drawing based on H.A.B.S. photographs by Cervin Robinson and Frederick Tilbury, Prints and Photographs Div., Library of Congress.

90. After a H.A.B.S. photograph, Prints and Photographs Div., Library of Congress.

91. After a photograph, Kilman Studio, Fredericksburg, Tex.

92. After a drawing, "Early Ste. Genevieve and Its Architecture," by Charles E. Peterson, *The Missouri Historical Review,* XXXV, Jan. 1941, p. 227.

93. After a drawing, "Early Ste. Genevieve and Its Architecture," by Charles E. Peterson, *The Missouri Historical Review,* XXXV, Jan. 1941, p. 227.

94. After a photograph, courtesy, the Illinois Department of Public Works and Buildings.

95. After an old photograph, *The Old St. Louis River Front.* St. Louis Art Room, St. Louis Public Library, 1938.

96. After an 1899 photograph copied for H.A.B.S. by Leslie Jones, Prints and Photographs Div., Library of Congress.

97. After a photograph by Frances Benjamin Johnston, Prints and Photographs Div., Library of Congress.

98. After a photograph by Frances Benjamin Johnston, Prints and Photographs Div., Library of Congress.

99. After a H.A.B.S. photograph by Richard Koch, Prints and Photographs Div., Library of Congress.

100. After a H.A.B.S. elevation drawing, Prints and Photographs Div., Library of Congress.

101. Based on a photograph by Thurman C. Smith, *Louisiana Plantation Homes,* by W. Darrell Overdyke. New York, Architectural Book Publishing Co., Inc., 1965; and a drawing, Leona M. Guirard, Acadian House Museum, Evangeline State Park.

102. After a drawing, *White Pillars,* by J. Frazer Smith, New York, Bramhall House, by arrangement with Wm. Helburn, Inc., 1941.

103. After a photograph from the collections of the National Trust for Historic Preservation.

104. After a photograph by Frances Benjamin Johnston, Prints and Photographs Division, Library of Congress.

105. After a photograph, "Early Ste. Genevieve and Its Architecture," by Charles E. Peterson, *The Missouri Historical Review* XXXV, Jan. 1941, opposite p. 222.

106. After a H.A.B.S. photograph by Frederick D. Nichols, Prints and Photographs Div., Library of Congress.

107. After a photograph and drawings, The Georgia Historical Commission.

108. After a H.A.B.S. photograph by C.O. Greene, Prints & Photographs Div., Library of Congress.

109. Based on a drawing, *The Houses of St. Augustine 1565-1821* by Albert Manucy. St. Augustine Historical Society, Jacksonville, The Convention Press, 1962.

110. Based on a photograph entitled ["Mapa de Pueblo, Fuerte y Caño de San Augustin de la Florida y del Pueblo y Caño de San Sebastian 1593."] (Lowery Collection No. 76), Geography and Map Division, Library of Congress; original in Archivo General de Indias, Seville, Spain.

111. After a drawing, *The Houses of St. Augustine 1565-1821,* by Albert Manucy. St. Augustine Historical Society, Jacksonville, The Convention Press, 1962.

112. Based on drawings, *The Houses of St. Augustine, 1565-1821,* by Albert Manucy. St. Augustine Historical Society, Jacksonville, The Convention Press, 1962.

113. After a photograph by Brian Paul Bowman, Historic Sites Specialist, St. Augustine, Florida.

114. After a photograph by Brian Paul Bowman, Historic Sites Specialist, St. Augustine, Florida.

115. Based on drawings, *The Houses of St. Augustine 1565-1821,* by Albert Manucy, St. Augustine Historical Society, Jacksonville, The Convention Press, 1962.

116. After a H.A.B.S. photograph by Prime A. Beaudoin, Prints and Photographs Div., Library of Congress.

117. Conjectural pictorial restoration based on descriptive material, collections in the Museum of New Mexico.

118. Based on photographs, collections in the Museum of New Mexico.

119. After a photograph by Riddle, collections in the Museum of New Mexico.

119a. After the plan, *Taos Adobes* by Bainbridge Bunting. Santa Fe, Museum of New Mexico Press, 1964.

120. After a photograph by Tony Perry, *Old Santa Fe Today,* The Historic Santa Fe Foundation, The School of American Research, Santa Fe, 1966.

121. After a photograph, courtesy of Mr. Leandro Martinez, as published in *Taos Adobes* by Bainbridge Bunting. Santa Fe, Museum of New Mexico Press, 1964.

122. A composite drawing based on a drawing, Rare Book Dept., The Huntington Library, San Marino, Calif.; photographs, Department of Parks and Recreation, The Resources Agency, State of California; text descriptions, *California's Architectural Frontier* by Harold Kirker. New York, Russell & Russell, 1960.

123. After a photograph, The Santa Barbara Historical Society.

124. After a photograph, the Monterey History and Art Association.

125. After a H.A.B.S. photograph by Ronald Partridge, Prints and Photographs Div., Library of Congress.

126. Design attributed to the Office of His Majesty's Works, London, 1706-20; Henry Cary, Supervisor of Construction, Williamsburg; Interiors and Grounds under the supervision of Gov. Alexander Spotswood, ca. 1710; Ballroom wing, 1749-51, Richard Taliaferro, arch.; destroyed by fire 1781; reconstructed as part of Colonial Williamsburg, 1931-34 after the plan drawn by Thomas Jefferson, a plate in the Bodleian Library, Oxford, and excavated foundations; Perry, Shaw & Hepburn, restoration architects. After a photograph, Colonial Williamsburg Inc.

127. After a photograph, Wentworth-Gardner and Tobias Lear House Association.

128. After a photograph by the author.

129. Based on a photograph, *A Hundred Pennsylvania Buildings* by Harold Edward Dickson. State College, Pa., Bald Eagle Press, 1954.

130. After a H.A.B.S. photograph by Ian McLaughlin, Prints and Photographs Div., Library of Congress.

131. Based on a photograph by Samuel Chamberlain, *Historic Deerfield; Houses and Interiors* by Samuel Chamberlain and Henry N. Flynt. New York, Hastings House, Publishers, 1972.

132. Based on a H.A.B.S. photograph by C. O. Greene, Prints and Photographs Div., Library of Congress and a drawing by D. Copeland, *Great Georgian Houses of America*, Vol. 1, Architects' Emergency Committee, New York, Dover Publications, Inc., 1970.

133. After a photograph, courtesy The Philadelphia Society for the Preservation of Landmarks.

134. After a drawing by John Mead Howells, *Great Georgian Houses of America*, Vol. I, Architects' Emergency Committee. New York, Dover Publications, Inc., 1970.

135. After a drawing by Wallace Heath, *Great Georgian Houses of America*, Vol. I, Architects' Emergency Committee. New York, Dover Publications, Inc., 1970.

136. After a drawing by W. M. Geety, *Great Georgian Houses of America*, Vol. I., Architects' Emergency Committee. New York, Dover Publications, Inc., 1970.

137. After a H.A.B.S. photograph by Arthur C. Haskell, Prints and Photographs Div., Library of Congress.

138. After a H.A.B.S. photograph, Prints and Photographs Div., Library of Congress.

139. After a photograph by the author.

140. After a drawing, *Advertect Homes*, 1927-28 edition. South Bend, Indiana. Advertect Inc., 1927.

141a-f. Based on photographs and drawings, Philadelphia City Archives and Prints and Photographs Div., Library of Congress.

142. Based on a restoration drawing by R. E. Collins from *The Dwellings of Colonial America* by Thomas Tileston Waterman. Chapel Hill, © 1950, The University of North Carolina Press. Details from *William Buckland 1734-1774* by Rosamond Randall Beirne and John Henry Scarff. Baltimore. The Maryland Historical Society, 1958.

143. After a photograph by Frances Benjamin Johnston, Prints and Photographs Div., Library of Congress.

144. After a drawing by John Loughnane, *Great Georgian Houses of America*, Vol. I., Architects' Emergency Committee. New York, Dover

Publications, Inc., 1970.

145. After a photograph by the author.

146. After a H.A.B.S. photograph by Arthur C. Haskell. Prints and Photographs Div., Library of Congress.

147. After a H.A.B.S. photograph by Arthur C. Haskell, Prints and Photographs Div., Library of Congress.

148. After a H.A.B.S. photograph by Arthur C. Haskell, Prints and Photographs Div., Library of Congress.

149. After a sketch attributed to Charles Bulfinch, the Otis Papers, courtesy, The Massachusetts Historical Society.

150. After a H.A.B.S. photograph by Frank O. Branzetti, Prints and Photographs Div., Library of Congress.

151. A composite drawing based on a photograph by Samuel Chamberlain, *Old Rooms for New Living* by Narcissa Chamberlain. New York, Hastings House, Publishers, 1953; and a photograph, *Mr. Samuel McIntire, Carver; Architect of Salem* by Fiske Kimball. The Essex Institute of Salem, Mass.; The Southworth-Anthoensen Press, 1940.

152. After a photograph by Richard Pratt, *The Golden Treasury of Early American Houses* by Richard Pratt. New York, Hawthorn Books, Inc., 1967.

152a. After a plan, *Great Georgian Houses of America*, Vol. I, Architects' Emergency Committee. New York, Dover Publications, Inc., 1970.

153. After a photograph, *The Octagon Library of Early American Architecture*, Vol. I, Edited by Albert Simons and Samuel Lapham. New York, The Press of the American Institute of Architects, 1927.

153a. After a drawing, *The Octagon Library of Early American Architecture*, Vol. I, Edited by Albert Simons and Samuel Lapham. New York, The Press of the American Institute of Architects, 1927.

154. After a drawing by Hugh A. Simpson, *Great Georgian Houses of America*, Vol. I, Architects' Emergency Committee. New York, Dover Publications Inc., 1970.

155. After a print from an old glass photographic plate, courtesy, Georgia Historical Society.

156. After a H.A.B.S. photograph by Edgar D. Tyler and a drawing variously attributed to Benjamin Henry Latrobe or James Hoban, arch., Prints and Photographs Div., Library of Congress.

157. After a drawing by Arthur H. Reilly, *Great Georgian Houses of America*, Vol. II, Architects' Emergency Committee, New York, Dover Publications, Inc., 1970.

158. After a H.A.B.S. photograph by Walter Smalling, Prints and Photographs Div., Library of Congress.

158a. Based on a drawing. courtesy, the Thomas Jefferson Memorial Foundation.

159. After a H.A.B.S. photograph by Charles E. Peterson, Prints and Photographs Div., Library of Congress.

160. After a photograph by Ezra Stoller, *A Treasury of Early American Homes*, The Curtis Pub. Co. New York, Whittlesey House, 1946.

161. After a drawing by Alexander Jackson Davis, engraved by Fenner Sears & Co., *Art and Life in America* by Oliver W. Larkin. New York, Holt, Rinehart & Winston, 1960.

162. After a drawing by Alexander Jackson Davis, courtesy The New-York Historical Soc.

163. After a H.A.B.S. photograph by Victor Stankiewicz, Prints and Photographs Div., Library of Congress.

164. After a H.A.B.S. photograph, Prints and Photographs Div., Library of Congress.

165. After a H.A.B.S. photograph by Roger Sturtevant, Prints and Photographs Div., Library of Congress.

166. After a photograph, *Cobblestone Architecture* by Carl F. Schmidt. Rochester, Great Lakes Press, 1944.

167. After a photograph, *Cobblestone Architecture* by Carl F. Schmidt. Rochester, Great Lakes Press, 1944.

168. After a H.A.B.S. photograph by R. Merritt Lacey, Prints and Photographs Div., Library of Congress.

169. After a H.A.B.S. photograph by William J. Bulger, Prints and Photographs Div., Library of Congress.

170. After a photograph by Wayne Andrews, *New York Landmarks* by Alan Burnham. Middletown, Conn., published under the auspices of the Municipal Art Society of New York, Wesleyan University Press, 1963.

171. After a photograph, Mississippi Agricultural and Industrial Board.

172. After a photograph by Frances Benjamin Johnston, Prints and Photographs Div., Library of Congress.

173. After a photograph by Walker Evans, Prints and Photographs Div., Library of Congress.

174. After a drawing by Alexander Jackson Davis, courtesy, the Metropolitan Museum of Art.

175. After a H.A.B.S. photograph by Jack E. Boucher, Prints and Photographs Div., Library of Congress.

176. After a H.A.B.S. photograph by Lester Jones, Prints and Photographs Div., Library of Congress.

177. After a photograph by John Maass, *The Gingerbread Age* by John Maass. New York, Holt, Rinehart & Winston, 1957.

178. After a photograph by Walker Evans, Prints and Photographs Div., Library of Congress.

179. After a drawing, *The Model Architect* by Samuel Sloan. Philadelphia, E. G. Jones & Co., 1852.

180. After a drawing, *The Model Architect* by Samuel Sloan. Philadelphia, E. G. Jones & Co., 1852.

181. After a drawing, *The Architecture of Country Houses* by Andrew Jackson Downing. New York, Dover Publications, Inc., 1969.

182. After a H.A.B.S. photograph by Cervin Robinson, Prints and Photographs Div., Library of Congress.

183. After a drawing, *Architectural Designs for Model Country Residences*, by John Riddell. Philadelphia, T. B. Peterson & Brothers, 1867.

184. Based on a photograph by Morgan Rieder.

185. After a photograph by the author.

186. After a photograph by the author and a drawing, courtesy, Yale University Library.

187. After a drawing, *The Octagon Fad* by Carl F. Schmidt. Scottsville, New York, 1958.

188. After a photograph, *The Octagon Fad* by Carl F. Schmidt. Scottsville, New York, 1958.

189. After a photograph, *The Octagon Fad* by Carl F. Schmidt. Scottsville, New York, 1958.

190. After a photograph, *The Octagon Fad* by Carl F. Schmidt. Scottsville, New York, 1958.

191. After a H.A.B.S. photograph by Frank O. Branzetti, Prints and Photographs Div., Library of Congress.

192. After a photograph by Katherine Driver.

193. After a photograph by Joseph P. Day, courtesy The New-York Historical Society.

194. After a photograph.

195. After a photograph, Massie-Missouri Commerce.

196. Based on a photograph by Berenice Abbott, courtesy, Museum of the City of New York.

197. After a photograph by Wayne Andrews, *Architecture in America* by Wayne Andrews. New York, Atheneum, 1960.

198. After a photograph by Robert Meservey, courtesy the Preservation Society of Newport County.

199. After a photograph by Robert Meservey, courtesy, The Preservation Society of Newport County.

200. After a print, collection of Professor Turpin C. Bannister.

201. After a photograph, Travel and Tourism Div., Department of Commerce, State of North Carolina, Raleigh, N.C.

202. Based on a photograph by V. & A. Hackett Photo, Mrs. Alice Hackett, ex-President, Walworth County Historical Society.

203. After a drawing, *Cheap Dwellings* by John C. Pelton, Jr. San Francisco, 1882; republished, *California's Architectural Frontier* by Harold Kirker. Huntington Library, San Marino, Calif.,1960.

204. After a photograph by Wayne Andrews from *The Architecture of H. H. Richardson and His Times* by Henry-Russell Hitchcock. © 1961, The Shoe String Press, Inc., Hamden, Conn.

205. After a photograph, *San Francisco Bay Cities* by Josef Muench; republished, *California's Architectural Frontier* by Harold Kirker. Huntington Library, San Marino, Calif., 1960.

206. After a drawing by John Maass, *The Gingerbread Age* by John Maass. New York, Holt, Rinehart & Winston, 1957.

207. After a photograph by Dorothy E. Henry, Director, Sussex County Library, Newton, N.J.

208. After a photograph, The picture collection, The Art Division, Martin Luther King Public Library, Washington, D.C.

209. After a drawing by Stanford White, *New York Sketch-Book of Architecture,* vol. 2, Jan.-Dec., 1875.

210. After a drawing by Stanford White, *New York Sketch-Book of Architecture,* vol. 2, Jan.-Dec., 1875.

211. After a photograph by Russell Lee, F.S.A./O.W.I. Collection, Prints and Photographs Div., Library of Congress.

212. After a photograph, *Indiana Houses of the Nineteenth Century* by Wilbur David Peat. Indianapolis, Indiana Historical Society, 1962.

213. After a photograph, *Henry Hobson Richardson and His Works* by Marianna Griswold Van Rensselaer (Mrs. Schuyler Van Rensselaer). New York, Dover Publications, Inc., 1969.

214. After a H.A.B.S. copy photograph from *J.J. Glessner, The Story of a House,* ca. 1923. Prints and Photographs Div., Library of Congress.

214a. After a drawing, *Henry Hobson Richardson and His Works* by Marianna Griswold Van Rensselaer (Mrs. Schuyler Van Rensselaer). New York, Dover Publications, Inc., 1969.

215. After an 1893 photograph, *Stately Homes in America* by Harry W. Desmond and Herbert Croly. New York, D. Appleton & Co., 1903.

216. After a photograph by Henry Fuermann, by permission Chicago Architectural Photographing Co., *Louis Sullivan, Prophet of Modern Architecture* by Hugh Morrison, from the collection of David R. Phillips.

217. After a photograph, *Indiana Houses of the Nineteenth Century* by Wilbur David Peat. Indianapolis, Indiana Historical Society, 1962.

218. After a photograph, *San Francisco Bay Cities* by Josef Muench; republished, *California's Architectural Frontier* by Harold Kirker. Huntington Library, San Marino, Calif., 1960.

219. After a photograph, courtesy, the Kuljian Corp.

220. After photographs by Katherine Driver.

221. After a photograph, Houghton Library, Harvard University; from *The Architecture of H. H. Richardson and His Times* by Henry-Russell Hitchcock. © 1961, The Shoe String Press, Inc., Hamden, Conn.

222. After a drawing, *Advertect Homes,* 1927-28 edition. South Bend, Ind., Advertect, Inc., 1927.

223. After a drawing by Maurice B. Adams, *Building News,* April 28, 1882, courtesy, *Architectural Record.*

224. Based on an elevation drawing by Henry Hobson Richardson, Houghton Library, Harvard University, as reproduced in *The Architecture of H. H. Richardson and His Times* by Henry-Russell Hitchcock. © 1961, The Shoe String Press, Inc., Hamden, Conn.

225. After a photograph, *Artistic Country Seats,* Section Two, by George C. Sheldon. New York, D. Appleton & Co., 1886.

226. After a photograph by Wayne Andrews, *Architecture in America* by Wayne Andrews. New York, Atheneum, 1960.

227. After a photograph by Bradlee Smith, *America's Arts and Skills* by the editors of *Life.* New York, E. P. Dutton, 1957.

228. By permission of Hawthorne Books, after a photograph, *In the Nature of Materials; The Buildings of Frank Lloyd Wright, 1887-1941* by Henry-Russell Hitchcock. Originally published by Duell, Sloan and Pearce, New York, 1942.

229. After a photograph, *A Monograph of the Works of McKim, Mead & White, 1879-1915.* New York, The Architectural Book Publishing Co., Inc., 1914-15.

230. After a photograph, *Frank Lloyd Wright to 1910* by Grant Carpenter Manson. New York Reinhold, 1958, by permission, Litton Educational Publishing Inc.

231. After a photograph by Carl Mydans, F.S.A./O.W.I. Collection, Prints and Photographs Div., Library of Congress.

232. After photographs by Katherine Driver.

233. After photographs, courtesy, Biltmore Estate.

234. After photographs, courtesy, Biltmore Estate.

235. After a photograph by Wayne Andrews, *Architecture in America* by Wayne Andrews. New York, Atheneum, 1960.

236. A composite drawing based on a photograph by Henry Fuermann, *Frank Lloyd Wright to 1910* by Grant Carpenter Manson. New York, Reinhold Publishing Co., 1958, by permission, Litton Educational Publishing Inc.; and a drawing, *Frank Lloyd Wright; A Study in Architectural Content* by Norris Kelly Smith. Englewood Cliffs, N.J., Prentice-Hall, Inc., 1966.

237. After a photograph by Wayne Andrews, *Architecture in America* by Wayne Andrews. New York, Atheneum, 1960.

238. After a photograph by John Hopf, courtesy, The Preservation Society of Newport County.

239. After a photograph, *Stately Homes in America* by Harry W. Desmond and Herbert Croly. New York, D. Appleton & Co., 1903.

240. After a photograph, Bain Collection, Prints and Photographs Div., Library of Congress.

241a. After a photograph, *American Architect and Building News,* July 25, 1900, courtesy, *Architectural Record.*

241b. After a photograph, *House & Garden,* Dec. 1901.

241c. After a photograph, *The American Architect,* Oct. 4, 1911, courtesy, *Architectural Record.*

241d. After a photograph, *The American Architect,* Feb. 12, 1913, courtesy, *Architectural Record.*

241e. After a photograph, *The American*

Architect, Feb. 12, 1913, courtesy, *Architectural Record.*

241f. *The American Architect,* Mar. 4, 1914, courtesy, *Architectural Record.*

242. After photographs taken for this book by Jarold D. Talbot, Curator, Hill-Stead Museum.

243. After a photograph, *The Architecture of John Russell Pope,* introductory text by Royal Cortissoz. New York, W. Helburn, 1924-30.

244. After a photograph, *The American Architect—The Architectural Review,* Mar. 12, 1924, courtesy, *Architectural Record.*

245. After a photograph, *American Country Houses of Today,* edited by Bernard Wells Close. New York, Architectural Book Publishing Co., Inc., 1922.

246. Based on photographs, *One Hundred Country Houses; Modern American Examples* by Aymar Embury II. New York, The Century Co., 1909; *Architectural Record,* Oct. 1904; *Architectural Record,* March 1906, courtesy, *Architectural Record.*

247. After a photograph, *The House Beautiful Building Annual, 1925,* by permission from *House Beautiful,* © 1925, the Hearst Corporation. All rights reserved.

248. After a photograph by Jay Sacks, *The American Heritage Book of Notable American Houses,* Marshall B. Davidson, author and editor in charge. New York, American Heritage Publishing Co., Inc., 1971.

249. After a photograph, *The Book of Building and Interior Decorating,* edited by Reginald T. Townsend. New York, Doubleday, 1923.

250. After a photograph, *American Country Houses of Today,* edited by Bernard Wells Close. New York, Architectural Book Publishing Co., Inc., 1922.

251. After an illustration, *Advertect Homes,* 1927-28 edition. South Bend, Ind., Advertect, Inc., 1927.

252. After a photograph, *Houses for Good Living* by Royal Barry Wills. New York, Architectural Book Publishing Co., Inc., 1946.

253. A composite drawing, based on photographs, The Library, National Housing Center, Washington, D.C.

254. After a photograph, The Library, National Housing Center, Washington, D.C.

255. After a photograph, courtesy, Levitt & Sons, Inc.

256. After a photograph by Henry Fuermann, Chicago Architectural Photographing Co., as published in *Frank Lloyd Wright to 1910* by Grant Carpenter Manson. New York, Reinhold, 1958; by permission, Litton Educational Publishing Inc.; and a measured drawing by Marion Mahoney.

257. After a drawing, *Advertect Homes,* 1927-28 edition. South Bend, Ind., Advertect Inc., 1927.

258. By permission of Hawthorne Books, after a photograph by Henry Fuermann, Chicago Architectural Photographing Co., from *The Buildings of Frank Lloyd Wright 1887-1941* by Henry-Russell Hitchcock. New York, originally published by Duell, Sloan & Pearce, 1942.

259. Based on drawing, *Advertect Homes,* 1927-28 edition. South Bend, Ind., Advertect Inc., 1927. Hip roof added as per text description.

260. After a photograph by Henry Fuermann, Chicago Architectural Photographing Company, as published in *Frank Lloyd Wright to 1910* by Grant Carpenter Manson. New York, Reinhold, 1958, by permission, Litton Educational Publishing Inc.

261. After a photograph, *Architecture in America* by Wayne Andrews. New York, Atheneum, 1960.

262. After an illustration, *Advertect Homes,* 1927-28 edition. South Bend, Ind., Advertect Inc., 1927.

263. After a photograph by Lloyd Yost, *Five California Architects* by Esther McCoy. New York, Praeger Publishers, 1975, by permission, Holt, Rinehart & Winston.

264. After a photograph, *The Ideal House,* Vol. III, No. 2, Sept. 1906. New York, T. A. Cawthra & Co. 1906.

265. After a photograph by Maynard L. Parker, collection of James Marston Fitch.

266. After a photograph by Roy Flamm, *Five California Architects* by Esther McCoy. New York, Praeger Publishers, 1975, by permission, Holt, Rinehart & Winston.

267. After a photograph by Wayne Andrews, *Architecture in America* by Wayne Andrews. New York, Atheneum, 1960.

268. After a drawing by Frank Lloyd Wright, "Frank Lloyd Wright: The Life Work of an American Architect," Introduction by Hendricus T. Wijdeveld, Wendigen (special issues), Santpoort, Holland; C.A. Mees, 1925, Rare Book Dept., Library of Congress.

269. After a photograph by Maynard L. Parker, by permission from *House Beautiful,* © Nov. 1955, the Hearst Corporation. All rights reserved.

270. After a photograph by Ezra Stoller, *You and Architecture* by Alfred Browning Parker. New York, Delacorte Press, 1965.

271. After a photograph by W. P. Woodcock, *Five California Architects* by Esther McCoy. New York, Praeger Publishers, 1975, by permission, Holt, Rinehart & Winston.

272. After a photograph by P. E. Guerrero, *Frank Lloyd Wright* by Vincent Scully. New York, George Braziller, Inc., 1940.

273. After a photograph by Ezra Stoller, *You and Architecture* by Alfred Browning Parker. New York, Delacorte Press, 1965.

274. After a photograph by Wayne Andrews, *Architecture in America* by Wayne Andrews. New York, Atheneum, 1960.

275. After a photograph by Marvin Rand, *Five California Architects* by Esther McCoy. New York, Praeger Publishers, 1975, by permission, Holt, Rinehart & Winston.

276. After a photograph, *Architecture U.S.A.* by Ian McCallum. London, The Architectural Press, 1959; New York, Reinhold Book Corp.

277. After a photograph, *Five California Architects* by Esther McCoy. New York, Praeger Publishers, 1975, by permission, Holt, Rinehart & Winston.

278. After a photograph by Bill Hedrich, as published in *Frank Lloyd Wright* by Vincent Scully. New York, George Braziller, Inc., 1940, by permission from Hedrich-Blessing.

279. After a photograph, collection of A. Lawrence Kocher, architect.

280. After a photograph by Maris-Ezra Stoller Assoc., courtesy, office of Edward Durrell Stone Assoc., P.C., archs.

281. After a photograph, the Exhibition of Contemporary Industrial Art, Metropolitan Museum of Art, 1934.

282. After a photograph, courtesy, The Architects Collaborative and Mrs. Walter Gropius.

283. After a photograph, courtesy, The Architects Collaborative and Mrs. Walter Gropius.

284. After a drawing, *Walter Gropius: Rebuilding Our Communities,* an Institute of Design book. Chicago, Paul Theobald & Co., 1945, p. 42.

285. After a photograph, New England Techbuilt Inc.

286. After a photograph from *R. Buckminster Fuller* by John McHale. New York, George Braziller, Inc., 1962, by permission, R. Buckminster Fuller Archives.

287. After a photograph from *R. Buckminster Fuller* by John McHale. New York, George Braziller, Inc., 1962, by permission, R. Buckminster Fuller Archives.

288. After a photograph by permission from Hedrich-Blessing, *Ludwig Mies van der Rohe* by Arthur Drexler. New York, George Braziller, 1960.

289. After a photograph by Wayne Andrews, *Architecture in America,* by Wayne Andrews. New York, Atheneum, 1960.

290. After a photograph by Charles Eames, *Modern California Houses* by Esther McCoy. New York, Praeger Publishers, 1975, by permission, Holt, Rinehart & Winston.

291. After a photograph by Ezra Stoller, *Second Treasury of Contemporary Houses, Architectural Record.* New York, F. W. Dodge Corp., 1959.

292. After a photograph by Ezra Stoller.

293. After a photograph, courtesy, Edward Durrell Stone Assoc., P.C., archs.

294. After a photograph by Michael Hare, architect, courtesy, Mrs. Michael Hare.

295. After a photograph, *Second Treasury of Contemporary Houses, Architectural Record.* New York, F. W. Dodge Corp., 1959, by permission from Hedrich-Blessing.

296. After a photograph by P. A. Dearborn, *Pencil Points,* May 1946.

297. After a photograph by Roger Sturtevant, courtesy, Wurster Bernardi & Emmons, archs.

298. After a photograph, Leavenworth's, *The Natural House* by Frank Lloyd Wright. New York, Horizon Press, 1954.

299. After a photograph, courtesy, Robert Damora.

300. After a photograph by John Ebstel, *Architectural Forum,* Sept., 1950.

301. After a photograph, courtesy, Ezra Stoller.

302. After a photograph by Ezra Stoller, *Second Treasury of Contemporary Houses, Architectural Record.* New York, F. W. Dodge Corp., 1959.

303. After a photograph by Phillip Harrington, *Look* Magazine.

304. After a photograph by Robert Damora.

305. After a photograph by Phillip Harrington, *Look,* January 16, 1962.

306. After a photograph, courtesy, Eduardo F. Catalano, architect.

307. After a photograph by Joseph W. Molitor, *The New York Times Magazine,* April 28, 1963.

308. After photographs and a drawing, courtesy, Tasso Katselas, architect/planner.

309. After a photograph by David Plowden, *Architectural Forum,* Nov. 1965.

310. Based on a staff drawing and photographs by Morley Baer, *Progressive Architecture,* June 1963.

311. After a photograph, courtesy, office of Hugh Newell Jacobsen, F.A.I.A., arch.

312. After a photograph by Stephen Hill, *Modern Movements in Architecture* by Charles Jencks. New York, Anchor Press/Doubleday, 1973.

313. After a photograph, courtesy, Venturi & Rauch, archs. and planners.

314. After a photograph by Ezra Stoller.

315. After a photograph, courtesy, Acorn Structures, Inc.

316. After a photograph, courtesy, James S. Kries, designer and builder.

317. Based on a drawing, *The Futurist,* Vol. X, No. 1, Feb. 1976 and photographs, courtesy, John E. Barnard, Jr., A.I.A. architect.

318. After a photograph, courtesy, Mr. Jesse Savell, Savell Systems International.

319. After a photograph, courtesy, Department of Architecture, University of California at Berkeley; under a grant, U.S. Department of Housing and Urban Development, 1969. Project Team: Henry Sanoff, chairman; Tyrus Porter, Amos Rapoport, Patrick Morreau.

320. After a staff photograph, *The Mother Earth News,* No. 56, March-April, 1979.

Major sources from which much of the information in the text was derived include the following:

Henry Chandlee Forman, *The Architecture of the Old South.* Harvard University Press, Cambridge, Massachusetts, 1948.
Thomas Tileston Waterman, *The Dwellings of Colonial America.* The University of North Carolina Press, Chapel Hill, 1950.
Albert Mauncy, *The Houses of St. Augustine: 1565-1821.* The St. Augustine Historical Society, Convention Press, Jacksonville, Florida, 1962.
Talbot Hamlin, *Greek Revival Architecture in America.* Oxford University Press, London and New York, 1944.
Henry-Russell Hitchcock, *The Architecture of H. H. Richardson and His Times.* The Museum of Modern Art, 1936.
Vincent Scully, *The Shingle Style.* Yale University Press, New Haven, 1955.

Index

About the Author

Mary Mix Foley has written numerous articles on architectural subjects, and is coauthor of two books, *Housing Choices and Housing Constraints* and *Modern Church Architecture.* She was an associate editor of *Architectural Forum,* and with architect Cloethial Woodard Smith, organized the American exhibit of architectural work for the VII Pan American Congress of Architects, which won the Gold Medal for the United States. She also served on the staff of the AIA for two years. She lives in Washington, D.C.

About the Artist

Madelaine Thatcher was on the staff of *Architectural Forum* for many years. Her drawings have appeared in numerous magazines.